And whatever you do ~~in word~~
word or deed,
name of the Lo
thanks to God
Him.

Colossians 3:17

Gary and Peggy   12/2009

Zig Ziglar

THE ONE YEAR®
DAILY INSIGHTS
with
ZIG ZIGLAR
& DR. IKE REIGHARD

TYNDALE HOUSE PUBLISHERS, INC.
CAROL STREAM, ILLINOIS

Visit Tyndale's exciting Web site at www.tyndale.com.

TYNDALE and Tyndale's quill logo are registered trademarks of Tyndale House Publishers, Inc.

The One Year is a registered trademark of Tyndale House Publishers, Inc.

The One Year Daily Insights with Zig Ziglar

Designed by Dan Farrell

Edited by Erin Gwynne

Published in association with Yates & Yates, LLP, Orange, CA.

ISBN 978-1-4143-1941-4

Printed in the United States of America

15   14   13   12   11   10   09
7   6   5   4   3   2   1

To Paige Patterson, my longtime friend and confidant,
who has had a major impact on my life as he's guided me
through some pitfalls along the way.
I love and respect Paige Patterson and am grateful
he took an interest in me as a new and growing Christian.

—ZIG ZIGLAR

I would like to thank Pat Springle, my writing partner for over ten years,
and Donna Monroe, my executive assistant and friend of over twenty years.
And to the four girls in my life: Robin—for over twenty-five years as my friend
and the best wife ever! Abigail—thanks for being my writing partner and thought
generator on this project. Danielle and Addi—thank you, my lovely daughter,
for blessing all of us with a granddaughter who delights us
each and every day!

—DR. IKE REIGHARD

INTRODUCTION

IN 1985, AS A GUEST SPEAKER at a megachurch in Dallas, Texas, I quoted Zig Ziglar from his book *See You at the Top* in my message on overcoming giants in your life. After the service, a tall, thin, immaculately dressed gentleman approached me and said, "I really liked what you had to say about Zig Ziglar." I replied by asking, "Oh, are you a Zig fan?" The "fan" paused for a moment before he said, "I *am* Zig Ziglar!" To my astonishment (and embarrassment), I had met one of my heroes!

Long before I ever met Zig Ziglar in person, his book *See You at the Top* inspired me to make significant changes in my life. I began setting goals. One of the first was to graduate from college. Zig's influence in my life through that book continued as I earned a bachelor's degree, a master's degree, and a doctorate.

After I had met Zig and as our friendship grew, I began receiving regular Saturday morning calls from him that have been a great blessing in my life. As Zig prepared to teach his Sunday morning Bible class, he would go over his ideas for his lesson. I soon became his "pastor in residence" and amateur theologian. As we spoke of the week's passage from Scripture, I would use my background in biblical studies to give him context and socioeconomic, geographical, and spiritual implications from my personal studies. Saturday mornings with Zig became not just a ritual but a blessing that I will treasure forever.

Our long-standing friendship has been featured in two books: *Sheltering Trees*, by Donna VanLiere and Eddie Carswell, and *Over the Top*, Zig's sequel to *See You at the Top*. Zig used my story of becoming "a meaningful specific" rather than "a wandering generality."

We bonded from the beginning, and what ensued was an unequaled relationship that—other than my relationship with Jesus Christ—has helped shape me as a husband, a father, a Christian, and an inspirational speaker.

—DR. IKE REIGHARD

I ASKED IKE to write this book with me because I have valued and trusted his spiritual discernment and his biblical counsel for many years now. I believe you will benefit, as I have, from the wisdom and knowledge that Ike Reighard brings to this book. Between the two of us, you will find quotes, memory verses, and thought-provoking daily insights into our beloved Word of God. It is our prayer that these daily devotions will encourage you and lead you into a more intimate relationship with our Lord and Savior, Jesus Christ.

—ZIG ZIGLAR

ONE THING

Brethren, I do not count myself to have apprehended; but one thing I do, forgetting those things which are behind and reaching forward to those things which are ahead, I press toward the goal for the prize of the upward call of God in Christ Jesus. PHILIPPIANS 3:13-14 { MEMORY VERSE

PAUL WAS THE GREATEST leader in the history of the church, but he wasn't cocky. He knew he was still a work in progress. Paul's days were filled with starting churches, managing leaders, and taking the gospel to everyone in the known world, but he reduced his job description to "one thing." We'd interpret his comments in management terms as *the rigorous commitment to a singular objective* that has two parts: not dwelling on the past, but reaching ahead to achieve the vision of the future.

The past can bog us down in two distinctly different ways: Some of us feel ashamed by failures in our personal lives or in business, and our minds are haunted by those memories. Every decision we make is colored by our grief and the fear that we'll make the same mistake again. Others of us, though, live in past glories. We've enjoyed stunning success, but instead of using our gains as a foundation for future growth, we keep reliving those memories. Living in the past, whether failed or successful, takes our lives out of focus. Paul says, "Forget the past and move on."

In which direction should we move? We should reach forward to fulfill the vision God has for us. Paul encourages us to uncover and embrace a God-sized cause, one that has a positive impact on people and expands His Kingdom. We can have causes like that at work, in our neighborhoods, and at home, as well as at church.

As you begin this New Year, focus on Paul's "one thing."

What are some past failures or successes you need to leave behind?

Is there a God-sized cause that has gripped your heart? Explain your answer.

"The day our memories become larger than our dreams is the day our soul begins to shrink." —IKE REIGHARD

"Discipline yourself to do the things you need to do when you need to do them, and the day will come when you will be able to do the things you want to do when you want to do them." —ZIG ZIGLAR

WRITE IT DOWN!

The LORD answered me and said: "Write the vision and make it plain on tablets, that he may run who reads it. For the vision is yet for an appointed time; but at the end it will speak, and it will not lie. Though it tarries, wait for it."

HABAKKUK 2:2-3

SOME OF US WANDER from one thing to another our whole lives. We're capable of so much more, but we have never clarified our purpose in life. An out-of-focus purpose can't inspire us, but a crystal-clear lens on God's purpose for us rivets our attention and gives us energy to keep going until we reach our goals. While the prophet Habakkuk was in prayer, God told him to write down the vision He was giving him. In that day, scribes used a stylus to etch words into blocks of clay. It took work, so they thought carefully about what they wanted to write in order to avoid wasting time and tablets.

We need to write our vision down in clear, compelling language so that it grips our hearts. A clearly written vision statement frees us from confusion so that we can "run" instead of wander, stumble, or go backward. A clear vision overcomes inertia and produces the inspiration to run toward our goals.

But the fulfillment of our vision, God tells the prophet, is in His timing, not ours. Seldom does anyone move in a straight line from the conception of a dream to its fulfillment. Far more often, we experience ups and downs, delays, and disappointments. These, though, won't stop us if we keep our eyes on our purpose and on the One who has given it to us.

Do you have a clear, compelling vision statement?

What would it (or does it) mean to you to have one?

"We grow by dreams. All big men are big dreamers. Some of us let dreams die, but others nourish and protect them, nurse them through bad days . . . to the sunshine and light which always comes." —**WOODROW WILSON**

GOD'S DREAM FOR OUR LIVES

King Agrippa, I was not disobedient to the heavenly vision. ACTS 26:19

MANY PEOPLE HAVE DREAMS of wealth, popularity, power, and ease, but there's another kind of dream that's even more powerful and far more fulfilling:

finding and following God's dream for our lives

When the apostle Paul stood before the king to explain why he had followed his path, he could have described the pros and cons of each decision along the way. But pros and cons didn't determine Paul's direction. Paul had a God-given vision, and he aligned his life to fulfill it. That was his defense before the king. A compelling dream will generate the obedience to push past our fears.

All pursuits promise to fill our lives with meaning, but only God can transform us, fill us, challenge us, and give our lives ultimate purpose. God gave His all, and He demands our all. In perhaps the most loved devotional book in the English language, Oswald Chambers wrote, "The only way to be obedient to the heavenly vision is to give our utmost for His highest—our best for His glory. This can be accomplished only when we make a determination to continually remember God's vision."* The paradox of the Christian life is that when we live unreservedly for God, we find true fulfillment ourselves. Don't be disobedient to the dream God has given you.

How clear is God's dream for your life right now?

Is any fear holding you back from accomplishing this dream? If so, what is it? How will you push past it?

"Attempt great things for God and expect great things from God." —WILLIAM CAREY

---

*Oswald Chambers, *My Utmost for His Highest* (Grand Rapids, MI: Discovery House, 1992), 71.

DISCOVER YOUR STRENGTHS

All the gifted artisans among them who worked on the tabernacle made ten curtains woven of fine linen, and of blue, purple, and scarlet thread; with artistic designs of cherubim they made them. EXODUS 36:8

THE "GIFTED ARTISANS" were able to use their God-given gifts to help build the Tabernacle. God has also given each of us abilities that we can use to fulfill our God-given dreams. Certainly, training is important, but we won't get too far if we rely only on training. All of us know people who received lots of training, but they don't have much competence for their jobs. They grind out work day after day, gritting their teeth until Friday afternoon and dreading Monday mornings. Some of us might be those people!

Don't focus on your weaknesses; focus on your strengths. When your work responsibilities fit your God-given abilities, you're in the jet stream of accomplishment. You're far more creative, more energetic, more relaxed, and more willing to help others who need a hand.

Some of us have been caught in dead-end jobs for years, and we've lost hope of ever finding something that fulfills us. Certainly, God can take us through valleys from time to time to teach us important lessons, but life need not be a perpetual valley. We cannot be passive. We need to take initiative to uncover our latent talents and use them with all our hearts. It's not optional. Someday, we will stand before God to give an account of our time here on earth. On that day, He will ask us how we used the talents He gave us. I want to hear Him say, "Well done!" Don't you?

What are the activities and responsibilities that rev your engine?

What do you need to do to refine your career so that your job fits your God-given talents?

"Quality is never an accident. It is always the result of intelligent effort. There must be a will to produce a superior thing." —JOHN RUSKIN

EXCELLENCE WHERE YOU ARE

Uzziel the son of Harhaiah, one of the goldsmiths, made repairs. Also next to him Hananiah, one of the perfumers, made repairs; and they fortified Jerusalem as far as the Broad Wall. NEHEMIAH 3:8

SOMETIMES, GOD'S DESIRE for us is to do our very best even though we don't quite fit the job. When Nehemiah went back to Jerusalem to rebuild the walls of the city and restore dignity to God's people, the place was in terrible shape. His job looked hopeless, but Nehemiah believed God could do the impossible. He rallied the people and put them to work carrying stones, framing doors, and defending one another from attacks.

Through the chapters of Nehemiah's story, we find people pitching in where they were needed. They didn't ask HR to fit them perfectly to their job; they just rolled up their sleeves and went to work. Uzziel was a master goldsmith, but when he was asked to carry huge rocks, he never complained. He just worked. And next to him, Hananiah carried stones too. This guy's regular work was making perfume, not slinging mortar, swinging a hammer, or lugging rocks! But he worked hard next to the goldsmith.

Perhaps those around you complain when their work doesn't perfectly match their skills. Don't let their attitude poison you. Instead, roll up your sleeves and do whatever it takes to get the job done. You'll win the trust of your boss and the respect of your peers—and you might even enjoy it! When you do more than you're paid to do, you'll be paid more for what you do.

What are you tempted to complain about at work?

How long should you do a job that doesn't fit you?

"Some people have greatness thrust upon them. Few have excellence thrust upon them.... They achieve it. They do not achieve it unwittingly by doing what comes naturally and they don't stumble into it in the course of amusing themselves. All excellence involves discipline and tenacity of purpose." —JOHN W. GARDNER

SECOND AND THIRD CHANCES

You, being dead in your trespasses and the uncircumcision of your flesh, He has made alive together with Him, having forgiven you all trespasses, having wiped out the handwriting of requirements that was against us, which was contrary to us. And He has taken it out of the way, having nailed it to the cross.

COLOSSIANS 2:13-14

A FEW YEARS AGO, Chuck Swindoll asked his sister, "What's your favorite emotion?" After a minute of reflection, she replied, "Relief." I agree. If we are honest with ourselves, we have to admit that we have some rotten thoughts, desires, and actions. Sure, we put on a mask of competence and respectability, but underneath, we hide some ugly traits. We often sin against God and against people at home and at work—and we feel terrible about it.

But we don't have to live under the guilt that comes as a result of our sin. The central, paramount truth of the Christian faith is that God, in His amazing grace, forgives us. He doesn't excuse our sin by saying, "Well, it's not that bad" or "It doesn't really matter." No, He calls it sin, and He has paid a high price to forgive us.

In his letter to the Colossians, Paul uses the metaphor of a Roman debtor's prison. When a person couldn't repay a debt, he was thrown into a cell, and a parchment scroll of all his debts was nailed to the cell door until the debts were paid. Jesus saw us in the prison of our guilt, and He took the list of our sinful debts and nailed them to the cross, where He paid for them in full.

Freedom is never free. Christ's grace is free to us, but it cost Him His life. His sacrifice shows us how much He loves us, and we are wise to gratefully accept His wonderful forgiveness. When we do, we're set free to experience relief, and we're motivated to honor the One who freed us.

What's the difference between excusing sin and forgiving it?

What are some things you've thought or done that need to be forgiven by Jesus?

"This is the mystery of the riches of divining grace for sinners; for by a wonderful exchange our sins are now not ours but Christ's, and Christ's righteousness is not Christ's but ours." —MARTIN LUTHER

COURAGEOUS CONVERSATIONS

They said to me, "The survivors who are left from the captivity in the province are there in great distress and reproach. The wall of Jerusalem is also broken down, and its gates are burned with fire." So it was, when I heard these words, that I sat down and wept, and mourned for many days; I was fasting and praying before the God of heaven. NEHEMIAH 1:3-4

MOST OF US SPEND OUR LIVES trying to project an image of beauty and competence. Certainly, we want others to think highly of us, but one of the things I respect most about people is their ruthless honesty—about themselves and their situations. Nehemiah had a plum job. He was working closely with the king, and he lived a life of luxury. His heart, though, beat in unison with God's heart. He cared about the things God cares about, and when he heard that the people in Jerusalem were suffering, his heart broke. He didn't minimize the problem, and he didn't fly into a panic of mindless activity. Instead, he let the brutal truth sink in, and he responded appropriately: He sat down and wept.

Nehemiah had a courageous conversation with the messenger, then he had a courageous conversation with God. Only courageous people are known for their honesty. It's a lot easier to look the other way when we see needs in our lives or in the lives of people around us. We can give the excuse that we've tried as hard as we can or that we don't have time to help a person in need. But excuses don't cut it. Like Nehemiah, we need to let the truth sink into our hearts so we can respond with genuine compassion.

This is just the first part of Nehemiah's story. He then took bold action to gather resources, inspire the people, and rebuild the walls of Jerusalem. Successful action, though, starts with ruthless honesty about the need.

What are some needs in your own life and in the lives of those around you?

How would being honest about those needs become a springboard for change?

"Men occasionally stumble over the truth. But most of them pick themselves up and hurry off as if nothing happened." —**WINSTON CHURCHILL**

CRAFTED

We are His workmanship, created in Christ Jesus for good works, which God prepared beforehand that we should walk in them. EPHESIANS 2:10 { MEMORY VERSE

OUR ABILITIES, PERSONALITIES, AND PHYSICAL FEATURES are no accident. God has crafted each of us just the way He wanted to. Paul wrote that we are God's "workmanship." The Greek word for workmanship is *poiema*, from which, of course, we get our word *poem*. Poetry is a beautiful expression of thought, carefully structured and meticulously worded. The meter of each line and the choice of each word come together to maximize the meaning. And these things don't just happen by chance. They are the product of the poet's skill, intention, and detail.

In the same way, God crafts each of us by using His skill to shape our personalities and give us the abilities and appearances He has chosen for us. No one is created just like another because no one has the same purpose God has given each of us. Paul also tells his readers that God's purpose isn't something He dreams up along the way. God prepared His purpose for us long ago, "before the foundation of the world" (Ephesians 1:4).

When we feel prideful because we've accomplished a lot, we need to realize where our abilities came from. On the other hand, if we're confused or discouraged because we can't seem to discover the meaning for our lives, we can rest assured that Almighty God has a divine purpose for us. Either way, we can remember that God is the poet, and we are His poems.

How do you respond to the fact that you are God's poem?

What are some ways God has used you to accomplish "good works"?

"God does not love us because we are valuable. We are valuable because God loves us." —FULTON J. SHEEN

"In my mind there is no doubt that those who use their talents to serve the Lord will truly enter into the joy of the Lord." —ZIG ZIGLAR

PERFORMANCE REVIEW

We must all appear before the judgment seat of Christ, that each one may receive the things done in the body, according to what he has done, whether good or bad. Knowing, therefore, the terror of the Lord, we persuade men.

2 CORINTHIANS 5:10-11

WHEN YOU KNOW you're going to meet with your boss in a couple of weeks for a performance review, how do you act? Most of us look at our list of responsibilities to be certain we get all our tasks accomplished, and we make sure we're pleasant to the people around us. The stakes can be pretty high. We may want a promotion or a raise, or we may just want to hear that we're doing a good job so we can stay employed. We do whatever it takes so that the review is as positive as possible. In other words, the reality of the review makes a difference in our choices.

The Bible tells us that we'll be called into the Boss's office one day for the ultimate performance review. We'll stand before Jesus Christ to give an account of our choices as Christians. This is called the Bema seat, which is named after the victory platform in the ancient Olympics. Many believers aren't aware this judgment seat is coming. They know there's going to be a judgment at the end of time for unbelievers, but they are unaware there's another one for those who have trusted in Christ. On that day, you and I will look Jesus in the eye as He reviews the times we made selfish choices and the times we were gracious to others, the moments we hoped no one was watching and the ones we hoped the world knew what we were doing. All our selfishness will burn up and vanish, and we'll be left with the reward we've earned by pleasing God.

And this is the only performance review by Christ we'll ever experience. For that reason, we need to get ready now by aligning our lives with God's purposes and His ways. I want that review to be a good experience for me. How about you?

If Jesus' review of your life happened today, what would He be pleased with, and what would He be unhappy about?

How does the future reality of this review change how you will act today?

"The most important thought I ever had was that of my individual responsibility to God." —DANIEL WEBSTER

DESIGNER LABEL

God said, "Let Us make man in Our image, according to Our likeness; let them have dominion over the fish of the sea, over the birds of the air, and over the cattle, over all the earth and over every creeping thing that creeps on the earth."

GENESIS 1:26

WHEN WE WERE GROWING UP, we got our sense of identity by receiving messages from our parents and later from our friends, teachers, and employers. But the most powerful message about who we are comes from God, our Heavenly Father, who crafted us with skill and love. No matter what anyone else says about us, we aren't accidents of nature, and we aren't mistakes. Almighty God has made us, and He has imprinted His image on us. To be sure, sin has tarnished that image, but we still possess a portion of the dignity God originally imparted to Adam and Eve in the Garden.

When you look in the mirror, what do you see? Do you see someone who was created by God, who is a descendant of royalty and a person of infinite worth? If we see ourselves that way, we instantly realize two things: We desperately need the grace of God to forgive us when we fail to live up to our identity, and we need to conform our lives to fit our status as the King's kids. We should stop monkeying around and begin to act like the children of the King so we will be a reflection of all He desires us to be!

When you look in the mirror, what do you see? Be honest.

How would it affect your attitude and choices today if you saw yourself as someone who has been skillfully crafted by Almighty God?

"If God exists and we are made in His image we can have real meaning, and we can have real knowledge through what He has communicated to us."
—FRANCIS A. SCHAEFFER

A HOLY PLACE

Do you not know that your body is the temple of the Holy Spirit who is in you, whom you have from God, and you are not your own? For you were bought at a price; therefore glorify God in your body and in your spirit, which are God's.

1 CORINTHIANS 6:19-20

"ME, GOD?" you might respond. "I don't feel like a 'temple of the Holy Spirit' most of the time."

One of the most amazing truths of the Christian life is that when we trust in Christ as our Savior, His Spirit takes up residence in us. He's not just "out there" any longer. He's living in us. In the same way that Christ stepped out of heaven and came to earth to communicate His love, forgiveness, and power to us, His Spirit steps into the life of each believer to impart wisdom, encouragement, and strength to us—every day. Always, He is literally as near as our breath.

The implications of this truth are stunning. We are never alone. In our times of celebration, we remember that He is the One who gave us success. In times of suffering, the One who comforted Mary and Martha when their brother died is with us, too (see John 11:5-44). When we are confused, we can trust Him for direction. And when He seems slow to answer, we can wait patiently because He has proven that we can trust His timing.

But housing the Holy Spirit also brings responsibility. We represent the King of kings to every person we meet, and we are His ambassadors to those around us (see 2 Corinthians 5:20). Realizing we are God's temples causes us to stop and think about what we say, what we do, and what we value.

As God's temple, do you need a remodeling job? Explain your answer.

How does this truth inspire you? How does it challenge you?

"Though every believer has the Holy Spirit, the Holy Spirit does not have every believer." —A. W. TOZER

BLESSED TO BLESS

The LORD bless you and keep you; the LORD make His face shine upon you, and be gracious to you; the LORD lift up His countenance upon you, and give you peace.   NUMBERS 6:24-26

EVERYBODY LOVES TO FEEL BLESSED. When God was in the process of transforming a nation of slaves into a culture of strength and joy, He gave Moses words of blessing to repeat over and over again for the people. They needed the blessing of God's protection, presence, and kindness—just as we need His blessing today. To bless is to grant favor, and we trust God to give us His favor. We don't just roll through our lives with no thought of God. Instead, we look to Him to give us wisdom in all we do, to guide us, and to give us success in our relationships and our work.

This prayer for blessing, though, doesn't guarantee a worry-free life. God's hand of protection keeps out countless calamities, but He allows enough difficulties to remind us that we need to trust Him. Problems show us again that God is faithful to provide for us. He is present with us every second of every day, and we can experience His peace because He understands our situations—even when we don't. When we trust God this way, we shine light on everyone around us. As we experience God's blessing, we bless others.

Does this prayer for blessing express the desire of your heart today? If it does, pray it for yourself and those you love.

What would it mean for you to be blessed and become a blessing for others today?

"My business is not to remake myself, but make the absolute best of what God made." —ROBERT BROWNING

OUR NEED FOR AWE

Listen to this, O Job; stand still and consider the wondrous works of God.

JOB 37:14

JOB HAD EVERY REASON, humanly speaking, to doubt God's goodness and power. His life had been turned upside down, and his friends blamed him for his problems. But into his pain God spoke. God said, in effect, "Hey, Job, pay attention. I know you're hurting, but your faith can be refreshed by looking at the wonders of all I've made." When our faith is shaken, we, too, can look at the awesome creation God has made, and our faith can be rekindled.

In *More than Meets the Eye*, Dr. Richard Swenson describes in vivid detail the macro- and micro-wonders of God's creation. The size of the universe is beyond comprehension. Light we see tonight from the nearest star has been in transit over four years . . . at 186,000 miles per second! And the universe contains hundreds of billions of galaxies, each containing one hundred to two hundred billion stars. But God's creation isn't only vast. The intricacies of DNA and the complexity of the nervous system and all the other parts of our bodies tell us that God is concerned about the minutiae as well as the big picture.

To notice God's power and delicate hand in Creation, we have to "stand still" and look. If we're rushing around in a panic trying to fix everything, we'll be focused only on our problems. Even in the most difficult times in our lives, faith is built by stopping and looking at the wonder of God's power and grace in the expanse and intricacies of nature.

When was the last time you were overwhelmed with a sense of wonder?

What's the connection between wonder and daily faith?

"The size of your success is determined by the size of your belief."
—LUCIUS ANNAEUS SENECA

PRISON OR CLASSROOM

We also glory in tribulations, knowing that tribulation produces perseverance; and perseverance, character; and character, hope. Now hope does not disappoint, because the love of God has been poured out in our hearts by the Holy Spirit who was given to us. ROMANS 5:3-5

LIFE IS ALL ABOUT PERSPECTIVE. If we see difficult people and painful situations as threats, they become prisons for our souls. Like inmates in medieval dungeons, we languish away for days and weeks, wishing the problems would just go away, or we try frantically to get out any way we can.

Whether our problems are caused by our own dumb mistakes, the sins of others, natural disasters, or anything else, our difficulties can, instead of dungeons, become classrooms where we learn life's greatest lessons—if we'll pay attention to them.

In some circles today, Christian leaders teach that God wants everybody to have peace and plenty, lots of money, and all the happiness in the world. That may sell books, but it doesn't help much when God allows difficulties to take us deeper into a relationship of trusting Him. In his letter to the Romans, Paul recommends a different perspective, one that sees problems not as prisons but as classrooms where God gets our attention, transforms our character, and gives us strong hope in the things that are most valuable—His will and His ways. Eventually, the lessons take us to the heart of God, where we experience His kindness and love more deeply than ever before.

We all experience difficulties. Will we see them as prisons or as classrooms?

What are some difficulties in your life right now?

How would it change your response to them if you could see them as God's classroom?

"There is nothing that touches my life that has not been filtered through the Father, the Son and the Holy Spirit." —ALAN REDPATH

A LAST RESORT?

Be anxious for nothing, but in everything by prayer and supplication, with thanksgiving, let your requests be made known to God.

PHILIPPIANS 4:6 { MEMORY VERSE

WORRY CAN EAT OUR LUNCH. During the day, we worry that we cannot do enough, and at night, we worry that everything we've done will fall apart. We replay conversations to find something we've said that could be misunderstood, and we beat ourselves up for being so stupid. We worry about our marriage or, if we aren't married, about never finding a spouse; we worry about money, sex, in-laws, and our kids. When we're at work, we're haunted about things at home, and when we're at home, we can't stop thinking about all the things that could go wrong at work.

Into this cesspool of destructive thinking Paul says, "Be anxious for nothing." "Yeah, right," we are tempted to say. "He doesn't understand what I'm going through." Well, actually he does. Paul had plenty to worry about, but he learned to fix his thoughts on the goodness and greatness of God (see Philippians 4:8), and he practiced the habit of prayer. Prayer can't coexist for long in the same mental space with worry; one will crowd the other out.

Many times we forget to pray, but when we fail to pray, we miss out on the source of peace, hope, and joy. When we pray about everything, thank God for His wisdom, and trust Him for His will to be done in His timing, we can experience God's amazing peace even in the most difficult circumstances. God will listen to every request.

What are some things you tend to worry about?

Take some time right now to pray about them, thank God for His wisdom and strength, and trust Him for His timing.

"You may give out, but never give up." —**MARY CROWLEY**

"As your positive confessions come forth, you will discover more blessings you will have to thank God for." —**ZIG ZIGLAR**

ONE NATION UNDER GOD

Blessed is the nation whose God is the LORD, the people He has chosen as His own inheritance. PSALM 33:12

HAS THERE EVER BEEN A NATION as blessed by God as the United States? Historians and pastors may argue about the intentions and beliefs of our founding fathers, but one thing is certain: God has given us incredible wealth, freedom, and protection throughout our history.

The question we must consider is, What are we doing with it? Far too often, we enjoy the benefits of God's blessings by spending them on today instead of investing them in the future. In biblical history, God blessed Israel so that they would be a blessing to the nations of the world. When Israel welcomed foreigners and supported widows and orphans, God continued to shower them with riches and freedom.

Today, Christians in our land have an unprecedented opportunity to rise up and make a difference. Some of us may choose to invest our freedom by getting active in the political process, or perhaps we choose issues of social justice or missions or global warming as the target of our attention. However God leads each of us, we can be sure of this: God always leads the rich to help the poor, directs the free to reach out to the oppressed, and empowers the wise to give hope to those who are confused.

We have phenomenal riches in this country, riches that come from the hand of God. We need to recognize the source of all our blessings and commit ourselves to use every resource to make a difference for Christ's sake.

What are some blessings we enjoy that other nations don't?

What are some specific ways you can invest your riches and freedom to make a difference in others' lives?

"On our National Day of Prayer, then, we join together as people of many faiths to petition God to show us His mercy and His love, to heal our weariness and uphold our hope, that we might live ever mindful of His justice and thankful for His blessings." —RONALD REAGAN

MODELING THE RIGHT STUFF

Meditate on these things; give yourself entirely to them, that your progress may be evident to all. 1 TIMOTHY 4:15

WHEN PEOPLE FOLLOW US, what are they looking for? The answer to that question may be as varied as the individuals themselves. Some want a parent figure, some want a big brother or sister, some want only to learn a few specific skills, and some want specific help in developing a new business plan. Most followers, though, want to follow leaders who know where they're going and have genuine passion about getting there. Those two traits aren't that complicated, but the combination is surprisingly rare.

In his letter, Paul had given Timothy a raft of instructions and the rationale to implement a strategy of leadership. However, he didn't want his young friend to just go through the motions. He gave him sound advice: Think long and hard about all that I've written to you so that it sinks deep below the surface and becomes an integral part of your life. And that's not all. Don't just think about these things; pour your life into them, everything you've got— body, mind, and soul! When people see that, they'll sit up and notice, and then they'll follow you.

Paul understood that leadership doesn't come from a manual. It comes from the heart. We may move bodies by our directions in staff meetings, but we move hearts only when they are convinced that we really understand the ins and outs of what we're talking about and only when we show them that we are devoted to the mission. Insight and passion—that's modeling the right stuff.

Describe the level of your understanding of your role and cause and your passion to accomplish your purpose.

What would "modeling the right stuff" look like in your life?

"My prayers seem to be more of an attitude than anything else. I indulge in no lip service but ask the great God, silently, daily and throughout the day to permit me to speak to Him. I ask for wisdom, understanding, and strength to carry out His will. As a result, I am asking and receiving all the time." —GEORGE WASHINGTON CARVER

THE SECRET OF CONTENTMENT

I have learned in whatever state I am, to be content: I know how to be abased, and I know how to abound. Everywhere and in all things I have learned both to be full and to be hungry, both to abound and to suffer need.

PHILIPPIANS 4:11-12

MANY OF US have some mixed-up ideas about contentment. We think that if we can ever have this good thing, our life will be better. If we can avoid that bad thing, then we'll be really happy. If we thought about it more than a nanosecond, though, we'd realize that we know plenty of people who have this or who have successfully avoided that but still aren't any happier than we are. There must be a secret we haven't discovered yet.

There is. Somewhere along the way, Paul learned the secret of contentment. He realized that possessions, fame, beauty, and other earthly things can be pleasant for a while, but they can never produce genuine contentment. That comes from the inside. We experience true contentment when external things lose their grip on our hearts and don't matter much anymore. Some of us get bent out of shape when we realize our favorite shirt is still at the cleaners or when we can't find the perfect pair of shoes. Paul's well of contentment was so deep that he could enjoy life with or without the most basic needs. He was content being full or going hungry, having many possessions or little to speak of, living a life of ease or suffering at the hands of evil men.

A poster in a college professor's office reads, "Happiness isn't having what you want; it's wanting what you have." Jealousy, envy, and greed suck the life—and any sense of contentment—out of us. Replace those joy killers with gratitude for what you have, and listen to your heart sing!

> What does this statement mean to you: "Happiness isn't having what you want; it's wanting what you have"?
>
> What are some steps you need to take to learn the secret of contentment?

> *"The only ultimate disaster that can befall us is to feel ourselves at home on this earth."* —MALCOLM MUGGERIDGE

PURE AND POWERFUL

The words of the LORD are pure words, like silver tried in a furnace of earth, purified seven times. PSALM 12:6

WITH ALL THE TECHNOLOGY surrounding us, we hear thousands of messages every day. Linda Stone, formerly of Apple and Microsoft, coined the term *continuous partial attention* to describe the constant distractions of e-mail, instant messaging, cell phones, and other devices. She observes, "To pay continuous partial attention is to pay partial attention—*continuously*.... We want to connect and be connected. We want to effectively scan for opportunity and optimize for the best opportunities, activities, and contacts, in any given moment."

Too often, we value all received messages equally. God's Word, though, is more precious and valuable than any other message sent to us. The psalmist describes God's message as "pure words" that are like silver processed "seven times" in the furnace. The number seven signifies completion and perfection throughout the Scriptures. God's Word is absolutely perfect and in alignment with the character of God. It is the supreme measure of truth, and it imparts light and life to those who treasure it.

When we read and hear God's Word, we need to sit up and take notice. If we don't understand it, we need to dig deeper until we find out what it means. And when God uses His Word to redirect our steps, we are wise to say, "Yes, Lord. I'm listening." God's Word directs us along God's path, and that way is perfect for us each day.

How do you treat letters or e-mails that are especially meaningful to you?

What would it mean for you to truly treasure God's Word?

"To know the will of God is the greatest knowledge! To do the will of God is the greatest achievement." —GEORGE W. TRUETT

SPIRITUAL ALIGNMENT

Let the words of my mouth and the meditation of my heart be acceptable in Your sight, O Lord, my strength and my Redeemer. PSALM 19:14

JESUS SAID, "Out of the abundance of the heart the mouth speaks" (Matthew 12:34). We may try to hide what we really think of a person or a situation, but sooner or later, our words will reflect our beliefs. For most of us, aligning our hearts and our words is difficult, and sometimes (maybe often), we dance around what we really believe and say things we don't really mean.

But for those who are serious about following Christ, alignment doesn't stop with our hearts and our mouths. We need to align both with the character and purposes of God so that what we say and what we believe reflect His heart and His direction for our lives.

What, then, is "acceptable" in God's sight? God delights in our acts of kindness to those in need, our forgiveness of those who hurt us, and our refraining from blurting out venomous words. God loves it when we are brutally honest with Him about our faults and broken hearts because He knows He has our attention. Then He can reveal the secrets of His love to us.

Our words serve as a thermometer, reflecting the content of our hearts and indicating the desire for change. The more we value God's grace, His wisdom, and His strength, the more we'll long for every part of us—especially our words and our hearts—to be in alignment with Him.

> **What did your words reflect about your heart in the past twenty-four hours?**
>
> **What are some things you can do to align your words and your heart with God's character and purposes?**

> *"The heart of a fool is in his mouth, but the mouth of the wise man is in his heart."* —BENJAMIN FRANKLIN

WHAT'S IN A NAME?

Some trust in chariots, and some in horses; but we will remember the name of the Lord our God. PSALM 20:7

IN MANY CULTURES, and especially in the ancient world, a name has represented the character or another significant aspect of a person. Throughout the Bible, the names of God give us insights into His greatness. For instance, *Elohim* tells us He is the Creator, *El Roi* says that He sees everything all the time, *Jehovah-jireh* promises that He will provide, and *Adonai* indicates that He is the sovereign Lord who rules over all. All these names (and many more) are like facets of a diamond, shimmering with the light of God's power, majesty, and goodness. They reinforce our awe of God and reenergize our faith in Him through the good times and the bad.

We tend to trust tangible things that are inherently strong, such as chariots and horses—or possessions and bank accounts. In fact, we often trust in our abilities, our status, our parents' money, our spouse's reputation, or a hundred other things before we trust in God. It's almost as if we try everything else and then realize, "Oh, I could have trusted God!" Precisely.

The psalmist recognized our tendency to trust in powerful things we can see instead of in a God we can't see. Those things have value, but they also have limitations. On the other hand, God's infinite love and awesome power—represented by His names in Scripture—make Him our first resort, not our last.

What are some visible things in your life that are easy for you to trust in?

What would it mean for God to be your first resort instead of your last?

"Who steals my purse steals trash . . . but he that filches from me my good name, robs me of that which not enriches him, and makes me poor indeed."
—WILLIAM SHAKESPEARE, *OTHELLO*

FIRST THINGS FIRST

Seek first the kingdom of God and His righteousness, and all these things shall be added to you. MATTHEW 6:33 { MEMORY VERSE

SOME WELL-MEANING BELIEVERS misunderstand Jesus' message in the verse above. They think He's telling us to focus exclusively on Him and not be concerned at all about anything else in our lives. While that interpretation is close to the truth, it's a bit off the mark. Jesus is telling us to pursue Him *primarily.* We still have to eat, sleep, raise our kids, pay our mortgages, and keep our cars running, but these things will flow far more easily if we make our relationship with Christ our first priority.

Many of us try to manage our lives as if we're trying to put a jigsaw puzzle together. All the pieces are there, but we are bewildered about where they go. We make attempt after attempt to make things work, but no matter how hard we try, all the pieces just don't fit together. We're frustrated and exhausted!

In our exasperation, Jesus calls to us and says, "Hold on a minute. I know you're trying hard, but your way is not working. There's a better way. Put Me in the center of your life, and then you'll see how the pieces fit together."

We may think, *How can I add one more thing to my schedule? Seek Christ first? No way!* But if we take His advice, He promises to lead us, bless us, and give us more meaning than ever before. Will we take the risk?

What do you think it means to put Jesus first in your life?

Will you take the risk? Why or why not?

"Build today, then, strong and sure with a firm and ample base; and ascending and secure shall tomorrow find its place." —HENRY WADSWORTH LONGFELLOW

"God showed me that He could and would replace everything that was missing in my life, but that nothing could replace Him in my life." —ZIG ZIGLAR

EVERYBODY NEEDS A SHEPHERD

The LORD is my shepherd; I shall not want. He makes me to lie down in green pastures; He leads me beside the still waters. PSALM 23:1-2

NATIVE TEXANS ARE PROUD of their heritage. They talk (for hours!) about the rugged individualism of their people and cite numerous examples of wildcatters in the oil business and trail drivers who led tens of thousands of cattle across the prairie. But independence isn't just a Texas trait; in all parts of the country, we admire people who go it alone.

Christians, however, are never alone. We have a Shepherd who guides us, and He has the authority to give us directions because He bought us out of slavery to our sins. His authority over us, though, is shaped by affection and attention.

David, who wrote today's Scripture, knew all about shepherding because he had tended sheep for years. As the king of Israel, he reflected on his experience in the fields and compared his work as an attentive shepherd to God's ownership and care for His people. As David did countless times with his sheep through every season of the year, God leads His people to food, water, and shelter. Sheep are notoriously panic prone, and they sometimes forget to trust their shepherd. We're just like them. But if we trust our Shepherd, He will lead us to plenty and peace.

As our Shepherd, what is God's authority over us?

As our Shepherd, what has God promised to do for us?

"This is wise, sane Christian faith: that a man commits himself, his life and his hopes to God. That God undertakes the special protection of that man; that therefore that man ought not to be afraid of anything!" —GEORGE MACDONALD

OPEN EYES, OPEN HANDS

Surely goodness and mercy shall follow me all the days of my life; and I will dwell in the house of the LORD forever. PSALM 23:6

GOD'S GOODNESS is His predisposition to show favor and His energy to bring about blessing. It's not just a static characteristic; God's goodness actively flows from Him to us. God's mercy has a different tone. His standard is perfection, but we fall short every day. Although we deserve punishment, God's mercy means that we *don't* get what we deserve. What a relief!

In his most beloved poem, David is overwhelmed with God's love, and he remarks that His goodness and mercy will be his companions every day of his life—not just on the days David goes to the Temple, and not just on the days that he is thankful and obedient. No, in this psalm, he's counting on God's goodness all day every day, even when he'll blow it and desperately need to experience God's mercy again.

David had tasted God's goodness and mercy, and he wanted to experience God's presence as much as possible. Before the coming of Christ, the presence of God dwelled in the Holy of Holies in the Temple. Today, instead of in the Holy of Holies, God's Spirit actually lives in each believer, so we are never alone. If our spiritual eyes are open, we'll notice God's goodness and mercy all around us, and we'll grasp His blessings with both hands. They're there; we just need to see them.

What are some evidences of God's goodness and mercy in your life today?

What are some things you can do to be more aware of God's presence?

"A mighty fortress is our God, a bulwark never failing: our helper He amid the flood of mortal ills prevailing." —MARTIN LUTHER

LIVE LIKE YOU MEAN IT!

The poor shall eat and be satisfied; those who seek Him will praise the LORD.
Let your heart live forever! PSALM 22:26

ONE OF THE MOST DESTRUCTIVE ATTITUDES in a person's life is to demand, "I deserve better." Psychologist and writer Larry Crabb observed that many Christians see themselves as the center of the universe, and to them, God exists only to make them happy and comfortable. Crabb said that we treat God like a "specially attentive waiter," giving Him our orders and tipping Him when He performs well, but complaining when we don't get exactly what we expected.*

A far more accurate perspective is that we are "poor, blind, and naked" (Revelation 3:17) before the majesty and holiness of Almighty God. Everything we are and everything we have are gifts from Him. If we grasp that fact, we, the poor, will be far more satisfied with the gifts and opportunities God gives us—instead of demanding our way and complaining when we don't get it.

With humility, we pursue God and delight to know Him. We increasingly realize that He is our most valuable treasure, and our hearts sing with gratitude. We are amazed that the Creator of the universe would love us and involve us in the greatest adventure people have ever known. That's when our hearts "live forever"!

How does seeing God as a "specially attentive waiter" ruin our relationship with Him?

Take a minute to reflect on God's greatness and grace, His love, and the privilege of being His partner in changing people's lives.

"Do you want to enter what people call 'the high life'? Then go a step lower down."
—**ANDREW MURRAY**

---

* Larry Crabb, *Finding God* (Grand Rapids, MI: Zondervan, 1993), 18.

OVERCOMING THE WORLD

*This is the love of God, that we keep His commandments. And His command-
ments are not burdensome. For whatever is born of God overcomes the world.
And this is the victory that has overcome the world—our faith. Who is he who
overcomes the world, but he who believes that Jesus is the Son of God?*

1 JOHN 5:3-5

IN THE NEW TESTAMENT, the word *world* is used in two different ways.
Sometimes it describes the earth and all its people ("Behold! The Lamb of
God who takes away the sin of the world!" John 1:29), and sometimes it refers
to sinful, self-absorbed patterns of life. When John says that believers "overcome the world," he has the second meaning in mind.

We live in a culture that promises far more than it can deliver. Each and
every day, we are barraged by promises of beauty, riches, success, fame, and
pleasure. They claim to be able to fill our hearts and give us ultimate happiness,
and quite often, we believe their lies. If these promises came to us dressed up
as demons in little red suits, we'd recognize them at once and refuse to trust
them, but because their lies appear, like Satan himself, as sources of light, we
are easily duped.

Why do we need to overcome the world? Because it can overwhelm us
and distract us from our relationship with God. These lies steal our attention, erode our faith in God, corrupt our motives, and strain our relationships. Every part of our lives is affected, if not ruined, if we believe the false
promises.

Overcoming the world doesn't happen by magic because we say a certain
thing or by osmosis because we attend church. Wars are won by carefully
planning, marshalling resources, being courageous in action, and especially
by following the directions of the commander. In our fight with the world, we
overcome when we stay close to Jesus, recognize and reject the lies we hear,
and walk in obedience to Him.

**What are some of the lies the world tells us? Why do we so readily
believe them?**

**How well are you overcoming the world at this point in your life? What
adjustments do you need to make?**

*"Christianity has died many times and risen again; for it has a God who knew
His way out of the grave."* —G. K. CHESTERTON

TAKE UP THE CROSS

Jesus, looking at him, loved him, and said to him, "One thing you lack: Go your way, sell whatever you have and give to the poor, and you will have treasure in heaven; and come, take up the cross, and follow Me." MARK 10:21

WHEN WE READ about the rich young ruler, we often picture him as self-righteous and greedy, but that doesn't seem to be the case at all. His pursuit of God was sincere. He ran to Jesus and fell on his knees in front of Him, and his questions reflected honest inquiry (see Mark 10:17).

Mark records that Jesus' famous directive to the man, to sell all his possessions and give to the poor, was motivated by His love, not by disgust. Jesus wants each of us to love Him wholeheartedly, but we can't love Him that way if our hearts are full of anything or anyone else. Idolatry isn't just about little statues. We can make anything an idol if it takes first place in our hearts: a spouse or children, work, hobbies, wealth, fame, beauty, or possessions. Jesus pinpointed the one thing that kept this young man from experiencing the richness of a relationship with God: money.

The remedy for idolatry isn't a halfway measure. Idols must be ripped out of our hearts and replaced with God Himself. Since money was this man's idol, Jesus didn't mince words: "Sell your stuff and give all the money to the poor." Jesus didn't tell anyone else to do this, but when He points out an idol in anyone's life, He requires radical surgery. Nothing less will do.

When we loosen our grip on our idols, we can then take up the cross of obedience and loyalty to Christ and follow Him wherever He leads. This is the "abundant life" in all its richness that only Christ can give; idols steal our hearts and leave us empty.

How would you have felt if you'd been the man that day?

Has the Spirit pointed out any idol in your heart today? If so, what will you do about it?

"There are no crown-wearers in heaven who were not cross-bearers here below."
—CHARLES HADDON SPURGEON

OWNER OR MANAGER?

The earth is the LORD's, and all its fullness, the world and those who dwell therein. PSALM 24:1

IN A CAPITALIST ECONOMY, ownership is a cornerstone of society. We earn money and buy things, and we consider those things to be ours. But the Bible has a different twist on capitalism. The earth and everything in it were created by God, and as the Creator, He is the rightful owner. He entrusts parts to us for a short time, but we're wise to see ourselves as managers instead of owners.

A consumer mentality values things and people for what they do for us. If they make us feel happy and strong, we like them, but if they don't make us feel good, we get rid of them. As God-appointed managers, we acknowledge that our money (and the skills God gave us to earn money) is the Lord's, and our first question is, Lord, how can I use this in a way that pleases You? If we ask that question often enough, we may change some of our spending habits, and we might devote more of our resources to the things that matter most to God.

Of course, people are what matter most to Him. Our families, friends, neighbors, and coworkers belong to God too. He has put us in relationships with them for a purpose, and again, we need to ask a similar, piercing question: Lord, how can I relate to these people in a way that encourages them and honors You?

How would it affect your management of money and other resources if you saw yourself as God's appointed manager?

How would it affect your relationships if you saw people as entrusted to you by God?

"Where your pleasure is, there is your treasure. Where your treasure is, there is your heart. Where your heart is, there is your happiness." —**SAINT AUGUSTINE**

ALL DAY, EVERY DAY

Whatever you do in word or deed, do all in the name of the Lord Jesus, giving thanks to God the Father through Him. COLOSSIANS 3:17 { MEMORY VERSE

MANY CHRISTIANS ATTEMPT to compartmentalize their lives into sacred and secular parts. They're aware of God for an hour on Sunday mornings and perhaps for a few minutes each day when they read the Bible and pray, but they hardly think of Him the rest of the time. One of the most life-transforming concepts is that we are in God's presence all day, every day. We can relate to Him, serve Him, and depend on Him every moment—at work and at home, in the car and on the golf course, in the bedroom and in the boardroom.

In his insightful and challenging book *The Call*, Os Guinness defines our purpose as "the truth that God calls us to himself so decisively that everything we are, everything we do, and everything we have is invested with a special devotion, dynamism, and direction lived out as a response to his summons and service."* This perspective gives meaning to every moment, and it challenges us to live with integrity in every choice and relationship because we represent God at all times.

Does this perspective inspire you to use every part of your day more effectively as God's servant, or does it threaten you because you realize some things in your life aren't what they should be? It should do both.

What are some negative consequences of compartmentalizing God into just a part of our lives?

What would it mean to you to live by Guinness's concept of our calling?

"Nothing great was ever achieved without enthusiasm." —RALPH WALDO EMERSON

"You've got to be before you can do, and do before you can have." —ZIG ZIGLAR

---

* Os Guinness, *The Call: Finding and Fulfilling the Central Purpose of Your Life* (Nashville: W Publishing, 1998), 9.

SURE-FOOTED

Vindicate me, O LORD, for I have walked in my integrity. I have also trusted in the LORD; I shall not slip. PSALM 26:1 {MEMORY VERSE}

A CLEAR CONSCIENCE is a glorious thing. When we can go to bed at night without having to relive situations and rethink conversations to make sure we don't get caught in lies, we can enjoy sweet sleep. And when we talk to our spouse and children or look at a colleague at work, we can look them in the eye because we don't have any fear of being caught in fabrications of the truth. Only then can we pray, "Vindicate me, O LORD," with confidence when someone challenges us.

Why do we lie (or as we might say, exaggerate the truth)? We may be trying to look good to someone else, we may want to avoid blame for something we've done, or we may have developed a habit of shading the truth. As followers of Christ, we are called by God to live in truth. Sometimes that truth is glorious, but sometimes it shows our dark side. Either way, King David (who knew a thing or two about both glory and shame) encourages us to speak truth, live truth, and be an example of truth to others. Trusting God gives us strength to face the sometimes painful facts of our lives. When we've failed, we can embrace God's forgiveness, confess our deception to the person we've lied to, and choose the path of truth again.

How clear is your conscience today?

What would it mean for you to walk in integrity?

"Integrity is when you are one with God, yourself, and your loved ones."
—IKE REIGHARD

HIS STRENGTH

Be strong in the Lord and in the power of His might. Put on the whole armor of God, that you may be able to stand against the wiles of the devil.

EPHESIANS 6:10-11

AUTHOR C. S. LEWIS SAID that we often make one of two mistakes about the devil: We either make too little of him or too much of him. We need to avoid those extremes. In the book of Ephesians, Paul writes beautifully about our new life in Christ and the way we work together as the body of Christ, and he gives us clear directions about how to relate to God, to our family members, to other believers, and to those who don't know Christ. Now, at the end of his letter, he addresses the issue of spiritual warfare.

"Don't be surprised to find yourself in a fight," Paul seems to be saying. "And remember all the rest of what I've written to you in this letter." Satan uses several different ploys to block our walks with God. He uses temptation—of sex, money, power, pleasure, and possessions—like a fishing lure to get us to chase something that looks good but is very harmful to us. He tries to confuse us with conflicting teaching about God and His will so that we stop moving forward and drift in a cloud of uncertainty. And he attacks us with accusations ("You're rotten," "God will never forgive that," or "How can you call yourself a Christian?") to try to make us doubt God's love and forgiveness.

God has given us powerful armor to protect us and the sword of the Spirit, the Scriptures, to enable us to fight back (see Ephesians 6:13-17). We need to prepare ourselves for the fight with truth, grace, and faith, so that in the heat of battle, we have the resources we need to fight effectively.

In what ways can you identify Satan's ploys of temptation, confusion, and accusation in your own life?

Are you fighting effectively? Why or why not?

"To the degree that God will use you, the devil—to an equal degree—will try to destroy you." —IKE REIGHARD

BE TRUE TO YOUR HEART

As he thinketh in his heart, so is he. PROVERBS 23:7, KJV { MEMORY VERSE

WHAT DO YOU SPEND most of your time thinking about? Many of us never step back and analyze what's running through our minds; we just go with the flow. But when we stop to take notice, we may find that our thoughts are dominated by daydreams of success and worries of failure. A snapshot of our thoughts gives us a picture of the content of our hearts, and what we hold in our hearts serves as the ground, seed, and fertilizer for what grows into our attitudes and actions.

A good analysis of our thoughts includes looking at both *what* we think about and *how* we think. We may be preoccupied with concerns about our children, conflict with our spouses, the expectations of a boss, or a hundred other worries. Or, we may daydream about escaping our problems by taking a cruise, playing the perfect game of golf, or finding a thrill in a secret affair.

All our thoughts, including our worries and desires to escape, can be filtered through faith, hope, and love. When we're worried, we can refocus our thoughts on the goodness and greatness of God so that we find faith to trust Him for wisdom. When we're bored and want to escape, we can choose to rivet our minds on the hope of God's purpose for us. And when we are thankful, we can let our thoughts roll on in gratitude and love for our Lord.

Some would say that we can't control our thoughts. To some extent, that's true, but Martin Luther once said, "We can't keep a bird from flying over our heads, but we can keep it from building a nest in our hair!"

Analyze your thoughts for the past twenty-four hours and put them into categories of worry, escape, determination to succeed, faith, hope, and love.

What can you do today to make better choices about what you think and how you think?

"A man is what he thinks about all day long." —RALPH WALDO EMERSON

"You are what you are and where you are because of what's gone into your mind. You can change what you are and where you are by changing what goes into your mind." —ZIG ZIGLAR

WHEN LIFE DOESN'T SEEM FAIR

He makes His sun rise on the evil and on the good, and sends rain on the just and on the unjust. MATTHEW 5:45

YOU WORKED HARD in the company for years, but someone else got the promotion. You invested your money in funds your broker recommended, but they plunged to the bottom of the Morningstar ratings. You did your best to be a good parent, but your kids turned out to be no better than the children whose parents didn't seem to care about them.

Many times, unbelievers do just as well in life as believers. What's that about? If we take out our measuring stick too often, we can become angry because we think we deserve more than we're getting from God.

Jesus spent a lot of His time explaining the grace of God to people. Grace is a foreign concept to most of us. We operate by standards, rewards, and punishments, so grace just doesn't fit. But in this passage, Jesus explains that the embracing arms of God's goodness reach out to everybody: the good and the evil, the righteous and the unrighteous, you and your neighbor, you and your spouse, you and the person who got the promotion instead of you.

When we see God's grace operate in the lives of people who we feel don't deserve it, we have a choice: Either we can complain and feel sorry for ourselves, or we can be thankful that the God of such goodness is the One we love and serve. Comparison kills because it always leaves us wanting more, but thankfulness brings life.

In your opinion, who are some people who are getting more than they deserve?

How does comparison kill, and how does thankfulness give life?

"Into each life some rain must fall." —HENRY WADSWORTH LONGFELLOW

WHEN OUR DISAPPOINTMENTS ARE GOD'S APPOINTMENTS

It is good for me that I have been afflicted, that I may learn Your statutes.

PSALM 119:71

THE VAST MAJORITY OF US avoid suffering at all costs. We spend lots of money on electronics, entertainment, and events that make us feel comfortable, and we've developed the expectation that life "should" be fun, easy, and pleasant. We now have more "conveniences" than any other time in history, yet we complain as much or more than the people who lived before us.

From time to time, the God of love and truth steps into our misplaced expectations and shakes us up. He doesn't do this to be mean—just the opposite. He knows that the best way for us to learn life's most important lessons is through suffering. Sometimes, God wants to get our attention to redirect us. Sometimes, He needs to discipline us so that we stop a self-destructive behavior. Sometimes, He wants to display our courageous faith to others around us, and suffering lets them see into our hearts. No matter what the cause, God always wants to teach us to depend on Him, and difficulties have a marvelous way of directing the eyes of our hearts to God's love, truth, wisdom, and power.

If we develop spiritual eyes to see that God is doing something rich and wonderful in the midst of our suffering, we won't avoid it. Instead, we'll say with King David, "It is good for me that I have been afflicted"—not because it was fun, but because suffering is one of the best ways to learn life's most important lessons.

What are some disappointments you've experienced lately?

Examine your heart to determine if God might be using these difficulties to redirect you, discipline you, display your courage to others, or teach you to depend more on Him.

"Afflictions are but the shadows of God's wings." —GEORGE MACDONALD

EVEN IF HE DOES NOT

Our God whom we serve is able to deliver us from the burning fiery furnace,
and He will deliver us from your hand, O king. But if not, let it be known
to you, O king, that we do not serve your gods, nor will we worship the gold
image which you have set up. DANIEL 3:17-18

SHADRACH, MESHACH, AND ABED-NEGO had stood up strong for God in
a hostile, foreign land, and now they were facing the consequences. A royal
decree demanded that they die for their faith. It was patently unfair. They
could have been really angry with God, but instead they trusted Him. The
statement they made in that critical moment articulates rock-solid faith in
God's abilities without demanding that He act in a certain way.

Could God rescue them from the fire? Certainly. He could fix the problem in a dozen different ways. Would He? They didn't know. They didn't put a
straitjacket on God and insist that He bail them out a certain way—or bail them
out at all. They believed not only in the power of God to rescue but also in the
wisdom of God to choose when, where, and how to demonstrate His power.

Church history tells us about countless men and women who have faced
the same challenges. They served God faithfully and well, and when they were
faced with persecution and death, they put themselves in God's hands to do
whatever He chose to do. Sometimes, they were miraculously rescued; more
often, they died for their faith. Either way, they were convinced that God is faithful. God was honored by their trust in Him, and that was enough for them.

When we stand up for God in our families, at work, and in our neighborhoods, we can expect some applause, but we can also expect opposition.
When we face the consequences of our faith, will we trust in God's wisdom
as well as in His power to rescue?

What kind of opposition do believers face today?

**Do you face opposition? If so, how do you handle it? If you don't face
opposition, why not?**

"It is much easier to tell your story than to live your story." —IKE REIGHARD

REALLY THANKFUL

Thanks be to God who always leads us in triumph in Christ, and through us diffuses the fragrance of His knowledge in every place.

2 CORINTHIANS 2:14

IT'S A DELIGHT to be around thankful people. They fill up a room with their optimism, thoughtfulness, and peace. In his letter to the believers in Corinth, Paul said that such people act as a fragrant perfume that brings pleasure to every corner of a room.

Grouchy people give off a fragrance, too, but they smell like something besides perfume! Each of us knows people who seldom have anything positive to say. Even when things go well, their cynicism sours people around them.

What makes people thankful? They are known for two connected actions: remembering God's past blessings and realizing that God still gives them wonderful gifts. They look forward to the future, trusting that the One who has abundantly provided will provide yet again. Don't assume that thankful people are blind to the often painful realities in life. In fact, they can be more honest about hurts and disappointments because they don't need to hide from those things. But their hope focuses their attention away from their hurts and disappointments and onto God's character. They are convinced that sooner or later He will give them the wisdom, strength, direction, and blessing they need. Looking back at God's past faithfulness gives them confidence in Him for the future.

Who is the best example in your life of someone who is an honest and thankful person?

As you look back as well as forward, what needs to happen for you to take steps to become more thankful?

"Each day came forth from the hand of God newly created and alive with opportunities to do His will. We for our part, can accept and offer back to God every prayer, work, and suffering of the day, no matter how insignificant or unspectacular they may seem to us. Between God and the individual soul, however, there are no insignificant moments: this is the mystery of divine providence." —WALTER CISZEK

LIVING SACRIFICES

I beseech you therefore, brethren, by the mercies of God, that you present your bodies a living sacrifice, holy, acceptable to God, which is your reasonable service. And do not be conformed to this world, but be transformed by the renewing of your mind, that you may prove what is that good and acceptable and perfect will of God. ROMANS 12:1-2

WE ALL MAKE DECISIONS that involve what we could call "opportunity costs": when we say yes to one choice, we're saying no to countless other options. The question we instinctively answer each time is, What gives me the most benefit? In this passage, Paul asks his readers to reflect on all he has written in the first eleven chapters of Romans about the incredible mercy of God to rescue us from sin and give us purpose, peace, and hope. In response to God's mercy, the only "reasonable" choice is to devote ourselves wholeheartedly to Him. Paul says this devotion takes the form of a "living sacrifice," a choice we have to make each moment of every day. Do we choose to follow a cause? Yes, but much more than that, we choose to follow a person, the One who loves us, forgives us, and calls us His own.

When we say yes to God each moment, we choose a lifestyle that reflects Christ's values. Paul tells us not to be squeezed into the world's mold of selfishness, but to let God transform us as our minds focus on God's truth. The result of saying yes to God each moment is the incalculable benefit of knowing and following God's perfect will for our lives. We join hands with Him to walk on the mountains and in the valleys of the adventure of life.

What are some of the opportunity costs when a person says yes to Christ each moment?

How is the world trying to squeeze you into its mold? What can you do to have your mind renewed by God's truth?

"Our service is to be a living sacrifice of devotion to Jesus. The secret of which is to identify with him in suffering, in death and in resurrection." —OSWALD CHAMBERS

KING OF THE MOUNTAIN

Who may ascend into the hill of the LORD? Or who may stand in His holy place? He who has clean hands and a pure heart, who has not lifted up his soul to an idol, nor sworn deceitfully. PSALM 24:3-4

IN THE BUSINESS WORLD, many people get to the top by climbing over others on the way. They want to be "king of the hill," and nothing or nobody is going to stop them. But in the spiritual world, the goal isn't to stand in power in front of shareholders; it's to stand in humility and inner strength before the Lord.

In the awkward time between his anointing and his coronation as king, David had many opportunities to take shortcuts and compromise his integrity. Saul chased David and his men through deserts and towns, and on several occasions, David could have killed Saul and taken the throne immediately. His most trusted and loyal followers urged him to do just that. But each time, David refused to rush to success. He trusted God to accomplish His purposes in His timing. Through times of being misunderstood, attacked, and betrayed, David had "clean hands and a pure heart." He trusted God even in the darkest days, and he kept telling the truth.

One of the most significant features of David's life was the loyalty of his men. In him they saw a man they could trust, a man who spoke the unvarnished truth and followed God with his whole heart. Even before David became king of Israel, his character won the hearts of his men.

What are some temptations to take shortcuts to gain promotions at work?

What does it take for someone to act like David did and keep "clean hands and a pure heart"?

"The greatest use of a life is to spend it for something that will outlast it."
—WILLIAM JAMES

THE PARADOX OF LEADERSHIP

Whoever desires to become great among you, let him be your servant.

MATTHEW 20:26 { MEMORY VERSE

IN HIS OUTSTANDING BOOK *Good to Great*, Jim Collins describes a mistake many companies make when they hire a CEO. Too often, they try to get a charismatic leader who becomes, in Collins's phrase, "a genius with a thousand helpers." This person demands to be the center of attention and receive all the praise. Others in the company are "peons," just helpers who deserve no recognition. In stark contrast, Collins observed that the most successful companies have leaders who are "humble visionaries." They lead with passion, but they are happy to give plenty of credit to anyone and everyone else.*

Collins's observations fit perfectly with Jesus' leadership strategy. In reaction to the natural, normal style of leaders to demand to be the center of attention, Jesus told His followers to show their greatness by serving. He then dispelled any misconceptions of what it means to be a servant by picking up a towel and washing the dirty feet of the men at the table, the job of the lowest servant in the home.

What does it mean for us to be servants of those under us in our families and on the organizational chart? If we follow Jesus' example, we take time to do the most humble tasks: washing dishes, cleaning, sweeping, helping an intern with a task, or stopping to talk to an employee in the shipping department to ask about her family.

Are you too busy for things like that? Don't be.

What impact do "geniuses with a thousand helpers" have on those under them?

What impact do "humble visionaries" have on people? What are two things you can do today to be a servant to those around you?

"No man has ever risen to the real stature of spiritual manhood until he has found that it is finer to serve somebody else than it is to serve himself."
—**WOODROW WILSON**

"Duty makes us do things well, but love makes us do them beautifully."
—**ZIG ZIGLAR**

---

* Jim Collins, *Good to Great: Why Some Companies Make the Leap . . . and Others Don't* (New York: HarperCollins, 2001).

LET ME TELL YOU A SECRET

The secret of the LORD is with those who fear Him, and He will show them His covenant. PSALM 25:14

WE LOVE SECRETS because they often promise to bring excitement into our lives. Getting the inside scoop is a delicious feeling, and the one who listens to a secret feels valued by the one who tells it.

In the spiritual world, many things seem to be hidden. We wander and stumble around, trying to figure out how to relate to God, how to follow His will, and how to relate to His people. King David understood that God doesn't share His secrets with everybody—just with those who fear Him. The term *fear of God* isn't very popular today because it's misunderstood as being afraid of Him. It actually implies wonder and awe, a sense that God is so powerful, so intelligent, and so loving that we can hardly imagine it!

People who are overwhelmed with the awesome nature of God become good listeners, and God delights in sharing His secrets with them. What are those secrets? They aren't the winning lottery numbers for this week's drawing, and seldom are they the specific directions for what to do in a situation. No, God's secrets focus on His character. We can trust Him even when we can't see His hand at work because He assures us that He is infinitely wise, loving, and strong. And ultimately, the biggest secret of all is that God has made us His own dearly beloved children in a covenant relationship with Him. But that's not a secret anymore.

Why do you think God withholds His secrets from people who don't have great respect for Him?

What does fearing God mean to you?

"God created man on purpose, and for a purpose." —ZIG ZIGLAR

GOD'S GENTLE TUG

He gives more grace. Therefore He says: "God resists the proud, but gives grace to the humble." JAMES 4:6

HUMILITY CAN BE a difficult concept for us to grasp. It is often thought of as being weak or spineless, but that is the wrong definition of humility. A fitting example of humility can be found in the responsiveness of a fine horse to the gentle tug of its rider on the reins. When the horse was acquired, it may have been a wild bronco, but it has been broken and now gladly responds to its master's care and guidance.

The Bible describes proud people as "stiff-necked" and "willful." They demand their own way, which focuses on their selfish purposes of success, pleasure, and approval. In His kindness, God allows difficulties into our lives to break us, not to harm us but to tame the selfishness in our hearts. As long as we buck, we fight against God and His gracious purposes for us, but when we finally give in and accept His leadership in our lives, we experience more encouragement, strength, freedom, and joy than we ever imagined.

The "freedom" of the proud is an illusion. Rebellion ultimately results in shattered dreams and shattered lives. But "a broken and a contrite heart" (Psalm 51:17), one that is open to God's discipline and leading, experiences the true riches of His grace.

What are some ways you've seen God resist the proud?

Would you say you have been broken, you are being broken, or you are still running wild? Explain your answer.

"It does not take great men to do great things: it only takes consecrated men."
—PHILLIPS BROOKS

EYES ON THE OUTCOME

Count it all joy when you fall into various trials, knowing that the testing of your faith produces patience. JAMES 1:2-3

MANY CHRISTIANS READ James's comment about suffering and simply don't believe it, and those who do believe often feel frustrated and defeated because they don't see the result he promised. *Count it all joy? Oh, come on!*

To see these trials produce results in our lives, we need to undergo a radical reorientation. Years ago, cultural critic Francis Schaeffer observed that most of us supremely value "personal peace and affluence."* Anything that gets in the way of those values is, to say the least, unwelcome. But in the Kingdom of God, those things aren't all that valuable, and in fact, they can get in the way of what God truly values. He treasures our faith in Him through thick and thin, but He knows faith is built most effectively in times of difficulty. For that reason, God, our loving and attentive Father, allows or orchestrates problems in our lives so that we learn to trust Him.

Author and speaker Elisabeth Elliot notes that suffering takes all kinds of forms. Her broad definition is, "Not having what you want, or having what you don't want." Every obstacle, every annoyance, and every genuine heartache in our lives is part of God's curriculum to produce persistent, tenacious, rich, deep trust in Him. Patience isn't killing time until we experience more personal peace and affluence. It's riveting our affections on God and His purposes every moment of every day.

> What are some ways the pursuit of "personal peace and affluence" erodes patient and persistent faith in God?
>
> How would it help you to realize that every difficulty in your life is part of God's curriculum to teach you faith and patience?

> *"It does not matter how great the pressure is. What matters is where does the pressure lie? Does it push you closer to the heart of God or away from God?"*
> **—HUDSON TAYLOR**

---

* Francis A. Schaeffer, *How Should We Then Live? The Rise and Decline of Western Thought and Culture* (Wheaton, IL: Crossway, 1976), 205.

GOD'S PEACE PLAN

The LORD will give strength to His people; the LORD will bless His people with peace. PSALM 29:11

MANY OF US HAVE an entirely wrong idea about peace. We think it can only be found in the absence of hassles, but that's not the way King David saw it. In this brief psalm, he recounts a few of the wonders of God's power. He describes a violent thunderstorm that breaks over Lebanon, north of Israel, its lightning shattering the sky and trees and its thunder frightening the animals in the forest. Finally, David reminds us that God showed the power of His hand and His righteous judgment against sin by sending the Flood to destroy the entire population except for Noah and his family.

Out of this power and majesty, God gives His people strength and peace. A heart at rest doesn't come only from the absence of problems. Far more significantly, God's peace can be ours any time we focus on His greatness, His involvement with His Creation, and His tender care. With that perception, we can experience God's peace even in the middle of the storms of life. That's God's peace plan. Our part is to fill our minds with the wonder of His strength, and as our faith grows, so will our sense of God's peace.

What's the connection between wonder and peace?

What are some things you can do to increase your sense of wonder at God's power?

"God takes life's broken pieces and gives us unbroken peace."
—**WILBERT DONALD GOUGH**

SPIRIT AND TRUTH

[Jesus said,] "The hour is coming, and now is, when the true worshipers will worship the Father in spirit and truth; for the Father is seeking such to worship Him. God is Spirit, and those who worship Him must worship in spirit and truth." JOHN 4:23-24

THE SAMARITAN WOMAN at the well thought that people could connect with God only at particular places and in particular ways (see John 4:20). Jesus gently told her that God is bigger than that—a lot bigger! Places and rituals aren't the essentials of a relationship with God. Jesus explains that, instead, there are two rails that keep us on track: spirit and truth. Both are necessary for a vibrant, growing relationship with God.

In today's verse, John quotes Jesus as saying, "God is Spirit." We operate in the physical world, but God has put eternity in our hearts (see Ecclesiastes 3:11) with an awareness of the unseen world. It's easy, though, to be attracted to any of the myriad of spiritual experiences promised by other religions and New Age philosophies. Jesus reminded the woman (and us) that the second rail in our pursuit of God is truth. The Scriptures tell us the truth about the nature of God, the way He relates to us, His instructions about life and relationships, and the consequences of turning our backs on Him.

Our expanding grasp of truth, though, can lead only to pride if we aren't sensitive to God's Spirit, who points out our selfishness and points us back to God again and again. Spirit and truth—both are essential in our walk with God.

Which are you more attracted to, spiritual experiences or biblical truth?

What would a strong blend of both look like in your life?

"Many times Christians state their love for the Lord and their willingness to die for Him. I will make no pretense of knowing the Lord's will in your life, but I do feel that in most cases the Lord is far more interested in our living for Him than He is in our dying for Him." —ZIG ZIGLAR

THE GOSPEL IN A NUTSHELL

God so loved the world that He gave His only begotten Son, that whoever believes in Him should not perish but have everlasting life. JOHN 3:16 { MEMORY VERSE

JOHN 3:16 is the most frequently quoted verse in the Bible. We see it sprayed on highway overpasses, held up on signs at football games, and printed on the bottom of cups at fast-food restaurants. Jesus' words are so familiar that we run the risk of forgetting their significance. We are wise to look at the verse as if we've never seen it before.

The statement is shocking! We had literally nothing to offer God—no bargaining chips to twist His arm and no virtue to win His acceptance—but God didn't wait for a better deal. Because He loved, He took the initiative to give, and His gift brought the cleansing of forgiveness and the promise of being with Him forever.

We can measure love by how much the lover gives, and in this one verse of Scripture, we find that God gave everything. Jesus had spent all eternity in Heaven being worshiped and served by a host of angels, but He stepped out of Heaven to earth for one purpose: not to live, but to die. And because He died for us, we don't have to experience the excruciating separation from Him for eternity that the Bible calls Hell.

Look at the words in the verse as if it's the first time you ever saw them. He loved, He gave, He forgives, and He rescues. That's the gospel in a nutshell.

How does it affect you to read this verse as if it's the first time you ever saw it?

Have you accepted His promise? Who else needs to hear it?

"In order to create there must be a dynamic force. And what force is greater than love?" —IGOR STRAVINSKY

"You are not saved by a feeling, but by trusting God and accepting Jesus Christ as your Savior." —ZIG ZIGLAR

WELL, SHUT MY MOUTH!

Whoever guards his mouth and tongue keeps his soul from troubles.

PROVERBS 21:23

THE PRINCIPLE TAUGHT in this verse is one of the most empirically obvious in God's creation, but most of us still need remedial classes to learn the lesson. How many times do we roll our eyes and think, *How could I have said something so stupid?*

We can keep our souls from trouble—the trouble that comes from others tormenting us for hurting them or from the nagging guilt from saying dumb things—only if we actively guard our mouths. Here are some commonsense suggestions that can change your life:

- Every morning, ask God for wisdom about your words.

- Before any significant conversation, take a minute to define your goals. Also, identify any topics or issues to avoid or treat diplomatically.

- Watch out for any temptation to use sarcasm to get a laugh. (Stopping that habit may severely limit the number of words some of us use!)

- In conversations, be aware that words can kill or cure. If you feel emotions rising, take a deep breath and don't let your words fly!

- From time to time, give yourself a progress report on how well you're guarding your mouth.

For all of us, learning a new skill takes time and effort. And for some of us, the learning curve for guarding our words is really steep. Still, the peace of mind and joy of relationships are worth the effort.

In what specific kinds of situations does your mouth get you in trouble?

What steps will you take today to guard your mouth?

"I have never had to apologize for something I did not say." —IKE REIGHARD

THE TURNAROUND ARTIST

You have turned for me my mourning into dancing; You have put off my sackcloth and clothed me with gladness. PSALM 30:11

KING DAVID'S LIFE was far from the life of ease we picture a king having. He dealt with enemies who were attacking him, poor health, and discouragement and hopelessness. In this psalm, he recounts a time when he felt especially depressed because, just after he had bragged about doing so well, it seemed God had abandoned him (see Psalm 30:7)! But David didn't stop looking for God. He cried out to Him, and eventually, He turned his life around.

Even a casual reading of David's psalms shows us that David wasn't afraid to be honest with God. Over and over again, he poured out his heart, sometimes in praise, but often in complaints that God seemed to be mistreating him or abandoning him. In almost every painfully honest psalm of David, we read in the end about God's resolution and relief.

The lesson for us is clear: God wants us to be honest with Him. He doesn't want us to be "plastic" Christians who always put on a happy face. David's example is that only through gut-level honesty, exposing our hurts and hopes to God, can we find Him. In this psalm and in many others, David doesn't tell us when or how the answers came. He just tells us they did come, and that's all we need to know. God delights in turning our mourning into dancing, but first we have to trust Him enough to be completely honest with Him.

Is it easy or hard for you to be genuinely honest with God? Explain your answer.

What are some things in your life right now that need to be turned from mourning to dancing?

"Extraordinary afflictions are not always the punishment of extraordinary sins, but sometimes the trial of extraordinary graces. Sanctified afflictions are spiritual promotions." —MATTHEW HENRY

COME NEXT SPRING

Agrippa said to Paul, "You almost persuade me to become a Christian."

ACTS 26:28

ALMOST. What a tragic word! It speaks of potential, desire, and possibility, but it also tells us about the devastation of hesitation. King Agrippa had listened to Paul explain the message of Christ's forgiveness in great detail. Everyone else, it seemed, was impressed with Paul's story and God's promise of eternal life. The king's faith, though, was blocked by reluctance, by "what ifs" and "but what abouts." His reaction was tragic, like the buds of early spring that promise new life but for some reason never flower.

It doesn't have to be that way. When Jesus spoke to Andrew and Peter, James and John, they listened intently, and then Jesus invited them to follow Him. Immediately, they dropped their fishing nets and went with Jesus (see Matthew 4:18-22; Mark 1:16-20), beginning the greatest adventure life has to offer.

Paul didn't invite Agrippa to respond until he had heard the full message of forgiveness and new life, and Jesus didn't invite the fishermen to follow Him until they had heard His story. But at a point, the offer was given and choices were made. Have you heard God's message? Did you hesitate and miss out on the adventure of a lifetime, or did you drop your nets and follow Jesus?

Why do you think some listen and respond but others listen and hesitate?

In what ways are you hesitating, and in what ways are you following Jesus with all your heart?

"Never put off until tomorrow what you can do today." —BENJAMIN FRANKLIN

THE PROMISE TO AN OVERCOMER

To him who overcomes I will grant to sit with Me on My throne, as I also overcame and sat down with My Father on His throne. REVELATION 3:21

EARLY IN JOHN'S ACCOUNT of his revelation from Christ, he tells of Jesus' observations of and directions for the seven churches. Some were following Him with integrity and faith, but some were struggling. The believers at Laodicea had some problems. Was it persecution for their faith? No. Were they suffering economic hardships? No. Had they experienced the devastation of a natural disaster? Not at all. Christ tells them that He isn't pleased with them because they are spiritually apathetic (see Revelation 3:14-16).

These believers were so wealthy that they didn't feel the need for God. Instead of seeing their riches as gifts from God and using their wealth to help others, they spent it on themselves. Jesus looked beneath their superficial riches into their hearts. He told them they were actually "wretched, miserable, poor, blind, and naked" (Revelation 3:17). The solution was to turn to Him for forgiveness and to change the direction of their lives.

God allows difficulties in our lives so we may overcome them. For some, it's poverty or an addiction or physical illness or a tragic accident or natural disaster. But for others, it's the burden of wealth. Some of the wealthy lack insight about where their wealth came from or how to use it. God calls all of us to trust Him in overcoming the problems in our lives, but those who are rich face the added difficulty of realizing that wealth can be a hindrance to vibrant faith.

In what ways can wealth be a serious obstacle to following Christ?

What do repentance and overcoming look like for a rich person?

"Our strength grows out of our weakness." —RALPH WALDO EMERSON

A SURE CURE FOR TROUBLED HEARTS

[Jesus said,] "Let not your heart be troubled; you believe in God, believe also in Me. In My Father's house are many mansions; if it were not so, I would have told you. I go to prepare a place for you. And if I go and prepare a place for you, I will come again and receive you to Myself; that where I am, there you may be also." JOHN 14:1-3

JESUS HAD JUST DELIVERED news to His disciples that rocked their world. Earlier, He had described a series of calamities that the world would experience in the last days. His men probably thought, *That sounds terrible, but at least Jesus will go through it with us.* But now He tells them, "I'm leaving. First I'll be killed, and then I'll be leaving you" (see John 12:23-24; 13:33). The looks on their faces probably told Jesus that He should give them some desperately needed perspective.

Our faith in God, He explained, gives us ultimate security. Though we may experience all kinds of difficulties and heartaches, we can count on God's love and on our place with Him in eternity. With that assurance, our hearts aren't nearly as troubled.

To give His disciples confidence, Jesus explained that each of them would have a permanent home in heaven. During the three years they had followed Him, the disciples had never had a place they could call home. Though Jesus was going away, His promise of a home must have meant a lot to them. Jesus also promised that He would be with them again, both in Heaven and when He would return to earth to rule during the Millennium.

When disturbing news troubles us, we can count on God's promises. In this case, Jesus promised the ultimate security of a home in heaven and the ultimate thrill of being with Him forever. That's a sure cure for troubled hearts.

What are things that sometimes (or often) trouble your heart?

How do these promises give you confidence and peace?

"Worry does not empty tomorrow of its sorrow; it empties today of its strength."
—CORRIE TEN BOOM

THE GOD OF THE VALLEYS

A man of God came and spoke to the king of Israel, and said, "Thus says the Lord: 'Because the Syrians have said, "The Lord is God of the hills, but He is not God of the valleys," therefore I will deliver all this great multitude into your hand, and you shall know that I am the Lord.'" 1 KINGS 20:28

THE SYRIANS WERE a lot like many of us. They believed that God was in control only on the mountains and was absent in the valleys. We often believe that God is attentive and active when times are good and we are on the "mountaintops" of life, but we often see difficulties, or "valleys," as a sign that God can't be trusted. In our age of affluence, many of us expect God to give us trouble-free lives of peace and plenty. But God often has a different agenda. He knows that faith is forged most often in the hot fires of difficulties, in the valleys of our lives, so He takes us into these valleys to build our trust in Him.

Will we find God when we've experienced a tragic loss through death, disease, divorce, or some other major setback in our families, at work, or in our health? Author C. S. Lewis famously observed, "God whispers to us in our pleasures, speaks in our conscience, but shouts in our pains: It is His megaphone to rouse a deaf world."* In the valleys, we may have to wait for an answer from God, but we can be sure an answer will come. God delights in revealing Himself to us. Sometimes He shows Himself quickly, and sometimes He delays for a while.

If you are in one of life's valleys and are tempted to assume that God has abandoned you, remember that He is the God of the valley just as much as the God of the mountain.

What do you normally think about God when you are in one of life's valleys?

How does Lewis's statement encourage you to keep pursuing God in times like that?

"He who offers God a second place offers Him no place." —JOHN RUSKIN

---

* C. S. Lewis, "Quote DB," http://www.quotedb.com/quotes/594.

SELF-FULFILLING PROPHECY

Fulfill my joy by being like-minded, having the same love, being of one accord, of one mind. Let nothing be done through selfish ambition or conceit, but in lowliness of mind let each esteem others better than himself. Let each of you look out not only for his own interests, but also for the interests of others. PHILIPPIANS 2:2-4

THE PARADOX OF LIFE is that by giving, we receive; by sacrificing, we gain; and by putting others first, we feel fulfilled. Some people get it. Newborn babies certainly don't have much success or many skills to offer, but they give their mothers and fathers tremendous joy. Employers who celebrate their people's successes more than their own reap the joy of their employees' smiles and greater productivity, the natural product of feeling affirmed.

We experience this paradox, however, only when we start at the right point: "lowliness of mind." Thinking properly about ourselves is the first step. Instead of selfish ambition to achieve status, we feel secure in God's love. Instead of conceit that we're better than others, we value others highly. Some people confuse humility with shame, but humility doesn't mean we despise ourselves and demean our abilities. Instead, it means that we see our abilities as gifts from God to be used to build others up and accomplish His purposes. As we see all we have and all we are as gifts from God, we can stop promoting or defending ourselves, and we can focus our attention on others around us. Their needs become important to us. That's how Christ lived, and as we walk with Him, that's how we'll live too.

Why, do you think, are most people (and even many Christians) so self-focused?

What would it take for you to live this paradox? How would it impact your relationships?

"You can have everything in life you want, if you will just help enough other people get what they want." —ZIG ZIGLAR

RUN TO WIN

Do you not know that those who run in a race all run, but one receives the prize? Run in such a way that you may obtain it. And everyone who competes for the prize is temperate in all things. Now they do it to obtain a perishable crown, but we for an imperishable crown. 1 CORINTHIANS 9:24-25 { MEMORY VERSE

THE APOSTLE PAUL was very familiar with Greek culture, including the Olympic Games. In this particular passage, he used the metaphor of a race to describe the Christian life. *Finishing* the race wasn't good enough for Paul. He wanted to *win* his race, and he wanted to inspire all of us to win our races too.

Athletes in ancient Greece were incredibly popular, just as athletes are today. They trained, worked, and labored under their coaches' instructions for one purpose: to be the one standing on the podium, wearing the laurel wreath of a champion. Everything in their lives was subjugated to that purpose, and everything was evaluated by how it contributed or detracted from winning the race. Dedication. Intensity. Passion. Focus. Those were the traits of athletes who strove to win, just as they are for athletes today.

Paul encourages us to run with the same fierce dedication to winning our race. We honor Christ with everything we are and everything we do. But our reward is different. The day after the race at the Olympic Games, the laurel wreath had already wilted, but our wreath is imperishable, lasting for all of eternity.

Some rewards don't mean much because we didn't work hard for them. The imperishable crown of victory we win for following Christ, though, matters because it is dearly won. It's worth the effort.

What do you think the "imperishable crown" symbolizes?

Is it worth fierce dedication in your life? Why or why not?

"God will not look you over for medals, degrees, or diplomas but for scars."
—ELBERT HUBBARD

"I win not because of my own efforts or my own goodness, but rather through the grace, love, and mercy of my Lord and Savior, Jesus Christ. He died so that I might win this game of life and live with Him forever." —ZIG ZIGLAR

FATHER KNOWS BEST

Thus says the LORD, your Redeemer, the Holy One of Israel: "I am the LORD your God, who teaches you to profit, who leads you by the way you should go."

ISAIAH 48:17

GOD SEEMS TO SPEND a lot of time in the book of Isaiah warning His people of the trouble they'll experience if they wander away from Him, but He also reminds them again and again of the benefits of following Him. The question for the people of Israel then and for us today is, Has God proven He is trustworthy?

Like little children, we may choose to obey God to avoid punishment and experience rewards. While those are certainly strong motivations, God appeals to us to respond in a more mature way, to enjoy a rich relationship instead of just the consequences of punishments and rewards. He reminds us of His role as our Redeemer, who paid a high price to forgive us, and He tells us again about His character as a God of infinite love and blinding holiness. By His actions and His nature, He has proven that we can trust Him.

Trust implies relationship and interaction. God will lead us as we stay connected to Him. We'll be attentive to the "still small voice" of the Spirit as He whispers to us, and we'll respond when He reminds us of passages of Scripture that give us guidance. That's what it means to be led by God, and when it comes to the direction of our lives, our Heavenly Father knows best. But if we are too busy to pray or too preoccupied to pay attention to the Spirit, we'll miss His leading.

What are some reasons people trust God's leadership in their lives?

What needs to happen so that you are more responsive to His leading?

"The hardness of God is kinder than the softness of men, and his compulsion is our liberation." —C. S. LEWIS

LOVE'S LITMUS TEST

[Jesus said,] "A new commandment I give to you, that you love one another; as I have loved you, that you also love one another. By this all will know that you are My disciples, if you have love for one another." JOHN 13:34-35

MAKE NO MISTAKE: Jesus was a revolutionary. He didn't overthrow the political establishment, but He turned the spiritual world upside down. In the culture of His day, people lived by the "law of retaliation," which is commonly stated as "an eye for an eye." This principle says that an injured person has the right to retaliate to the same extent as the offense. Jesus, though, told His followers that He had a different law: Forgive your enemies.

In the final week before He was killed, Jesus gave instructions to His men, and His directive for believers' relationships with one another was just as revolutionary as His message about enemies. He instructed them to "love one another; as I have loved you." We can imagine the power of that statement to men who had been with Jesus for over three years. They had seen Him overlook a thousand offenses, they had watched Him forgive a thousand sarcastic remarks, and they had witnessed Him return kindness for coldness a thousand times. Suddenly, they realized He was telling them to love one another with the same patience, forgiveness, and kindness He had shown toward them countless times.

Loving people comes down to choices. When we're tempted to compete with people to show we're superior, to compare ourselves with them, or to engage in petty jealousies and gossip, we need to stop, think about the way Jesus loved, and choose a different course. Love doesn't happen because we use flowery words or express good intentions. It becomes real in our difficult choices every day.

How would you describe Jesus' love for His followers?

Who is one person to whom you need to show more of Christ's love?

"The fundamental issue in life and Scripture is the ability and willingness to forgive like God." —**IKE REIGHARD**

SPIRITUAL REDWOODS

Behold, how good and how pleasant it is for brethren to dwell together in unity! PSALM 133:1

WE'VE ALL HEARD STORIES (too many stories) of organizations, companies, and churches that disintegrated into bitter conflict. Quite often, the conflict began with someone shifting blame for a failure, petty gossip that caused hurt, envy that someone else was treated better, or fierce competition that produced genuine bitterness. Whatever the cause, people took their eyes off the common goal and started protecting themselves. That's no way to build a team!

But unity isn't the goal. Rather, unity is a result, one of a shared vision and cooperative efforts. In families, companies, churches, or any other organization, leaders can build unity by living for and pointing people toward a purpose that transcends each individual. With that goal in mind, they can identify and affirm each person's abilities and contributions, overlook petty issues, and communicate with clarity and compassion. When each person feels valued and included, incredible things can happen! People develop their skills, grow more committed to the cause, and encourage one another. In this environment, they grow as tall and strong as redwoods!

What's the temperature of your family or organization? If you aren't "dwelling together in unity," don't try to force it. Instead, focus your energies on clarifying a purpose and enlisting cooperation to achieve a common goal. It'll make a difference in those around you . . . and in you.

> **Describe the climate in your family, company, church, or other organization.**
>
> **What can you do to clarify the purpose and enlist cooperation?**

> *"Leadership is the ability to organize the spiritual gifts and limitations of others."*
> —J. OSWALD SANDERS

DOING GOD'S WILL

This Book of the Law shall not depart from your mouth, but you shall meditate in it day and night, that you may observe to do according to all that is written in it. For then you will make your way prosperous, and then you will have good success. JOSHUA 1:8

MANY SINCERE BELIEVERS are confused about the will of God. They've heard stories of God speaking to others to tell them what to do, and they've read accounts of God giving someone a chain of circumstances providing an unmistakable path through one of life's quagmires. Voices and signs, these confused believers assume, should be the norm in knowing God's will.

God can use any method He chooses to lead His children, but certainly His Word is the surest, yet most neglected, compass. The Scriptures are referred to as a "lamp to my feet and a light to my path" by the psalmist in Psalm 119:105. They are the source of wisdom to sort out black, white, and gray in our lives, and they expose the heart of God. In addition, they sometimes painfully expose our own hearts so that we can admit we are headed in the wrong direction and repent.

If the Bible is such a wonderful source of insight, encouragement, and direction, why do we spend so little time in its pages and expect God to lead us in some other way? Because studying the Bible takes work. It contains vast riches, but only a few of them are on the surface. The bigger veins of gold require effort to dig out. But for those of us who mine these treasures and follow their leading, God promises wisdom and success in relationships with Him and others. If we are wise, we cultivate the habit of internalizing God's truth so that we meditate in it day and night (see Psalm 1:2). That's a lot more productive than many other ways we spend our time.

Describe the blend of how God uses circumstances, the Spirit's whisper, and His Word to guide us.

What would it take (in motivation, discipline, and time) for you to make internalizing God's Word a habit in your life?

"When we want to know God's will there are three things which always concur. The inward impulse, the word of God, and the trend of circumstances. Never act until these three things agree." —F. B. MEYER

APPROVED BY GOD

Be diligent to present yourself approved to God, a worker who does not need to be ashamed, rightly dividing the word of truth. 2 TIMOTHY 2:15

NOT EVERY SPEAKER who talks about God is godly, and not every author who writes about spiritual life is writing about God's truth. In Timothy's world, as in ours, a lot of popular teaching about God sounded good but was at least "a half bubble off center." In the first century, some teachers said that man's spirit is entirely good and the body is entirely wicked. Those teachers claimed to have special knowledge beyond what was written in the Bible, but their teaching resulted in confusion and rampant sin. Today, far too many of us simply accept what a teacher says about God and spirituality. Paul told Timothy to study and to dig deep in order to find out what's true and what can't be trusted.

One of the most common messages we hear is that God wants all of us to be rich and healthy. All we need to do is ask Him—and perhaps give a wad of money to the teacher's ministry—and God will give us everything we want. To many people, this sounds very attractive; however, those who have read the Scriptures know that, while God promises blessings, they are often spiritual ones—not necessarily financial and physical blessings—and they often are experienced in the crucible of suffering. That's a very different message!

We are wise to follow Paul's advice to Timothy to study the Scriptures diligently. They are the source of truth, and we discover this truth by reading verses in the context of longer passages, by using trusted resources like study Bibles, and by listening to respected teachers.

Does it really matter that we dig deeper? Only if we want to pursue God and live by His truth instead of a counterfeit, and only if we want to be approved by Him.

What are some popular teachings that you suspect might not be the full and accurate truth?

What would it mean for you to be diligent in studying God's Word? What are some resources you can use?

"Happiness is neither virtue nor pleasure, nor this thing or that, but simple growth. We are happy when we are growing." —W. B. YEATS

HEALING TOUCH

[The Lord] heals the brokenhearted and binds up their wounds.

PSALM 147:3

WHEN WE EXPERIENCE the trauma of loss—through death, disease, rejection, or any other kind of major setback—we naturally and instantly ask why. That's not an idle question. We desperately want to find an answer because we believe that the answer will help us regain control of our lives. However, those of us who have found restoration and healing through grief know "Why?" is the wrong question. In most cases, we may be able to point to a human cause for our pain, but we can't figure out why God allowed it or caused it, and we are left angry, confused, and bitter. A far better question is, "What now?"

When Elisabeth Elliot experienced the devastation of losing her beloved husband when he was killed by the Auca Indians, she recognized that she couldn't dwell on all her grief all the time. It was simply overwhelming. So she determined to do "the next thing," even and especially if it was only sweeping or cleaning or cooking dinner. Focusing on the next thing gave her a tangible step to take in her grief, and eventually, God healed her broken heart and bound up her wounds.

We live in the information age, and we expect to know the answers to our questions immediately. But God will not be rushed. We are wise to change our question from "Why?" to "What now?" and choose to do the next thing. As we look to Him, in time God will touch our hearts to heal and restore.

What might be the outcome in our faith if we insist on knowing why something happened?

Describe how God has healed your broken heart.

"I do not pray for a lighter load, but for a stronger back." —PHILLIPS BROOKS

CALLED WITH A PURPOSE

We know that all things work together for good to those who love God, to those who are the called according to His purpose. ROMANS 8:28 {MEMORY VERSE}

PAUL'S ASSURANCE in his letter to the Romans is one of the most quoted and least understood passages in the New Testament. When some people hear the verse, they flare up in anger because they think Paul is saying that the traumatic event they've just experienced is good. But that's not at all what he's saying.

Paul is inviting us to remember—in every situation, even the most painful ones—the final result of our lives' tapestry. We should remember that the God of love, wisdom, and strength has the ability to weave the dark threads of our lives in with the light-colored ones to produce something beautiful. In our pain, all we can see is the back of the fabric, but we can be assured that God will produce something fine out of it.

Although God promises to work things for our good, the promise of this verse isn't that things will work out the way we want them to. God is the weaver, and events are the threads. Our lives are just the loom on which He works to create His masterpiece. In many cases, we find that God's design is quite different from what we hoped, dreamed, or even contemplated. We can either follow the design He has planned, or we can continue to demand our own way. One leads to life and peace; the other, to anger and despair. Choose wisely, with faith in God and His design.

What are some difficult things you've been facing?

What difference would it make for you to believe that God can weave those painful experiences into the fabric of your life and create something beautiful?

"God is too good to be unkind; too wise to be mistaken. When you cannot trace His hand, you can trust His heart." —CHARLES HADDON SPURGEON

"Mankind is all too often inclined to take credit for his accomplishments, but when things go wrong, he blames God." —ZIG ZIGLAR

BE REALLY HAPPY!

[Jesus said,] "Blessed are the poor in spirit, for theirs is the kingdom of heaven."

MATTHEW 5:3

IN HIS MOST FAMOUS MESSAGE, Jesus addressed a large crowd of people who had come to a hillside to hear Him. As He began to speak, the things He said were so different from anything the people had ever heard that He must have sounded as if He were from another planet! We call this list of statements "the Beatitudes." Each one begins with the description of people being "blessed," a word that means to be happy—really happy. People had never been taught that they could experience joy like this, so Jesus' words almost certainly startled them. Happiness, Jesus explained in each one, comes from the most unlikely sources.

First, Jesus told the crowd that those who are "poor in spirit" can be really happy. Ironically, genuine joy comes from the soul-jarring insight that we are spiritually bankrupt, with nothing to offer. This isn't a false modesty. It's the real thing! Pride ruins relationships—with God and with everybody else. When we measure ourselves by other people, we might look pretty good, but when we compare our motives and our behavior to the fierce purity, perfection, and majesty of Almighty God, we quickly become aware that we fall short—way short.

This painful realization, though, opens the door to God's forgiveness, His purpose, and His presence. That's what the Kingdom of Heaven is all about—the experience of God in our lives on earth and in Heaven.

Few of us long to be spiritually bankrupt, but a gripping sense of need as we stand before God is the first and most important step for us to gain insight about what really matters. Then we can experience the wonder of knowing God.

Has there ever been a time when you felt "poor in spirit"? If so, describe it.

In what way is the reality of our spiritual need an open door to experiencing God?

"Jesus clothed the Beatitudes with His own life." —CARL F. HENRY

"I must recognize that the enemy within the camp—the flesh, the old nature, self, I, the old Adam—is a usurper. By faith I must reckon him to be in the place that God put him—crucified with Christ. I must realize that now my life is hid with Christ in God; that He is my life." —MAJOR IAN THOMAS

COMFORT WHEN IT COUNTS

[Jesus said,] "Blessed are those who mourn, for they shall be comforted."

MATTHEW 5:4

MOST OF US immediately think of the death of a loved one when we identify things we grieve for, but we also grieve over other losses in life, such as the death of a dream, the loss of companionship, betrayal by friends, or chronic health problems. Yet our deepest sense of loss is of a spiritual nature. We mourn when we feel a sense of personal spiritual bankruptcy, realize our own sinfulness, and see our need to repent.

People today aren't good at mourning and repenting. We live in a society that promises immediate answers to problems and quick relief from pain. Gradually, most of us have come to believe that mourning is somehow sub-human. We've concluded that life should always be pleasant, but that's not the way it works. We live in a fallen world with fallen people. Hurts happen, and quite often they happen to us!

In this beatitude, Jesus tells us that genuine comfort occurs only when we are honest about our spiritual condition. When we repent and express our disillusionment to God, we become receptive to His forgiveness. We may begin by demanding to know why the sin happened, but sooner or later, we'll realize that God knows, God cares, and God has a gracious purpose that is far bigger than whatever sin we have committed. We stop asking, "Why?" We put our hands in His hand, and we ask, "What now?" Repentance is taking the first step back toward God's very best purpose for our lives.

What are some events in which you need closure on a spiritual level?

What does it (or would it) mean for you to genuinely experience God's forgiveness for your failures?

"It's not what happens to you that determines how far you will go in life; it's how you handle what happens to you." —ZIG ZIGLAR

MEEK AIN'T WEAK

[Jesus said,] "Blessed are the meek, for they shall inherit the earth."

MATTHEW 5:5

THE WORD MEEK has a bad reputation. Most people hear it and think of someone cowering in timidity, but that's not what the word means. It actually means "power under control," like the strength and beauty of a champion racehorse under the direction of an expert jockey.

Meekness doesn't come naturally. Often, we see the opposite extreme of angry defiance or wilting fear. Meekness isn't a blend of those two traits; it's altogether different. God has given all of us a set of abilities and character qualities. We are gifted in relationships, tasks, goals, or reasoning, and our personalities shape the way we interact with people and the way we fulfill our responsibilities. Desire is completely normal, but too often, our desires control us instead of our controlling them.

Meekness acknowledges that all our abilities and qualities are gifts from the hand of God, but we also recognize that we distort God's original intentions when we pursue selfish aims. We thank God for all He has given us, and we put it all in His hands. Like the horse responding to the jockey's directions, we move in concert with God's instruction. And like the horse, we may sometimes need a little stronger motivation! The Scriptures tell us that the humble will be exalted (see Luke 18:14). When we allow God's Spirit to direct us, a world of possibilities opens up to us. That's what it means to "inherit the earth."

How would you define meekness?

What would your life look like if your strengths were under God's guidance?

"A man can counterfeit love, he can counterfeit faith, he can counterfeit hope, and all the other graces, but it is very difficult to counterfeit humility." —D. L. MOODY

FILL 'ER UP

[Jesus said,] "Blessed are those who hunger and thirst for righteousness, for they shall be filled." MATTHEW 5:6

NOTHING SATISFIES like a good meal. All day, we anticipate dinner with friends, and it turns out to be as good as we'd imagined! When we finish the dessert and the last cup of coffee, we push back our chairs and relax with our friends. We're "filled" in every way.

A fine dinner with good friends is perfect imagery for the satisfaction we experience when we hunger and thirst for God and His purposes. Hunger and thirst aren't aberrations in life; they are, in fact, signs of life. When we long, want, and desire the things of God, our hearts fill with His wisdom, love, and peace.

Jesus makes a point of saying that we experience real satisfaction when we long for righteousness. That word isn't used often today because it sounds, well, too churchy. Think of righteousness as a plumb line—a device that indicates when something is exactly vertical. Surveyors and builders use plumb lines, and we should too. The plumb line of righteousness in our lives isn't somebody's arbitrary list of dos and don'ts. Instead, it's a sign of our passion to please God in everything we say and do. If we care that much about God, we won't have to worry about the details.

> **What do you hunger and thirst for—to please yourself, to please God, or some combination? Explain your answer.**
>
> **How would it change your life if you realized that true satisfaction comes from a deep desire to please God?**

> *"The true value of anything is known only when it is wanted."* —J. N. DARBY

A LITTLE KINDNESS, PLEASE!

[Jesus said,] "Blessed are the merciful, for they shall obtain mercy."

MATTHEW 5:7

JESUS COULD HARDLY have made it any clearer: If you want to be on the receiving end of kindness, you have to show kindness to others first. It's the law of sowing and reaping. Mercy is responding compassionately to someone's hurt, going the extra mile to help people in need, and being willing to listen when someone wants to talk. Some of us are naturally predisposed to be merciful, but for others, it's a tough task!

Those who delight in justice want to see the guilty punished, wrongs righted, and boxes checked off so that they can move on to more pleasant things in life. But hurting people are all around us, and they'll always be here. Some are obvious, some are hidden, and some live in the same house as we do. We won't have a prayer of being merciful unless we notice people in need.

If our instant response to others in need is, "Well, they get what they deserve," then we haven't realized that, by God's grace, we *don't* get what we really deserve. If we have difficulty showing mercy—and some of us show it everywhere but at home—then we first need to go to the Cross to realize the wealth of God's grace, mercy, kindness, and forgiveness given to us. With this realization fresh on our hearts, we'll be quicker to extend mercy to others in need around us.

We don't have to wait for someone else to begin the reciprocity of mercy. God has already started it. We just need to respond to Him . . . and to people in need.

Describe a time when someone extended mercy to you. How did it affect you?

How would it affect your most difficult relationship if you were merciful to that person?

"Constant kindness can accomplish much. As the sun makes the ice melt, kindness causes misunderstandings, mistrust and hostility to evaporate."
—ALBERT SCHWEITZER

NO DISTRACTIONS

[Jesus said,] "Blessed are the pure in heart, for they shall see God."

MATTHEW 5:8

"ARE YOU KIDDING?" someone might ask. "All of us have selfish *thoughts* even if we hide our selfish *behaviors*. How can anyone be 'pure in heart'?"

Good question. It was tough in Jesus' day to have a pure heart—which is a heart that overcomes selfishness and is riveted on the greatness and the purposes of God—and it's just as difficult now. When our eyes wander to look at beautiful and tempting things, our hearts quickly follow. We make solemn vows to change, but we fail again and again.

Purity of heart isn't perfection. Instead, it's the passionate desire to know and follow Christ. In this life, we'll experience all kinds of temptations, distractions, and detours, but God is looking for men and women who will keep pursuing Him, even if we stumble from time to time.

Jesus promises that we will be richly rewarded for pursuing God with all our hearts. We'll see God as He speaks to us through the Scriptures, as He works in us to change our hearts, and as He works through us to have an impact on others. As our hearts become more pure, we will care less and less about how much money, fame, or power we possess, and we'll care more and more about pleasing the One who loves us so much.

What would a passionate pursuit of God look like in your life?

What are you willing to abandon in order to truly see God?

"Let the seeking man reach a place where life and lips join to say continually, 'Be thou exalted,' and a thousand minor problems will be solved at once. His Christian life ceases to be the complicated thing it had been before and becomes the very essence of simplicity." —A. W. TOZER

BUILDING BRIDGES

[Jesus said,] "Blessed are the peacemakers, for they shall be called sons of God."

MATTHEW 5:9

CONFLICT IS SO COMMON in our culture that we barely notice it anymore. But simmering anger soon turns into destructive bitterness, hatred, and the desire to take revenge, which destroy relationships. Some of us use more subtle means to hurt others. We put them down, and when they challenge us, we say, "Hey, I was only kidding!" Yeah, right.

In conflict, some of us clench our fists, raise our voices, make demands, and try to intimidate people. Others look down to avoid eye contact, barely mumble above a whisper, and give in to stop the argument. Neither of these poses, though, builds bridges of trust and understanding.

A peacemaker is someone who treasures relationships based on mutual respect and works hard to help people take steps in that direction. In some cases, a simple misunderstanding can be resolved fairly easily, but long-standing, deep wounds take time and attention to heal. Gradually, suspicion turns to understanding, and bitterness gives way to forgiveness.

When we've benefited from a peacemaker who stepped in to build bridges between us and someone we've despised, we are amazed and grateful for the peacemaker's work. Peacemakers are, indeed, "sons of God," who follow the pattern of the Prince of Peace by offering hope, trust, and relief to people whose relationships have been shredded by hatred.

How has conflict affected your stress levels, your happiness, and your relationships?

Where and how might you be a peacemaker to build bridges between people in conflict?

"The meek man will attain a place of soul rest. As he walks on in meekness, he will be happy to let God defend him. The old struggle to defend himself is over. He has found a peace which meekness brings." —A. W. TOZER

SLAMMED

[Jesus said,] "Blessed are those who are persecuted for righteousness' sake, for theirs is the kingdom of heaven." MATTHEW 5:10

JESUS TAUGHT this beatitude early in His career, but perhaps He was already thinking about the last week of His life, when He would be killed by religious leaders who felt threatened by His life and teachings. Jesus told those who followed Him, "A disciple is not above his teacher" (Matthew 10:24). Those who follow Jesus can expect to be attacked by people who feel threatened by the truth.

Today, thousands of believers around the world experience severe beatings, imprisonment, and even death because they stand up for Christ. In our culture, our lives are seldom threatened, but we may suffer ridicule when we stand up for righteousness' sake. What does this look like? A man refuses to pad his expense account as his coworker does. When both are asked about the difference in their reimbursement request, the truth comes out. The other employee begins a smear campaign against the one who refused to lie. A woman won't join in when her friends insist on gossiping, only to be ridiculed by those she cares about. A young single man is still a virgin when he's twenty-seven years old, and he feels as if he's the only virgin left. A man insists on paying his full share of taxes, while his brother skimps a little bit here and there. The examples are almost endless. When we choose to do right for Christ's sake, many will cheer, but some will ridicule us unmercifully.

For the second time in this hillside message, Jesus promises "the kingdom of heaven" to those who follow His example. In this case, He tells us that when we are ridiculed—or worse—for following Him, we will experience His presence, peace, and strength. The price of obedience is sometimes steep, but the reward is sweet.

Have you or someone you know ever been ridiculed for doing the right thing? Describe the experience.

Based on this passage, is it worth it to be persecuted for Christ's sake? Why or why not?

"If you haven't met Satan face to face, it's because you are running in the same direction." —ZIG ZIGLAR

IN CASE YOU MISSED IT …

[Jesus said,] "Blessed are you when they revile and persecute you, and say all kinds of evil against you falsely for My sake. Rejoice and be exceedingly glad, for great is your reward in heaven, for so they persecuted the prophets who were before you." MATTHEW 5:11-12

DOING THE RIGHT THING no matter what others may do to you must be an important point, because Jesus goes back a second time to address the issue of persecution for believers. This time, He elaborates on the types of attacks we may experience when we follow Him. We may be reviled, evil things may be said about us, and we may be falsely accused when we stand strong in our faith. Make no mistake: Jesus didn't promise a walk in the park. Other times, He warned His followers that their enemies would become enraged by their message and try to kill them!

Jesus wasn't kidding. The history of the church tells us that all the original disciples died as martyrs. James was killed with a sword, Peter was crucified upside down, and John died in exile. In the Gospel of John, he tells us that people "loved darkness" (see John 3:19-20). In fact, they loved it so much that they hated people who shined as God's light. In our culture, people still love darkness as much as ever, but often they ignore us instead of actively attacking us.

In the Old Testament, Moses and the other prophets were sometimes mocked and hated for bringing God's message to the people. In today's verse, Jesus compares their sacrifice for God with the sacrifice we make when we stand up for Him today. Our reward, too, parallels the one the prophets received, and for that, we can be thrilled.

For some of us, the blessing of rewards for being persecuted seems foreign and, to be honest, really bizarre. It's just not our experience. If you have stood strong for Christ but escaped persecution, be thankful, and realize that today men and women around the globe experience severe treatment because they stand up for Christ.

What does it mean to you that Jesus compared us to the Old Testament prophets?

In this passage, Jesus promised great reward for our faith. What do you think He meant?

"The ultimate measure of a man is not where he stands in moments of comfort and convenience, but where he stands at times of challenge and controversy."
—**MARTIN LUTHER KING JR.**

INCREASE YOUR POWER

[The Lord] gives power to the weak, and to those who have no might He increases strength. ISAIAH 40:29 {MEMORY VERSE}

THE CHRISTIAN LIFE—and especially the nature of spiritual growth—is a paradox: To grow strong, we have to admit our weaknesses. This paradox may seem odd, but it permeates the life and teaching of Christ. He was Almighty God, who became a helpless infant. He was the Ruler of the universe who allowed sinful people to kill Him. He told His followers that to become great they needed to become servants of all (see Matthew 20:26).

Most people spend their lives trying to avoid weakness in every area of life, and when they feel most vulnerable, they try to act powerful to fool people. For those who follow Christ, though, the unwillingness to admit weakness is a serious flaw that short-circuits God's transforming power. Honesty about our weaknesses may threaten us, but it opens the door to God's liberating truth, stunning freedom, and real change.

We can learn the habit of being honest with God about our weaknesses, but most of us are honest only in a crisis. At a point where we have tried everything else and failed, we're finally ready to admit we need God's help. We admit we are weak, and we trust in God's guidance and strength. When the crisis is over, though, many of us go back to trusting in ourselves. Real growth comes when we can admit, every day, "Lord, I need your wisdom and strength in these situations today. Please help me." And He will.

How is admitting our weaknesses the doorway to experiencing God's strength?

What are some areas of weakness in your life today?

"God uses men who are weak and feeble enough to lean on Him." —HUDSON TAYLOR

"God did not promise us a trouble free, griefless life. He did promise us that all our sins and griefs He would bear, if we would take them to the Lord in prayer." —ZIG ZIGLAR

TRUST IS A MUST

Let all those rejoice who put their trust in You; let them ever shout for joy,
because You defend them; let those also who love Your name be joyful in You.

PSALM 5:11

SOMETIMES, THE STRESSES and struggles of life take their toll on our emotions and on our outlook. We never intend for it to happen, but gradually, our sense of joy is washed away in a sea of demands and conflicts. King David experienced the pressures of leadership, but even in the middle of these pressures, he found great joy in his relationship with God.

In Psalm 5, David reports that he endured the lies of "bloodthirsty and deceitful" men who made themselves his enemies. He couldn't trust them, but he realized he could put his life in the hands of a good and kind God who loved him.

To David, God wasn't just a cosmic principle or a distant deity to be worshiped during certain times of the week in order to conform his life to a religious pattern. No, God was a person—a wonderful, trustworthy person he could delight in. David deeply appreciated God's deliverance and His wisdom. In response to God's personal intervention and care, David voiced the response of all believers who are thrilled with God: We "shout for joy"!

Our task is to turn our struggles into steps toward God instead of away from Him. We all experience difficulties at home and at work (or in David's case, in running the kingdom), but if we turn our gaze toward God, we'll find Him to be a rock we can stand on in those times of stress. When we realize that He genuinely cares, we, too, will shout for joy.

Whom do you know whose relationship with God becomes stronger during times of struggle?

What about God's love, care, and provision causes you to shout for joy?

"Courage is nothing more than fear that said its prayers this morning."
—ADRIAN ROGERS

HOW TO SEE CLEARLY

The statutes of the LORD are right, rejoicing the heart; the commandment of the LORD is pure, enlightening the eyes. PSALM 19:8

IT'S THE STRANGEST THING: Millions of Christians say they really want to be wise in their decisions. They want to follow God in their personal lives, jobs, and families and to experience God's blessings, but they often fail to do the one thing God promises will give them that wisdom: soak up the truths in His Word.

People who devour God's truth (and that's the image we get from Jeremiah 15:16, NLT) gradually develop a new set of eyes, one that sees beyond the tangible to the eternal. But that doesn't mean they're clairvoyant. They can't see into the future or know exactly what God is doing all the time. Rather, they gain insight about the ways and the will of God. They aren't shocked when roadblocks occur, because they've learned that God often uses detours to redirect them. They don't pout when God doesn't answer their prayer, because they know God sometimes has a different agenda that is much bigger than theirs. And they aren't caught off guard when people disappoint them, because they have more insight about the selfishness that's in their own hearts too.

Learning to see through the lens of Scripture takes time and effort, but most of us gladly expend time and effort on a host of other activities that promise far less. A writer once asked, "Do you spend as much time in God's Word as you spend reading the newspaper?" Today we might ask, "Do we spend as much time reading Scripture as we do watching YouTube or checking weather or sports online?"

Is having God "enlighten your eyes" attractive to you or just ho-hum? Explain your answer.

What would feasting on God's truth look like in your life?

"Read God's Word daily and get ready—you are about to experience the life you can't wait to live." —ZIG ZIGLAR

THE HARDEST WORD
TO HEAR

Wait on the LORD; be of good courage, and He shall strengthen your heart; wait, I say, on the LORD! PSALM 27:14

WAITING IS INCREDIBLY DIFFICULT. Author and pastor Charles Swindoll says it's the hardest thing Christians have to do. Because we live in an instant society, we're not used to waiting for anything. But God uses the discipline of waiting to teach us lessons we can't learn any other way.

Sometimes God puts the brakes on our plans because He wants to teach us an important lesson and He has to get our attention. Occasionally, God puts up a stop sign to keep us from going in a certain direction because he wants to redirect us. Quite often, we're so sure we're headed the right way that we won't listen unless He stops us dead in our tracks. Of course, we sometimes need God to grab us and stop the runaway train of our lives because we've sinned and we need to repent.

Waiting can be especially difficult when it seems as if everything in our lives is stuck at a red light, but He may be preparing a person or a situation so that when we proceed again He can work even more powerfully.

To us, waiting seems like a waste—or worse, it feels like things will never be right again. When we have to wait, we shouldn't just sit and fritter away the time. We should pursue God with all our hearts, try to determine the reason God wants us to wait, and trust His goodness and timing because He is, after all, God.

Describe the last time you experienced waiting on God.

Which of the reasons above might have been God's purpose in this experience?

"Though God take the sun out of the heaven yet you must have patience."
—GEORGE HERBERT

FULL OF HOPE

I know the thoughts that I think toward you, says the LORD, thoughts of peace and not of evil, to give you a future and a hope. JEREMIAH 29:11 { MEMORY VERSE

THE PROPHET JEREMIAH shared this message from the Lord after the people of Israel had experienced crushing disappointments. God wanted to remind them that He is the author of peace and hope.

Our dreams can take a beating too. We get excited when we feel that God has called us to do something important, then find we may not be ready to face the inevitable setbacks and criticism. We end up getting discouraged and wanting to quit.

For some of us, delays in fulfilling our dreams throw cold water on our enthusiasm. Instead of persevering, we become distracted by other things—often good things—and we lose focus on the thing God had burned into our hearts. Our impatience short-circuits the plan, and we settle for less than God's best. Keep in mind that the enemy of *the best* is settling for *something good.*

Imagine how refreshing God's words were when Jeremiah spoke them to the people! He reminded them that they weren't alone—God hadn't abandoned them. They had experienced severe problems and had doubted Him again and again. But in His great grace, God would even weave their problems into His plans for them. God's faithfulness is never dependent on our perception of our current situation.

Most of the greatest leaders we find in the Bible went through times of struggle and doubt. Abraham lied about his wife to save his own skin. Moses gave up on God and hit the rock to get water for the people. Peter proclaimed his loyalty to Jesus and a few hours later denied Him three times. But God reminded each of them of the hope they could have in their future because He is faithful and forgiving. As long as there is hope in the future, we'll have power in the present to persevere.

Are you discouraged that God's vision for your life doesn't seem to be making headway?

What do God's words of hope mean to you today?

"That the Almighty does make use of human agencies and directly intervenes in human affairs is one of the plainest statements in the Bible. I have so many evidences of His direction, so many instances when I have been controlled by some other power than my own will, that I cannot doubt that this power comes from above." —ABRAHAM LINCOLN

CAMPING OUT
WITH AN ANGEL

The angel of the LORD *encamps all around those who fear Him, and delivers them.* PSALM 34:7

THE FEAR OF GOD is a strange term in the ears of many modern people. In ancient times, kings ruled with absolute sovereignty. They could bestow riches or remove someone's cranium on a whim. Their supreme power and authority made people afraid of them—and rightly so! With God, though, we don't have to worry about capricious actions. His infinite wisdom, mercy, and justice always guide His actions.

Ah, justice. That's the problem. God isn't a Santa Claus who only gives us good gifts. He is a strong, loving Father who requires loyalty from His children. If we are loyal, God pulls out all the stops to bless us and encourage us. He also continues to strengthen our relationship with Him when we are faced with difficult situations so that our roots go down deep into Him.

In this wonderful psalm, David describes a miraculous deliverance when it looked as though he was going to be killed. He ascribed God's protection to an angel's presence camping around him. Angels aren't chubby little babies with cute wings and bare bottoms. When we see them in the Scriptures, they are terrifying creatures who inspire awe! They are the ones who camp out with you and me all day every day. They act in concert with God's purposes to direct us and provide for us.

Today, realize that you are camping out with an angel.

What is an angel's role in your life?

Why do you think angels only camp out with people who trust in God?

"When God contemplates some great work, He begins it by the hand of some poor, weak, human creature, to whom He afterwards gives aid, so that enemies who seek to obstruct it are overcome." —MARTIN LUTHER

I'LL BE WATCHING YOU

Behold, the eye of the LORD is on those who fear Him, on those who hope in His mercy. PSALM 33:18

HOW WOULD WE LIVE differently if we were convinced that Almighty God watches us every moment of every day? Many of us would make much better choices!

Of course, God doesn't watch just His children. He is omnipresent and omniscient, meaning He is everywhere at all times and knowing everything to the smallest detail about everyone and everything. But in this verse, the poet wants us to reflect on the fact that not only is God watching us; He's *watching out* for us.

To be honest, many of us don't have a daily, genuine sense of need for God's intervention. The modern world has made food, homes, and comfort standard equipment, and we've learned to expect these things. We look to God only when something happens that rocks our world. God may not have caused the calamities that bring us pain, but He uses them to remind us that He is infinitely powerful and good, and we can trust Him.

In times of desperation, we come face-to-face with our inadequacy. We may be highly competent executives or successful in other areas of life, but when we feel desperate, we cry out for His mercy. We need Him to do for us what we realize we can't do for ourselves.

And that's right where He wants us.

Does it encourage you or terrify you that God is watching you 24/7? Explain your answer.

In what kinds of circumstances are you most aware of God's presence?

"If the Lord be with us, we have no cause of fear. His eye is upon us, His arm over us, His ear open to our prayer—His grace is sufficient. His promise unchangeable." —JOHN NEWTON

THE CURSE OF MEDIOCRITY

Because you are lukewarm, and neither cold nor hot, I will vomit you out of My mouth. REVELATION 3:16

DO YOU EVER FEEL as if you're just going through the motions? Some of us, for any number of reasons, have lost our passion for work, God, our families, and everything else in our lives. We drag ourselves in after a long day and collapse on the sofa only to tune out in front of the television. We no longer want to change the world. The most we can muster is changing the channel.

Even if the stress levels in our lives are only slightly above optimum, our minds, hearts, and bodies eventually wear down, and all forms of energy in our lives dissipate. We used to be excited about this goal or that purpose, but no longer. We used to care deeply about this person or that cause, but not anymore. All we want is to be left alone or to find somebody or something that will give us a few moments' pleasure. The curse of mediocrity ruins us and everyone we touch.

In the letters to the seven churches in the opening chapters of Revelation, John writes to the church at Laodicea that the Lord is, to say the least, dissatisfied with its lack of passion. The church was located near the hot springs of Hierapolis, so the reference to "hot" may be about the steamy, healing, medicinal baths. The "cold" may reference the water that refreshed tired workers and travelers. But the church didn't have any cold water, either. All it had was tepid, bland water that couldn't heal and didn't refresh—the kind we'd spit out!

If your heart is lukewarm, step back, take stock of your stress level, notice any negative habits you've allowed to develop—and make changes. Don't settle for mediocrity any longer, but don't just add more activity to your life. To become fully alive again, you may have to eliminate even more than you add.

What activities, purposes, or people bring passion and purpose to your life?

To what extent has your life become mediocre? What do you need to do about it?

*"As I read my Scriptures today, the words ring loud and clear that the most miserable creature on earth is the fence-straddler trying to please God and man. He fails to do either and ends up not even pleasing himself, much less his fellow man or his God." —*ZIG ZIGLAR

ONE MORE NIGHT WITH THE FROGS

Moses said to Pharaoh, "Accept the honor of saying when I shall intercede for you, for your servants, and for your people, to destroy the frogs from you and your houses, that they may remain in the river only." So he said, "Tomorrow." And he said, "Let it be according to your word, that you may know that there is no one like the LORD our God." EXODUS 8:9-10

IF WE WANT TO DELAY making a decision, we can always find an excuse. And some of us are board-certified experts! After all, we don't want to decide now because

- the situation might change,

- the problem might completely go away,

- somebody may come up with a better solution, or

- we might win the lottery or a tornado might blow us away—either way, we won't have to make that decision!

Sometimes, we put up with an incredible mess because we're afraid of making a mistake. During the plagues, God sent frogs to torment Pharaoh so that he would set God's people free. Now, one or two frogs aren't a problem, but millions of them—in your shirt and squished under your feet—are big trouble! Moses offered to stop the plague, but Pharaoh said, "Well, let's wait until tomorrow." (I'm sure his wife pitched a fit!)

Certainly, we need to think through decisions so we choose the best option, but sooner or later, it's time to act. Procrastination is paralysis by fear, not astute planning. If you regularly have difficulty making decisions, look below the surface to identify your fears, and address them. Until you do, you'll be spending a lot of nights with the frogs.

What are some fears that can lead to procrastination?

How can someone address those fears so that they no longer interfere with life?

"You cannot escape the responsibility of tomorrow by evading it today."
—ABRAHAM LINCOLN

THE ONE TRADE YOU SHOULD NEVER MAKE

What will it profit a man if he gains the whole world, and loses his own soul?

MARK 8:36

GOD HAS CREATED US to live in two worlds, and while the spiritual is most important, our culture tends to value the tangible. We devote our time to making more money, and we spend our money getting more and more stuff. Some of us use our wealth as chips to show that we're smarter and sharper than others. We want to win, and possessions are the way we keep score. Others, though, don't really care what somebody else has. We just want as much as we can get to make our lives as pleasant as possible.

Jesus made the stark, sobering observation that the value of a single soul is greater than all the gold, oil, real estate, jewels, stocks, cars, and everything else of value on the planet. Jesus died to rescue our souls from eternal death. He died for our family members, our neighbors, the cranky old guy down the street, and the natives in the middle of the Amazon basin.

One of our most important, and yet one of the most difficult, tasks is to shift our attention from what is visible to what is invisible, from the tangible to the eternal, from what will rust and rot to what will last forever.

Souls are that important.

What's the lure of stuff? Why do we let it rule (or at least shape) our lives?

How would your life be different if you were gripped with the reality that a single soul is more important than all the world's wealth?

"The meaning of life is the most urgent of questions." —ALBERT CAMUS

WHEN GOD KNOCKS YOU DOWN

As [Saul] journeyed he came near Damascus, and suddenly a light shone around him from heaven. Then he fell to the ground, and heard a voice saying to him, "Saul, Saul, why are you persecuting Me?" . . . Then Saul arose from the ground, and when his eyes were opened he saw no one. But they led him by the hand and brought him into Damascus. ACTS 9:3-4, 8

SAUL, who later became known as Paul, was a member of the religious elite of Israel. He was trained by the best teachers, and his passion led him to capture and persecute members of a new sect: Christians. Saul was one of those people who are thoroughly convinced they're always right. (You know the type.)

On the road to Damascus, God met Saul in blinding light. In an instant, Saul realized that all he had believed had been false and that his life had been a lie. That moment was the pivotal point in this strong leader's life.

Was he devastated? Yes and no. He was literally and figuratively knocked down. His pride was shattered, his confidence blown away. But he submitted himself to Christ and to Christ's gospel, and God rebuilt him to become the most influential leader the church has ever known.

Great leaders often have great pride. To become useful to God, their pride has to be crushed. God can then use the broken pieces to create new, humble people whose consummate abilities are under the leading of the Spirit instead of driven by selfish ambition.

When God knocks you down, don't shake your fist at Him. Instead, let God reform your passions and redirect your path so that you can use all your God-given abilities for Him and for others instead of for yourself.

How can you tell if it's God who's knocking you down?

Does it encourage you or depress you that God is willing to crush your pride to reform you? Explain your answer.

"Until a man has found God and been found by God, he begins at no beginning, he works to no end. He may have friendships, his partial loyalties, his scraps of honor, but all these will fall into place, and life falls into place, only with God." —H. G. WELLS

BORN AGAIN

Jesus answered and said to him, "Most assuredly, I say to you, unless one is born again, he cannot see the kingdom of God." JOHN 3:3 { MEMORY VERSE

WE CAN IMAGINE Nicodemus scratching his head as he leaned in and listened to Jesus the night they met up to chat. Nicodemus was one of the top religious leaders of the country, respected and admired by everyone who knew him. He was devoted to keeping a rigid set of religious rules to prove to God that he was worthy. That's what all his friends taught, and that's the system he had known all his life.

But then Jesus rocked his world. Probably with a twinkle in His eye because He knew He was stretching Nicodemus's mind, Jesus announced a revolutionary new way of relating to God. It wasn't through all those rules and rituals Nicodemus had been following. This new way was through the Spirit of God transforming people's hearts and making them alive as they'd never been before. It was so radical that Jesus called it being "born again."

All of us long for a rich, full, meaningful life. God promises that kind of life as the result of experiencing His forgiveness and transformation. But some of us can't accept the fact that it's a gift. We still want to prove ourselves by following some set of rules, so we push Jesus' offer away instead of gratefully accepting it.

Jesus is incredibly patient. Though Nicodemus didn't seem to understand that night, he eventually grasped the fact that he could never follow enough rules to impress God. Sometime later, Nicodemus believed, and he was born again.

Why do some people cling to their hope of proving they are good enough to be accepted by God? {

What does it mean to be born again? Is that true for you?

"God doesn't have any grandchildren." —E. STANLEY JONES {

"To be good in the eyes of the world is one thing. To be saved is another matter."
—ZIG ZIGLAR

AN EXAMPLE TO FOLLOW

[Jesus said,] "You call Me Teacher and Lord, and you say well, for so I am. If I then, your Lord and Teacher, have washed your feet, you also ought to wash one another's feet. For I have given you an example, that you should do as I have done to you." JOHN 13:13-15

THE DISCIPLES could sense that this night was different. The whole week had been intense. It began with the crowds shouting and waving palm branches as Jesus rode into Jerusalem on a donkey's colt, but the days since then had been a checkerboard of arguments, miracles, debates, and challenges. Now, on the night of Passover, they gathered in a room to be together. Jesus had told them He would be arrested and killed. Would it happen soon?

In the thick air of anticipation, Jesus did something totally bizarre. He ceremoniously washed each of the men's feet. They watched in amazement as He went from one disciple to the next. When He was finished, He sat down and explained that He had done this as an example for them to follow after He was gone. Washing their feet was a simple act of service, usually performed by the lowest-ranking servant in a home. "Serve one another," Jesus was telling and showing them. "If you think you're too good to serve one another this way, just remember that I did it, and I'm your Lord and Teacher."

Washing their feet also symbolized forgiveness. Just as He forgave the disciples—and they would need His forgiveness again in an hour or so when they abandoned Him to the soldiers—He wanted them to forgive one another.

We can all think we're too cool, too good, too sophisticated, or too something else to stoop to serve others around us, but Jesus wants managers, officials, parents, and any others in authority to lead by serving.

How do you think the disciples felt that night when they watched Jesus wash their feet and heard His explanation?

What are some ways you can serve people who report to you?

"I don't know what your destiny will be, but one thing I do know: the only ones among you who will be really happy are those who have sought and found how to serve." —ALBERT SCHWEITZER

THE RESULTS OF TRULY TRUSTING

The LORD is my strength and my shield; my heart trusted in Him, and I am helped; therefore my heart greatly rejoices, and with my song I will praise Him.

PSALM 28:7

TRUSTING GOD MAY BEGIN as the desire for Him to meet a need in a particular situation, but it ends in a richer, stronger relationship with Him. Difficulties aren't aberrations of life; they are an integral part of life. Sometimes, to be sure, we bring them on ourselves by doing something foolish and destructive, and sometimes others wound us by their selfishness. Whatever the cause—by people or natural disasters or demonic activity—difficulties drive us to God with cries for help.

The answer may come instantly, but far more often, God takes His time to work more deeply in our hearts to purify our motives. Then, when the answer comes, we don't even think of claiming credit. We gladly point people to God as the source of the solution.

But a strange thing happens. When the answer comes, we're glad; however, something much deeper has happened in our hearts. We realize that we know God better than before, and that makes our rejoicing even sweeter.

Whenever a friend comes through for us when we're in trouble, we tell everybody we know, and we praise our friend's virtues. It's the same in our friendship with God. When we're convinced that He has come through for us, we can't stop talking about Him, and in fact, we sing His praises.

When God answers prayer, are we ever tempted to ascribe the solution to our own brilliance or to other people instead of God?

How has God been your "strength and shield" lately? Whom do you want to tell about Him?

"I looked at God and He looked at me, and we were one forever."
—CHARLES HADDON SPURGEON

GUIDANCE FROM ABOVE

Oh, let the nations be glad and sing for joy! For You shall judge the people righteously, and govern the nations on earth. PSALM 67:4

AT CERTAIN TIMES IN HISTORY, we see the hand of God moving very clearly and powerfully. Accounts of the formative years of our nation show time and again how God inspired people to pursue freedom. When freedom was realized after the Revolution, He gave our leaders incredible wisdom to structure the three branches of government as checks and balances. Today, we still enjoy the benefits of God's guidance in those crucial days of deliberation.

At other times in history, however, we can't see God's hand moving at all. Tyrants and dictators seize power over foreign lands and murder millions, and in our own country, scandals threaten to destroy our values. Things seem to be out of control—out of our control for sure, and seemingly out of God's control, as well.

A day will come, though, when we'll see how God orchestrated all the events of human history to accomplish His sovereign design for mankind. We'll see that God used even the events and leaders that appeared out of control to accomplish His grand purposes. On that day, God will show us how He governed the nations, directing events and leading people, but He'll also judge those who fought against Him.

In our nation's history—and in our own lives—God reigns supreme, guiding, directing, and shaping events to accomplish good things. Though at times He seems to be a million miles away, He's present, active, and engaged. We can count on it.

What are some ways you've seen God direct our nation and your life?

Take a few minutes to praise Him for His leading.

"The highest story of the American Revolution is this: it connected in one indissolvable bond the principles of civil government with the principles of Christianity." —JOHN ADAMS

THE 365 PLAN

God has not given us a spirit of fear, but of power and of love and of a sound mind. 2 TIMOTHY 1:7

PEPPERED THROUGHOUT THE SCRIPTURES, we hear a message spoken repeatedly by God, prophets, and angels: "Fear not." In fact, this encouragement is found 365 times. A coincidence? I don't think so. God wants us to know that we can trust Him every day, even in the most threatening situations or with the most difficult people.

Why does God give us the command to "fear not" so many times? Because we are so prone to let circumstances overwhelm us. When we feel out of control, our first instinct (sad to say) isn't to trust God but to run away in fear or fight back in defiance. God reminds us, instead, to first look to Him, remember His greatness and grace, and cling to His ability to do the impossible.

Paul's bold statement to Timothy arrests our attention like a slap in the face. He is saying, "Hey, if you're afraid, it's not from God. He's the author of power and love and right thinking. Count on it."

So, what about you and me? What are the recurring situations when we feel threatened, out of control, or overwhelmed? In those—even those—situations, God tells us to stop, look to Him, and listen for the assurance of His Spirit that He will guide us. If we keep focusing our attention on the problem, we'll be afraid and act to protect ourselves, but if we turn quickly to God and reflect on His love and strength, we'll keep trusting Him.

What are some recurring situations that cause you to run away in fear or fight back in defiance?

When that happens again, what about God do you need to remember? How will this reflection help you in critical moments?

"He who is not everyday conquering some fear has not learned the secret of life."
—RALPH WALDO EMERSON

UPRIGHT OR UPTIGHT?

Many sorrows shall be to the wicked; but he who trusts in the LORD, mercy shall surround him. Be glad in the LORD and rejoice, you righteous; and shout for joy, all you upright in heart! PSALM 32:10-11

BAD DECISIONS, especially those that are caused by our selfishness and that result in others' pain, create tremendous stress. If we don't turn to God quickly, we can multiply our "sorrows" with outbursts of anger when others point out our faults, with lies as we try to cover them up, and with ruined relationships because people can't trust us.

God doesn't demand perfection from us—just honesty. This beautiful psalm is David's confession of sin. In it, he bluntly describes the pain and anguish he endured when he kept silent about his sin, but when he embraced God's forgiveness, he experienced cleansing and hope. Perhaps as much as anyone who ever lived, David had good reason to be grateful for God's lavish mercy.

Thankfulness is one of the chief characteristics of a person who walks with God. We can be thankful for all manner of things: our homes, our health, our family and friends, our nation, and countless other blessings. But if we're honest about the darkness in our hearts, perhaps one blessing stands out above the rest: the infinite mercy of God.

We can't attain "upright hearts" by self-effort. Having a clean and pure heart comes only from the kindness of God to look at the worst of our sins and choose to forgive us. It's enough to make us shout for joy!

What are some selfish choices in your life that have made you uptight?

Take those to God and thank Him for His wonderful mercy and forgiveness.

"The Christian Church is a society of sinners. It is the only society in the world in which membership is based upon the single qualification that the candidate be unworthy of membership." —CHARLES C. MORRISON

PAYBACKS

Oh, love the LORD, all you His saints! For the LORD preserves the faithful, and fully repays the proud person. PSALM 31:23

WE'VE GOT GOOD NEWS and bad news. Actually the news is the same, but the one receiving it will determine if it's good or bad. The news is that God gives people what they deserve. In the Scriptures, we see this in two scenes. In his first letter to the Corinthians, Paul teaches us that all believers will stand before God one day to give an account of our faithfulness (see 1 Corinthians 3:13-15). On that day, God will review everything we've done since the day we trusted Christ. We'll be rewarded for all eternity for the things that we did to honor Him, and the rest of our actions, the ones done for selfish motives, will burn up and turn to ashes. At the end of Revelation we find the Great White Throne Judgment, where believers are rewarded and unbelievers are punished for eternity (see Revelation 20:11-15).

These scenes in the Scriptures aren't put there just to fill up space. They are important lessons God wants to impart to us. The choices we make today are very important. In fact, we'll receive a report card at the end of our lives, and we'll live with the results for all eternity.

Even in this life, we're given what we deserve. God rewards our faithfulness in many ways. He preserves us, blesses us richly, and gives us lives of meaning and peace. But we also pay for wrongdoing. In this life, arrogant, self-absorbed people often pay the price of strained relationships and other heartaches.

Both in this life and in the one to come, God gives us exactly what we deserve. Count on it.

How does God's grace fit into the teaching about God paying people back?

What choices do you need to make so that you'll get a good report card on that day when you stand before Christ?

"If you are sincere, praise is effective. If you are insincere, it is manipulative."
—ZIG ZIGLAR

DELIGHT = DESIRES

Delight yourself also in the LORD, and He shall give you the desires of your heart. Commit your way to the LORD, trust also in Him, and He shall bring it to pass.

PSALM 37:4-5 { MEMORY VERSE

THIS PASSAGE in the Psalms is sometimes misunderstood. Some have thought that it means God will give us all the things we desire in exchange for delighting in Him. Instead, He works in our hearts to change what we desire.

The source of our delight shapes the nature of our desires. If we delight in someone, we genuinely want that person to be happy. If we delight in acquiring bigger and better possessions, we won't be able to stop until we have enough to satisfy us—which never happens. And if we delight in God, our interactions with Him shape our hearts so that we gradually desire what He desires and value what He values.

Author and pastor John Piper has said, "God is most glorified in us when we are most satisfied in him."* To delight in God is to be satisfied and, in fact, thrilled with His love, forgiveness, and purpose for us. As we know and love Him more, we want to pursue His will, we make choices to follow His leading, and we take action to accomplish things He has directed us to do.

It doesn't take a psychologist to unlock the secrets of our desires. We need only to look at what excites us, what frustrates us, and what hopes and fears fill our minds. We can choose, though, to focus on God, to delight in Him so that He gradually changes the desires of our hearts to fit more with His.

What do your joys, frustrations, hopes, and fears say about your desires?

To what degree would you say you genuinely delight in God?

"If we will make the choice, God will make the change." —IKE REIGHARD

"Ability can take you to the top, but it takes character to keep you there." — ZIG ZIGLAR

---

* John Piper, *When I Don't Desire God* (Wheaton, IL: Crossway, 2004), 143.

WALKING AS JESUS WALKED

He who says he abides in Him ought himself also to walk just as He walked.

1 JOHN 2:6

YOU CAN'T JUST TALK the talk; you've also got to walk the walk. This statement about authenticity is true in every area of life, but none more than in our spiritual lives. What does it mean to "walk just as He walked"? Some of us might think it means performing miracles, and to that we may say, "Well, I don't think that's going to happen!" Probably not, but that's not what John is talking about. The hallmarks of the Christian experience, John says in verse 5, are obedience and love.

How did Jesus walk in obedience? From childhood, He dedicated Himself to the Father's will. When Jesus might have been tempted to stay where He was very popular, He said, "No, I have to go where the Father has sent Me." When He was criticized and condemned for following God, He didn't flinch. He stayed true to the Father's purpose for Him. When Satan offered Him the whole world, He said no. Nothing could keep Him from following the narrow path of doing what pleased the Father.

How did Jesus walk in love? To the amazement (and often, the dismay) of His closest friends, Jesus reached out to people at the "bottom of the barrel" over and over again. He didn't care what others thought of Him. He loved the prostitutes, the lepers, the blind, the paralyzed, the sick, the tax gatherers, the foreigners, and all the other outcasts in society. And of course, He loved everybody else, too.

When we walk as Jesus walked, our hearts are increasingly riveted on God's purposes instead of on our selfish desires and self-protection, and we reach out to care for the people no one else even notices. If we truly know Christ, He changes our hearts, and His love will overflow from us to touch others.

What do you need to do to align your life more completely with God's purposes for you?

Who are some people no one else notices who need your love?

"What would Jesus do?" —CHARLES SHELDON

A DESPERATE PRAYER FOR DESPERATE TIMES

Do not forsake me, O LORD; O my God, be not far from me! Make haste to help me, O Lord, my salvation! PSALM 38:21-22

YOU MAY THINK you've had a bad day, but it's nothing compared to the heartache David felt when writing Psalm 38. In this psalm, David describes one of the darkest points of his life. With blunt transparency, he admits that some of his pain and confusion comes from his own sins and foolish decisions. In addition, his cup of heartache is filled up with the accusations and attacks of his enemies; even worse, his family and friends have turned their backs on him when he needed them most.

Where could he turn now? In a desperate cry for help, David turned to God. "You won't forsake me, too, will You?" he seems to plead. Everything in his life had gone wrong, and everyone had turned against him. In this moment of hopelessness, David asked for help and found hope in God.

Our troubles may come from a wide variety of sources, but we don't want to experience them all at once the way David did! Whenever we feel hopeless, abandoned, misunderstood, betrayed, or incompetent, we can always turn to the One who is faithful to listen, to care, and to restore hope. This time of desperation wasn't the end of the road for David, and times of desperation aren't the end for us either—if we'll turn our attention to God and express our trust that He will come through.

When was the last time you felt hopeless, trapped, or abandoned?

How does God use those times to get your attention?

"When God is all we have left, we then realize that God is all we need."
—IKE REIGHARD

DO YOU GET IT?

The message of the cross is foolishness to those who are perishing, but to us who are being saved it is the power of God. 1 CORINTHIANS 1:18 { MEMORY VERSE

THE CROSS OF JESUS CHRIST is the most unifying—and the most divisive—event in all of history. People can easily talk about all kinds of philosophies and religions, but when someone brings up Christ's death on the cross, the conversation often radically changes. Some people get angry, some scoff, and some feel confused. Invariably, they ask questions: Why did a good man like Jesus have to die? Who was He, anyway? It happened so long ago; what difference does it make to me today?

People in Paul's day were no different. The Greeks loved to debate philosophies, but they didn't have a category for God becoming a human and dying for us. That concept simply didn't compute. It was foolish to them, just as it seems foolish to the people of our day who don't understand the message of the gospel.

But we get it. We grasp the phenomenal truth that Christ came to find us because we were lost and that He died for our sins as our substitute. Without Him, we had no hope. With Him, we have the most valuable possession in the universe: a relationship with Almighty God. We are well aware that it was grace and only grace that saved us. We had no power to accomplish anything toward forgiveness and eternal life, but God exercised His enormous strength to reach into our hearts, transform us, and make us new people.

We get it, not because we're smarter than the philosophers, but because God first took hold of us. For that we can be thankful.

Why do you think some people get it but others don't?

In light of people's spiritual blindness, take some time to pray for those you know who don't know Christ yet.

"I am not what I ought to be, I am not what I wish to be. I am not even what I hope to be. But by the cross of Christ, I am not what I was." —JOHN NEWTON

"To me, love is knowing that Jesus Christ died on the cross so that I might live forever. To me, happiness is knowing now that my eternity with Christ is irrevocably guaranteed, that He did it all, and all I have to do is believe and accept His grace." —ZIG ZIGLAR

"FATHER, FORGIVE THEM"

Jesus said, "Father, forgive them, for they do not know what they do."

LUKE 23:34

OVER THE NEXT SEVERAL DAYS, we'll look at Jesus' seven statements from the cross. In the first one, the depth of His grace toward the people putting Him to death is amazing.

We need to remember that when Jesus said, "Father, forgive them," it was after He had experienced excruciating stress during the previous week. The authorities had been looking for a way to kill Him. One of His followers had betrayed Him, and another one had denied he even knew Him. All the rest had fled when He was arrested, leaving Him completely alone. He had been beaten in the face so that He was unrecognizable and had been whipped with a cat-o'-nine-tails until His back was a bloody mess. On the streets of Jerusalem, He carried the timber that would be part of His cross until He stumbled and fell from exhaustion. When He arrived at the hill, guards drove spikes through His wrists and His feet, and He was hoisted up as a spectacle to the world.

If anyone ever had reason to be bitter, Jesus did. And if anyone ever had the power to execute vengeance on those who hurt him, Jesus did. One account says that He could have called down legions of mighty angels to slay the entire human race—which we deserved.

But there He hung, between two common criminals, to be executed like a slave or traitor though He had done nothing deserving of this fate. As He looked at the scene—angry, self-righteous religious leaders, disinterested Roman guards, masses of people who had come for the spectacle of blood and death—He turned instinctively to the Father and prayed for all those people. Has God's grace ever been more evident than at that moment?

How would you have responded if you had heard Jesus pray for those people?

What does His prayer of forgiveness for those people mean to you today?

"Forgiveness is a beautiful word, until you have something to forgive." —C. S. LEWIS

TODAY IN PARADISE

Jesus said to him, "Assuredly, I say to you, today you will be with Me in Paradise." LUKE 23:43

THREE MEN—two thieves and Jesus—hung on crosses, suspended in mid-air above the soldiers, religious leaders, and curious onlookers. The sense of hopelessness caused one of the thieves to bark at Jesus in derision, "If You are the Christ, save Yourself and us" (Luke 23:39).

The other criminal, though, saw things very differently. Somehow, he had heard about Jesus, and he corrected the other man, "Do you not even fear God, seeing you are under the same condemnation? And we indeed justly, for we receive the due reward of our deeds; but this Man has done nothing wrong" (Luke 23:40-41).

The man then turned to Jesus and said, "Lord, remember me when You come into Your kingdom" (Luke 23:42).

Many people had abandoned Jesus, and many had betrayed Him. This man's simple request must have sounded gratifying to Him. He turned to the man and promised, "Assuredly, I say to you, today you will be with Me in Paradise" (Luke 23:43).

Jesus didn't go into a long diatribe about the afterlife. He didn't bring out charts and graphs, explaining what happens to the soul and the spirit when a person dies. He didn't try to define terms or conjugate verbs. He simply spoke an unmistakable, clear promise that because the man believed, he would be in paradise that very day, the moment he died.

Before this conversation with Jesus, the man's life had been a train wreck. He had resorted to theft, been caught, and condemned to die a horrible death. At that moment, though, only one thing mattered: His identity and eternal destiny had changed forever.

How does the promise of paradise affect your perspective about death?

How does it shape your view of life today?

"The ultimate victory is eternity with Jesus Christ." —ZIG ZIGLAR

"WOMAN, BEHOLD YOUR SON"

When Jesus ... saw His mother, and the disciple whom He loved standing by, He said to His mother, "Woman, behold your son!" JOHN 19:26

JESUS HAD EVERY REASON in the world to be self-absorbed and bitter as He hung on the cross. He had been betrayed by two friends, abandoned by others, falsely accused, wrongly convicted, beaten to a pulp, and crucified as a traitor. But in His supreme moment of agony, His tenderness shone like a beacon to everyone at the foot of the cross. Jesus hung between heaven and earth, dying for the sins of the world in the single most crucial event in all of history; in that pivotal moment, He looked at those He loved and made sure His mother would be cared for. He was leaving to go back to the Father, so He put her in the hands of a friend He trusted. Jesus didn't ask John to be Mary's guardian to manage her estate. Instead, he assured her that John would care for her as a loving son cares for his mother.

In times of crisis, do we withdraw, or do we reach out? We may be tempted to become self-absorbed, but we can follow Christ's example by looking beyond our own pain to care for others.

What do you think this statement meant to Mary that day? to John? to Jesus?

In times of crisis, how do you want to care for those you love?

"For the sake of each of us he laid down his life worth no less than the universe. He demands of us in return our lives for the sake of each other."
—CLEMENT OF ALEXANDRIA

"WHY HAVE YOU FORSAKEN ME?"

About the ninth hour Jesus cried out with a loud voice, saying, "Eli, Eli, lama sabachthani?" that is, "My God, My God, why have You forsaken Me?"

MATTHEW 27:46

WE TALK ABOUT THE CROSS, sing about it, and hear messages about it all the time, but it remains the most awe-inspiring event in all of history. Jesus wasn't just a good man who died for a cause He believed in. He wasn't a soldier who died for the guy next to Him in a foxhole. He wasn't simply a misunderstood martyr or a teacher who said too much. He was Almighty God, who had stepped out of heaven to earth for one unique purpose: to give His life for you and me.

When Jesus hung on the cross, He was taking our place. Because of our sins, we deserved death. As He hung there, all the sins of every person who had ever lived and would ever live were piled on Him. At that moment, He became our substitute. His death gave us forgiveness, right standing with God, and eternal life.

Did God the Father turn His back on Jesus in that awful hour? Yes, He backed away so that all the punishment we deserve could be poured out on Jesus. All the wrath, judgment, and penalty for every sin became Jesus' at that moment, and the Father had to abandon Him for that to happen.

But the Father's abandonment was over when Jesus breathed His last. And three days later, He rose from the grave in the fullness of resurrected life. That moment on the cross, though, is the clearest picture of the matchless grace of God that we'll ever see: Jesus hung alone, abandoned and condemned, for you and me.

What do you think that moment was like for Jesus?

What does it tell you about His grace and His love for you?

"The only question Jesus ever asked God is 'Why have you forsaken me?' This is the *same question most every believer asks at some point in their spiritual journey."*
—IKE REIGHARD

"I THIRST"

Jesus, knowing that all things were now accomplished, that the Scripture might be fulfilled, said, "I thirst!" JOHN 19:28

EVEN IN HIS AGONY, Jesus maintained an unclouded mind. As a student of Scripture, He knew that the prophets had predicted that the Messiah's death throes would produce a dry mouth so that His "tongue sticks to the roof of [His] mouth" (Psalm 22:15, NIV), and those attending the execution would offer "vinegar for [His] thirst" (Psalm 69:21, NIV). Crucifixion is one of the most excruciating forms of torture in human history. Intense pain leaves a person gasping for air, which produces tremendous thirst.

John tells us that Jesus was acutely aware of every detail of His execution. For centuries, people have argued about who killed Jesus. Was it the Jews or the Romans? Actually, it wasn't either group of people. Jesus freely gave Himself to die so that we might live. He offered His own life to secure eternal life for us, and He died willingly as the substitute for the death we deserved.

As the moment neared for Him to die, Jesus made sure not a single detail would be overlooked. He wanted us to know that every *i* was dotted and every *t* crossed so that we might marvel at His great love—and believe.

Why was it important to Jesus—and to us—that every detail of prophecy be fulfilled?

How do these fulfilled prophecies strengthen our faith?

"In the Cross of Christ, excess in men is met by excess in God; excess of evil is mastered by excess of love." —LOUIS BOURDALOUE

"IT IS FINISHED"

When Jesus had received the sour wine, He said, "It is finished!" And bowing His head, He gave up His spirit. JOHN 19:30

TO FULFILL THE LAST PROPHECY, Jesus drank a little vinegar to quench His raging thirst, and then it was over. From the point of view of all the people around Him, the culmination of His life came suddenly and unexpectedly. Usually, people writhed in pain for days on the cross while people watched, but Jesus had been beaten so badly and had lost so much blood when He was flogged that He died within a few hours.

His statement "It is finished" is a translation of a Greek phrase that means "paid in full." The reason Jesus came to earth was to pay the terrible price for our sins. From the moment He was born, every interaction and every decision pointed to this moment. Now, the price was paid. Totally. Completely. Once for all.

Surveys show that about half the people who attend church aren't sure they are forgiven or whether they'll spend eternity with God in heaven. How can that be? Many of us sit in churches week after week listening to the message of God's grace, but perhaps we secretly cling to the hope that we don't really need grace. We think that we can do enough to earn God's favor, and if we can do just enough, we can pat ourselves on the back. But sooner or later, in this life or the one to come, we will realize that we can never do enough to earn God's approval. Our selfishness and arrogance separate us from God, and there's only one solution: the death of Christ to pay for our sins. Not some of them; all of them. Not to make us good enough to earn acceptance; but because we can never be good enough on our own. Christ's words "paid in full" confront our pride and remind us of His grace.

How does secretly hoping we can earn God's favor by being good enough affect our relationship with God?

Take some time now to let the grace of Christ sink deep into your heart, and thank Him for it.

"The greatness of a man's power is the measure of his surrender." —WILLIAM BOOTH

"INTO YOUR HANDS"

When Jesus had cried out with a loud voice, He said, "Father, 'into Your hands I commit My spirit.'" Having said this, He breathed His last. LUKE 23:46

EARLIER, JESUS HAD EXPERIENCED the Father's abandonment as the weight of mankind's sins crushed Him. He had moaned, "Oh, God, why have You forsaken Me?" (see Matthew 27:46). But now, in the last seconds of His earthly life, Jesus expressed His utter, complete trust in the Father: "I put Myself in Your hands." Then He died.

When we are in trouble and don't know what to do, we can turn to God for comfort and direction. When it seems as if God has led us into a dark tunnel that has no light at the end of it, we may be tempted to despair, to give up and blame God for not coming through the way we wanted Him to. In those painful times, we can follow Christ's example. At the most difficult times in our lives, perhaps all we can do is acknowledge the unseen and unfelt presence of the Father and express our trust in Him. In times of struggle in marriage, with children, in finances, with health problems, and in all the other times of darkness, we may not know what to do, but we can pray, "Father, I'm in Your hands."

This statement of faith pleases God, and it may be the beginning of answers and blessings that we never expected. Sometimes, the greatest blessing is simply knowing that God cares and is present with us—even in our darkest moments.

What have been some dark times in your life?

When we acknowledge that we are in God's hands, what can we expect from Him?

"You can trust the man who died for you." —LETTIE COWMAN

CHRIST IN YOU

I have been crucified with Christ; it is no longer I who live, but Christ lives in me; and the life which I now live in the flesh I live by faith in the Son of God, who loved me and gave Himself for me. GALATIANS 2:20 { MEMORY VERSE

THE CHRISTIAN LIFE isn't a self-help program. We aren't given a set of exercises to perform in order to achieve results. Instead, God works in our hearts and changes us from the inside out, transforming our desires and motives so that our new choices in behavior will be genuine and not contrived.

Our role in this transformation, though, isn't completely passive. Paul reminds us that the first step in this transformation process is a fresh perspective on death and life. He considered himself to be "crucified with Christ," which means that he applied Christ's sacrifice on the cross to his own selfish sins and, as many times as necessary, counted his selfish desires as dead. In place of Paul's selfish desires in residence, Christ Himself lived in his heart, transforming him little by little, day after day.

Even though Christ transforms our hearts, we take responsibility to recognize selfish motives and actions, consider them to be dead, and replace them with God-honoring thoughts and behaviors. The Christian life, then, is lived at the moment of choice when we pick life over death and Christ over our selfish demands.

We may be confused from time to time, and we may be disappointed that we aren't changing as fast as we'd like, but we can take heart that Christ Himself has taken up residence inside us. As we pay closer attention to His instructions and trust Him to use us, we'll gradually take on more of His character. We'll love people with His love, serve with His humility, and stand strong in hope of the future because we remember the promise of the Resurrection.

Describe what it means for Christ to live in you.

What's your responsibility for change, and what's Christ's responsibility to change you?

{

"People who are crucified with Christ have three distinct marks: (1) They are facing only one direction, (2) they can never turn back, and (3) they no longer have plans of their own." —A. W. TOZER

{

"When your number one goal in life is to die to yourself and put God first, you can rest assured you have a goal that will last a lifetime." —ZIG ZIGLAR

A CAUSE WORTH DYING FOR

Let them shout for joy and be glad, who favor my righteous cause; and let them say continually, "Let the LORD be magnified, who has pleasure in the prosperity of His servant." PSALM 35:27

IN OUR CULTURE, many self-absorbed people focus their energies on doing the newest activity that promises the most pleasure and on getting the latest technology that's supposed to make life easier. But those things don't satisfy for very long. God made us so that our hearts long for a transcendent purpose. We want to live for something much bigger than ourselves.

Causes come in every stripe and color. Some people get energized for a political candidate who promises to change a city, state, or nation. Others devote themselves to preserving the planet or helping the homeless. In war, soldiers fight and die for the freedom of those back home.

Many causes are noble, but most of them have only temporary results. Taking the message of Christ's love not only to the ends of the earth but to the family members in our homes and coworkers at our jobs is important, eternal work. Beyond even those noble intentions and actions, however, the cause for every believer is to know Christ and to honor Him in everything we do. While the cause of Christ involves reaching the lost and changing lives, ultimately the goal is to please the One who gave His life for us. That's the cause that makes us shout for joy!

What are some causes your friends are excited about?

If an objective observer looked at your life, what would he or she conclude that you are devoted to? Explain your answer.

"Many persons have a wrong idea of what constitutes true happiness. It is not attained through self-gratification but through fidelity to a worthy purpose."
—HELEN KELLER

WINGMAN

How precious is Your lovingkindness, O God! Therefore the children of men put their trust under the shadow of Your wings. PSALM 36:7

SINCE GOD ISN'T LIKE ANYONE or anything else in the universe, the writers of the Bible used many different analogies to explain His amazing attributes. In this psalm, David praises God for His mercy, faithfulness, righteousness, and justice (see 36:5-6). The tender care God gives each of us is precious to David. He seems carried away by the greatness and goodness of the Infinite God. It seems to him that God is like an eagle protecting its eaglets under its enormous wings in the nest.

In a fallen world, bad things happen to all of us. Some Christians believe that God should protect them from any trouble, and they are devastated when they experience even relatively mild difficulties. Like a mighty eagle, God is dedicated to the growth and strength of His "eaglets," and He uses our difficulties to help us grow stronger. In fact, struggles are stepping-stones of growth, so God wouldn't be a loving parent if He protected us from all problems.

But consider the many difficulties we don't experience. Every minute of every day, God protects us from all kinds of pains, from attacks by the enemy of our souls to "accidents" that we barely escape. Most of us enjoy prosperity, pleasure, and health far beyond anything known in earlier generations.

We live "under the shadow" of God's mighty wings, and He protects us with His love and power, but sometimes He nudges us out of the nest so we can learn to fly.

What are some ways God has protected you?

How has God nudged you out of the nest?

"To gain that which is worth having, it may be necessary to lose everything else."
—BERNADETTE DEVLIN

WHAT ARE YOU WAITING FOR?

Now, Lord, what do I wait for? My hope is in You. PSALM 39:7

THROUGHOUT THE BIBLE, we see many examples of waiting on God. We see Abraham waiting on God to bless him with a son. We see the nation of Israel waiting for someone to deliver them from slavery in Egypt, then waiting for hundreds of years for the promised Savior. In the New Testament, we see the disciples waiting for Jesus to become King (they didn't understand that He had to die first), and we see the church waiting for Christ to return. Waiting, it appears, is an integral part of God's design for our lives.

Why, then, do we hate waiting so much? Waiting requires us to trust in the unseen, to be assured that the invisible God will accomplish something good in the physical world. And we have to trust that He will do it when He is ready, not when we want Him to do it. Waiting demands trust, and we'd much rather have our blessings right now, thank you.

As we wait, God purifies and refocuses our hearts. We may have longed for a particular answer from God; however, as He delays, His Spirit works deep in us to change our desires. Our hope may have been in a person, a promotion, or a pleasure; but in the crucible of waiting, God shifts our hearts' attention to Him so that we desire to know Him above all else. Then we can say with David, "Lord, my hope is in You!"

> **How does God change our desires and focus them on Him by causing us to wait?**
>
> **Are you waiting on God for something right now? If you are, how much of your hope is in Him?**

> *"Faith is to believe what you do not see; the reward of this faith is to see what you believe."* —SAINT AUGUSTINE

MAGNIFIED TO BE GLORIFIED

Let all those who seek You rejoice and be glad in You; let such as love Your salvation say continually, "The LORD be magnified!" PSALM 40:16

WHEN WE VALUE SOMETHING, we want everybody to see what we see in it. A musician turns up the volume, gets bigger speakers, and blows the doors off at a concert! A gallery owner selects just the right frame for a beautiful painting and then puts it in the perfect setting in the shop, with the right light to show the artist's creative flair. A jeweler cuts a diamond to maximize the weight and brilliance of the stone and then puts it on a background of black velvet to magnify its luster.

In the same way, we "magnify" people's perceptions of God when we portray Him as wonderful, beautiful, and awesome. We may carefully orchestrate our words, or we may spontaneously shout our praise for God. Either way, our delight in His magnificent greatness and goodness and our amazement that He loves us so much show others how awesome He is.

But that's not all that happens. Have you ever watched someone who has shown you something wonderful or beautiful? Something happens in the hearts of those who magnify music, art, a diamond, or anything else they treasure. They are transformed by praising it. Their love for the musician, artist, craftsman, or creator grows, and their loyalty soars.

When we magnify God, we give Him the praise for which He is completely worthy, and as we praise Him, our love for Him grows.

Describe something beautiful or wonderful that you treasure.

What happens in our hearts as we magnify God?

"I feel it is far better to begin with God, to see His face first, to get my soul near Him before it is near another." —E. M. BOUNDS

WHAT GOES AROUND COMES AROUND

Blessed is he who considers the poor; the LORD will deliver him in time of trouble. PSALM 41:1

IT'S TECHNICALLY CALLED "the law of the harvest," but we commonly say "What goes around comes around" to refer to the law of reaping what we sow. We see the effects of this "law" every day. When we're angry and snap at people, they often snap back at us. (What a surprise!) When we help someone, the one we helped sometimes comes to our rescue when we are in need.

In this verse, though, the law of the harvest takes on a different twist. When we give to someone who is poor, that person can't pay us back, but blessings seem to come our way from out of the blue. It's God. He's the One who sees what we've done and takes care of us in return. That's like Him. Jesus said that it's no big deal to give to those who can give back to us (see Luke 14:12-14). The really big deal is to give to those who can't repay us. He loves that!

Who are the poor around us? Most of us have spent a small fortune buying homes in nice neighborhoods to protect our families from poor people. When we encounter them on drives through their parts of town, we hardly notice them—or worse, we make fun of them.

They're there, and they're real people with real needs and real hopes and dreams. First, God wants us to consider them, to imagine what their lives are like so that we learn to genuinely care. When we care, we'll find a way to take action.

Consider the poor. Who are they? What are their lives like?

What is one thing you can do to care for one of them?

"God's boomerang of blessing occurs when we do something for someone else who can do absolutely nothing for us in return." —IKE REIGHARD

TURNING A CAREER INTO A CALLING

Whatever you do, do it heartily, as to the Lord and not to men, knowing that from the Lord you will receive the reward of the inheritance; for you serve the Lord Christ. COLOSSIANS 3:23-24 {MEMORY VERSE

WHY DO WE GO TO WORK each day? Most of us get out of bed and head to the office for a number of good reasons: to provide for our families, to use our God-given abilities, and to enjoy interaction, creativity, and success. But when we face the inevitable difficulties of an unreasonable boss, a downturn in the economy, a heavy workload, or genuine failure, where can we find our motivation?

In his letter to the Colossians, Paul gives instructions to husbands, wives, fathers, and children. Then he turns his attention to another segment of society: slaves (see Colossians 3:18-22). If any group has cause to complain and be discouraged, it's slaves. They are asked to do the most but are given the least praise. Paul doesn't tell them just to work harder. He goes far beyond that, encouraging them to do their tedious, menial work "heartily," with real enthusiasm as they remember that they are working first for God Himself, not their human masters. But Paul also assures them that God will eventually reward their honest work. They may not see these rewards "today," but like an overperforming 401(k), someday the results will be thrilling!

We can get out of bed each day with the assurance that we are working for the Lord and that our good attitude and hard work will be richly rewarded—if not by our employers now, they will be someday by the God of the universe. That perspective changes our motivation and attitude at work!

What difference would it make for you to realize that you are working primarily for Christ, not for your boss or your company?

What needs to happen in your thoughts, attitudes, and actions to reflect this perspective?

"May he who is highest serve best." —ROBERT THIBODEAU

"We fear not because, when we put on the whole armor of truth and hide behind Jesus Christ, we know in Whom we've believed and we are secure in that belief. We then will serve without fear, and our effectiveness and productivity increase greatly." —ZIG ZIGLAR

RUNNING OVER

Give, and it will be given to you: good measure, pressed down, shaken together, and running over will be put into your bosom. For with the same measure that you use, it will be measured back to you. LUKE 6:38

JESUS' MOST FAMOUS MESSAGE, the Sermon on the Mount, is a beautiful message about Kingdom living (see 6:20-49). Those who trust in God, Jesus tells us, exhibit the life of God in their attitudes, actions, and relationships—in opposition to how the world normally works. He tells us to love those who don't love us, to do good to those who hurt us, and to give to those who can't or won't pay us back. It's revolutionary stuff!

On an intensely personal level, Jesus gives four promises in the form of two "don'ts" and two "dos": Don't judge people and you won't be judged, don't condemn and you won't be condemned, forgive and you'll be forgiven, and give and you'll receive (see 6:37-38). We often look at the promise of giving in isolation, but it's in every aspect of Kingdom life.

Trusting God transforms us inside and out. As our behavior toward others changes, He promises to pour—not trickle, not dab on, not squeeze out a drop or two—His blessings on us. Our trust in God's ability to provide for us results in our giving generously to God and His causes. Then, God opens the storehouses of heaven to bless us. How much? Jesus couldn't have been more expressive: It's so much that it has to be packed in, and it still runs over the top!

If we are stingy, we won't enjoy giving the little we give, and God withholds His abundant blessings. But if we give generously and joyfully, we'd better look out!

Many people say the tithe (10 percent) is the "training wheels" of giving. Do you agree or disagree?

What motivates you to give to God and His work? What about God would you need to know and trust in order for you to give even more?

"I can testify that the Lord is as good as His Word, that if we trust and believe and bring our tithes into the storehouse, He will 'pour out His blessings' of all kinds, including financial." —ZIG ZIGLAR

WHAT'S IN YOUR BOX?

No one can serve two masters; for either he will hate the one and love the other, or else he will be loyal to the one and despise the other. You cannot serve God and mammon. MATTHEW 6:24

AT THE STORE, a father gave his son an empty box and said, "Son, you can have anything you want, but you can have only *one* thing. Make a good choice." In a sense, God gives each of us the same opportunity. A million things compete for our affections and our attention, but only one can be on the throne of our hearts.

All these things make promises. Some promise to give us pleasure, some promise to thrill us, some promise to give us a status that will impress people, and some promise to help us escape pain. We hear voices whispering or shouting these promises all the time. Conversations at work, ads on television and billboards, chats with friends, and all other forms of communication promise to fulfill our dreams. All these things are like competing hawkers at a flea market, trying to convince us to come to their tent to buy what they're selling.

But we can choose only one thing to put in our box.

Amid the din of all these voices, we have to listen hard to hear another voice that says, "I am the way, the truth, and the life" (John 14:6) and offers us an adventure and an abundant life—if we allow this thing in our box.

What are you putting in your box?

Identify some of the competing voices and their promises in your life.

What have you had in your box in the past year or so? What are you putting in your box now?

"Whatever you choose to serve becomes that which you worship." —IKE REIGHARD

MAKING THE IMPOSSIBLE A REALITY

Jesus said to the centurion, "Go your way; and as you have believed, so let it be done for you." And his servant was healed that same hour.

MATTHEW 8:13

ON A FEW OCCASIONS, Jesus was astonished by someone's faith in Him. In this case, a God-fearing Roman centurion asked Jesus to heal his sick servant. Jesus told the centurion that He'd go to his home to heal the man, but the soldier replied, "Lord, I am not worthy that You should come under my roof. But only speak a word, and my servant will be healed" (Matthew 8:8).

Jesus had been among the Jewish people as he taught and healed. Some had believed, but many doubted. The leaders among His own race felt particularly threatened, and they later plotted to kill Him. But here was a Roman officer who believed that Jesus' power was so immense that He didn't even have to see or touch his servant to heal. His faith amazed Jesus.

What did the Roman see in Christ that others didn't see? Why was his faith so strong? The centurion explained that he understood the nature of authority because he exercised it in the military world (see Matthew 8:9). His experience gave him insight into God's authority, so the centurion felt sure that Jesus had authority to heal his servant—or do anything else, for that matter—from a distance.

In each of our lives, God has given us experiences to help us to believe Him more fully. For some, it's authority; for others, it's mercy and kindness. All of us can look for patterns of past experience that strengthen present faith.

Do you have a great respect for authority or perhaps a deep appreciation for grace and kindness? Describe it.

How can your past, positive experiences strengthen your faith for today?

"I used to ask God to help me. Then I asked if I might help Him. I ended up asking Him to do His work through me." —HUDSON TAYLOR

COMMIT TO CONNECT

She said to herself, "If only I may touch His garment, I shall be made well."

MATTHEW 9:21

MAYBE SHE HAD HEARD all the stories of the itinerant Preacher who had the power to heal people, and for the first time in a while, her hope was rekindled. She had been sick for twelve long years, and she had spent all her money on doctors. Nothing had helped. She still felt miserable, and worse, sickness was considered a sign of moral failure in her culture, so she was also an outcast.

We can imagine the conflicting emotions of hope and shame that must have fought in her soul that day as she made her way through the crowd. This, she was convinced, was her last hope. She saw a crowd—someone said Jesus was there! She stepped forward to get as close as she could. There He was! But it looked as if He was leaving. Suddenly, she fell to the ground and reached out between dusty legs and feet to touch the hem of His cloak.

It was an imperfect, impulsive act to connect with Jesus, but it was enough. Suddenly, the power of God surged into her body and healed her, but something even more amazing also happened: Jesus stopped, turned, and singled her out. She had tried to remain incognito. Now she was the center of attention. Only one pair of eyes, though, mattered to her. She had reached out to connect with Jesus, and He reached back to establish a real relationship with her.

What's the difference between really connecting with Jesus and going through the motions of church and other religious activities?

What are some ways you can reach out to connect with Jesus today?

"Hope is the foundational quality for all of life." —**ALFRED ADLER**

THE POWER OF THE LORD

Be exalted, O LORD, in Your own strength! We will sing and praise Your power.

PSALM 21:13

WE MAKE A HUGE MISTAKE when we think that God is only a little bigger than we are. He is far greater and more powerful than our wildest imaginations. Creation gives us a glimpse of His awesome power. The Bible tells us that God merely spoke a word and all the stars were flung into space.

How immense is the universe? The first astronomer, Ptolemy, counted 1,056 stars. With the magnification of a one-inch telescope, we can see 225,000 stars. A 100-inch telescope enables us to see 1.5 billion stars, and with a 200-inch telescope, we can see a billion galaxies, each with about 100 billion stars. The Hubble telescope has enabled astronomers to see 100 billion galaxies. Here's some help to put these numbers in perspective: 100 billion stars in each of 100 billion galaxies is roughly equal to the number of grains of sand on every shore on every beach throughout the entire world!

What difference does this make to us? Our trust in God is a reflection of our grasp of His greatness and grace. If we think He's just a little stronger or nicer than we are, our trust in Him will be meager. But if we marvel at His greatness, we'll trust Him more with every decision, every relationship, and every purpose in our lives.

How does it affect our capacity to trust God when we see Him only as a kind of superman instead of infinitely great and good?

What aspects of your life could benefit from a refreshed trust in the God of infinite power and grace?

"God is an infinite circle whose center is every where and whose circumference is no where." —SAINT AUGUSTINE

WALK WITH INTEGRITY

He who walks with integrity walks securely, but he who perverts his ways will become known. PROVERBS 10:9

INTEGRITY HAS BEEN DESCRIBED as "doing the right thing even when nobody is looking." When we try to hide our sinful behavior behind a mask of lies, we live with the constant fear of somebody finding out. All of us know this experience to some degree. Some of us stay on track most of the time and only occasionally have to fear being found out, but others have lied so much to cover their tracks that they don't remember what's true anymore.

A clear conscience is a treasure, but it doesn't just happen. We can experience the peace of a clean heart and an uncluttered mind only if we make a rigorous commitment to live our lives in the presence of God and, when we fail, make things right quickly. There's nothing quite as chilling as knowing that you're being watched. When we live with the confidence that everything we do passes under the eyes of God, we will make sure we don't stray off track. But we're human, and our sinful nature gets the best of us from time to time. When that happens, the Holy Spirit taps us on the shoulder and says, "Hey, I saw what you did, and it was wrong." We have a choice of saying, in effect, "Go away!" or "Yes, Lord, You're right. That was sin, and I thank You for forgiving me."

Everything we do is already known to God, and someday, everything will be revealed to those we have tried to fool. It's a much wiser course to walk with integrity now.

What happens to you and your relationships when you try to wear a mask to hide your sin?

What would it (or does it) take for you to live with a clear conscience?

"Every choice has a consequence; we can determine our choices, but we do not determine the consequence." —IKE REIGHARD

ANSWERED PRAYER

Jabez called on the God of Israel saying, "Oh, that You would bless me indeed, and enlarge my territory, that Your hand would be with me, and that You would keep me from evil, that I may not cause pain!" So God granted him what he requested. 1 CHRONICLES 4:10 { MEMORY VERSE

WE COULD SAY JABEZ PRACTICED the spiritual principle "You don't have because you don't ask" (see James 4:2) when he asked God for a lot. Boldness in prayer delights God's heart. He is thrilled when His children barge into the throne room and trust Him to be generous with them.

Some would wisely warn us to watch out for wrong motives. Certainly, our selfishness can distort any prayer or longing, but too much caution can cripple our spiritual lives. If we are bold enough to enter the throne room and ask for great things, we open ourselves to God so He can correct impure motives. Interaction with God is the open door for both blessing and correction, and to be honest, most of us need both!

Notice the content of Jabez's prayer. He asked God to enlarge his territory. In that day, land and livestock were signs of wealth, and Jabez unapologetically asked God to bless him. But he didn't just want to be rich; he wanted to experience God's presence and pleasure. He prayed that he would sense the hand of God on his life, and he also asked that God's hand would direct him and protect him from evil. The part of Jabez's request that tells us the most about his heart is the last part: "that I may not cause pain." He was a humble man who recognized his sinful nature's penchant for selfish gain at others' expense, so he asked God to guide him away from anything that might harm anyone else.

The writer tells us that God answered Jabez's prayer. It doesn't say when or how, but we learn that God, like any loving father, delights in giving good gifts to grateful children. Boldness and humility—those are the ingredients of prayers that delight our Father.

How does Jabez's prayer express your desires?

How can you develop more of that blend of boldness and humility?

"Prayers are heard in heaven very much in proportion to our faith. Little faith will get very great mercies, but great faith still greater." —CHARLES HADDON SPURGEON

"You don't pay the price for success; you enjoy the benefits of success." —ZIG ZIGLAR

REVERSING THE LEARNING CURVE

Jesus . . . said, "I thank You, Father, Lord of heaven and earth, that You have hidden these things from the wise and prudent and have revealed them to babes." MATTHEW 11:25

IN GOD'S KINGDOM, many things are the opposite of what you'd expect. To be great, be a humble servant. To be strong, recognize your weakness. To be close to God, admit the darkness and depravity in your heart. In this passage, Jesus gives another startling fact of the Kingdom: God reveals Himself and His truth to "babes" and hides from those who think they know it all. To learn spiritual truth, He explains, you need to go back to the basics.

As we look at how Jesus related to people in the Gospels, we see this reversed learning curve again and again. The highly educated religious leaders argued with Jesus, hardened their hearts, and eventually plotted to have Him executed. Only a couple of them opened their hearts to Him. But the unlearned, the outcasts, and the simple flocked to Him. They listened with wide-open hearts, and many trusted in Him. Virtually all His miracles were reserved for these people.

In our world, people pride themselves on what they know because "knowledge is power." But in the spiritual world, degrees and vast learning don't matter. They don't necessarily prevent insight, but they can easily get in the way. God values a humble heart, and He delights to teach those who will say to Him, "Lord, I don't get it. Will You help me?"

What are some ways pride can prevent us from learning spiritual truth from God?

Where are you on the reverse learning curve? Explain your answer.

"When you know the author of the Book, the Book will have meaning to you."
—ZIG ZIGLAR

WHEN YOU ARE SO TIRED

[Jesus said,] "Come to Me, all you who labor and are heavy laden, and I will give you rest." MATTHEW 11:28

IN A RECENT POLL, a large segment of Americans were asked the simple question, "How are you doing?" The number one answer given by thousands of respondents was simply, "Tired."

We've been had. Years ago, technology promised to make us more efficient so we could have more leisure time and more time with our families, but it hasn't worked out that way. Amazing advances in technology have made us far more efficient and productive, but our thirst for more has caused us to cram our schedules full of additional activities. Many families are so busy that they don't even have one dinner together each week! No wonder we're so tired.

The solution, we've tried to tell ourselves, is better time management or the latest technology, but that hasn't worked either. No, we need something radically different—a new focus with new priorities. Jesus invites us to come to Him. He doesn't promise to give us twenty-five-hour days or magically enable us to get everything checked off our lists each day. Instead, He invites us to trust Him and rest, to enjoy His love and let Him lead us so that we distinguish the *genuinely important* from the *seemingly urgent*. Trusting in Him makes a difference, a big difference.

What (if any) are some evidences in your life of chronic tiredness?

What would it look like for you to respond to Jesus' invitation?

"What worries you, masters you." —HADDON W. ROBINSON

REST FOR THE SOUL

[Jesus said,] "Take My yoke upon you and learn from Me, for I am gentle and lowly in heart, and you will find rest for your souls. For My yoke is easy and My burden is light." MATTHEW 11:29-30

SOME OF US ARE SO BURDENED by life's pressures that our concept of rest is complete escape from all responsibilities. Although that's not a bad idea for some of us, passivity and escape aren't what Jesus had in mind when He was speaking to His followers.

To illustrate his concept of rest, Jesus, in Matthew 11, paints a word picture of a pair of oxen pulling a wagon. Typically, a pair consists of a mature, experienced ox and a young one just learning how to work. The mature ox does far more of the actual work to pull the load. The young animal's task is to figure out how to walk in tandem with the older ox so that they don't pull against each other. The more it learns to cooperate, the easier the task is.

In the same way, Christ invites us to get in the yoke with Him and learn to pull alongside Him. When we have difficulties figuring out how to pull our weight and how to walk along with Him, He doesn't scold us. He's gentle and humble, patiently reminding us of who's pulling most of the load. Many of us are so tired because we've been pulling our own wagons, or we haven't yet learned to walk in tandem with Christ as we pull together. Learning this lesson brings peace, relief, rest, and a heart full of thankfulness for God's leading and strength.

How are you doing in the yoke as you learn to pull with Jesus?

What changes do you need to make? How will these affect your life?

"I have a great need for Christ; I have a great Christ for my need."
—CHARLES HADDON SPURGEON

GOD OF DELIVERANCE

Because he has set his love upon Me, therefore I will deliver him; I will set him on high, because he has known My name. PSALM 91:14

GOD ALWAYS DELIVERS. That's His nature. But God doesn't always deliver us in the way we expect or when we hope the answer will come. When we ask Him to deliver us from sickness, a conflict, or any other difficulty in our lives, we need to avoid demanding that He answer the way we want Him to. If we demand a certain answer, we set ourselves up for disappointment, and if disappointment isn't arrested, it will soon lead to discouragement.

The mark of true faith is steadfast trust in God when we don't see what He's doing or how He's doing it. In spite of what we see with our physical eyes, we cling to the truth that God's purposes, ways, and timing are higher than our ways, as "the heavens are higher than the earth" (Isaiah 55:9). With that kind of faith, God sets us "on high" even in the middle of our trouble. No, we aren't oblivious to our problems, but we hang on tightly to God through thick and thin with the confidence that sooner or later, in one way or another, He will deliver us.

We learn some of life's lessons only by taking the path through life's valleys. It would be great if we could learn all the important lessons on the mountaintops, but we don't. Valleys are part of the path for every believer. When we're there, we can be sure that we have a Guide we can trust and that the path will eventually lead us to higher ground.

When we experience difficulties, what are some differences between demanding answers from God and trusting that He will deliver us in His way and in His time?

What are some of the lessons we learn in life's valleys?

"Faith for my deliverance is not faith in God. Faith means, whether I am visibly delivered or not, I will stick to my belief that God is love." —OSWALD CHAMBERS

COURSE CORRECTION

There are many plans in a man's heart, nevertheless the LORD's counsel—that will stand. PROVERBS 19:21

WHEN WE'RE YOUNG, we plan to take the world by storm. When we're in our middle years, we wonder how we got where we are, and we plan to take it easy one day. When we're older, we plan to leave a legacy. Many of us spend our lives making great and glorious plans, but only a few focus on what's really important. To do that, we need a consultant; we need "the LORD's counsel."

One of the marks of maturity at any age is the ability to see through the urgent to discern what's really important. In our younger years, it seems that everything is urgent. We rush from one goal to another, seldom enjoying life along the way. Sooner or later, we learn that we shouldn't trust ourselves or some of our friends. We need a higher authority, and we turn to God for direction. We search the Scriptures and find that some of the things that seemed so important aren't, and some that seemed trivial are vital in God's view. Money, prestige, power, and possessions are measuring sticks of our culture, but God shakes His head at our compulsive pursuit of these things. They aren't wrong; they just aren't central.

First things first. If we discover God's purposes and pursue them with our whole hearts, our plans will follow His leading. And in the end, our plans—and the positive impact of a life lived for Him—will stand.

What are some things most people think are really important today?

What does God say is really important? How do your pursuits match up with God's purposes?

"Never be afraid to trust an unknown future to a known God." —CORRIE TEN BOOM

IGNORANCE IS NO EXCUSE

If you say, "Surely we did not know this," does not He who weighs the hearts consider it? He who keeps your soul, does He not know it? And will He not render to each man according to his deeds? PROVERBS 24:12

HUMAN BEINGS MAY NOT DO a lot of things well, but we excel at making excuses. One man observed accurately, "The prisons are full of people who insist they are innocent!" And whenever we do anything wrong, we quickly point to someone else to blame, or we describe a circumstance so we can say, "See, I couldn't help it."

God is incredibly gracious and forgiving, but He's not blind. He's not like a kindly old grandfather who lets his grandchildren run wild with impunity. God knows how much we know, and He considers our grasp of situations when He evaluates culpability for our failures. Each of us will give an account of our choices and actions. Each of us will stand before a just and gracious God while He evaluates our behavior, and we'll be rewarded (or not) based on truth and justice. In many cases, pleas to be excused because of ignorance will be discarded because God will say, "I gave you a conscience, but you disregarded it. I gave you the Scriptures, but you didn't read them. I gave you Christian friends, but you spent time with other people instead. I gave you My Spirit, but you didn't listen."

The day of reckoning for Christians will be an evaluation of our deeds and motives as believers, not the judgment of heaven and hell. On the day of reckoning, each of us will give an account, and no excuse will work. All of us want to hear Him say, "Well done, good and faithful servant. Enter into the joy of your Master" (see Matthew 25:21, 23).

Why is it so easy to make excuses instead of taking responsibility?

What needs to change so that standing before Christ will be a joy for you?

"What you get by reaching your destination is not nearly as important as what you will become by reaching your destination." —ZIG ZIGLAR

THE RIGHT WORD AT THE RIGHT TIME

A word fitly spoken is like apples of gold in settings of silver.

PROVERBS 25:11

THE WISEST, MOST MATURE, and most effective people are those who capture a moment by saying the right thing in the right way. Quite often, their statements seem to come from out of the blue because the tone of voice and the actual words speak a very different message from what most people expect. Instead of returning anger for anger and backing people into a corner, they calmly speak truth and give options. Instead of being annoyed by a boring person and walking away, they engage in deeper conversation. Instead of using a person's fears to control him or her, they soothe fear by speaking words of hope.

Researchers tell us that communication is largely nonverbal. Only 7 percent of the impact is in actual words. Facial expressions, gestures, and the tone of voice make up the rest. Words can be "fitly spoken" only if we say them with authenticity, really meaning what we say, and letting our faces, hands, and tone of voice carry the message too.

Messages have incredible power. They can build or destroy, instill hope or take it away. Think about the people you will see today. Some of them are hurting, some are angry, and some have lost hope. What would it mean for you to communicate powerful, life-giving messages of faith, hope, and love to those dear people?

Who are the people who have most often and most powerfully affirmed you and given you hope when you felt hopeless?

What are some messages you can give to particular people today?

"Colors fade, temples crumble, empires fall, but wise words endure."
—EDWARD L. THORNDIKE

TIME IS RUNNING OUT

Teach us to number our days, that we may gain a heart of wisdom.

PSALM 90:12 ⟨ MEMORY VERSE

BY THE TIME MOSES WROTE THIS PSALM, he was growing old. As he reflected on his life, he realized that life passes really quickly. When we're young, life seems to crawl, but in old age, it flies by! To an eternal God, however, time is meaningless. A thousand years, Moses knew, is like a day to God.

The rapid pace and brevity of life, though, isn't a cause for despair but for wisdom. Moses asked God for insight: "Teach us to number our days." He didn't mean to count them one after another, but to value each one individually so we don't waste a single one.

With a sense of urgency, some people feel compelled to fill up each moment of each day with as much activity as possible, but this isn't the model of life Jesus gave us. He lived each moment with the certainty that His life counted, and He made choices to speak, work, rest, and engage others because His heart was focused on the Father's will, not some arbitrary standard of achievement.

Life is short, but it's full of meaning, love, and hope if we "number" our days and live them for Christ instead of wasting them on empty pursuits. With Him in the center of our lives, we can rest, laugh, work hard, serve, and engage people in conversations that matter. That's what Jesus did. We can too.

What does it mean to "number our days"?

What does (or would) the fruit of a "heart of wisdom" look like in your life?

"Time stands still for no man." —LEONARD REISS

"You can earn more money, but when time is spent it is gone." —ZIG ZIGLAR

THE POWER OF VISION

Where there is no vision, the people perish: but he that keepeth the law, happy is he. PROVERBS 29:18, KJV {MEMORY VERSE

SOME PEOPLE HAVE A CLEAR VISION for their lives, and they gladly subject every aspect of their lives to fulfill their life purpose. Most of us, though, muddle through with only a vague sense of meaning and direction. Some of us dream too much, and some dream too little. Of the two, the latter is worse than the first. If people are moving, they can be steered in a better direction, but if they're stuck, no amount of steering will do any good.

Where does vision originate? Some of us have a personality type that naturally identifies goals and pushes us to achieve them. Others have grown up with parents or other mentors who saw latent potential in us and inflamed the embers of desire to accomplish great things. An imparted vision is just as powerful as one we develop on our own. If we don't have a clear, compelling sense of purpose, we need to hang around people who can rub off on us.

If you look for these people, you'll find them in almost any organization. But be careful of whom you hang out with. Many people have powerful goals, but they are almost completely self-absorbed. Find someone whose purpose in life is to love and serve and build others up—and camp out with that person!

Describe someone you know whose vision is clear, compelling, and centered on others.

Does your sense of purpose need an overhaul? Explain your answer.

"A vision without the ability to execute it is called hallucinating! Every God-given vision will result in being fulfilled; every man-concocted vision will be a dead end." —IKE REIGHARD

"Go as far as you can see, and when you get there, you will always see farther." —ZIG ZIGLAR

FULLY ACQUAINTED

O Lord, You have searched me and known me. You know my sitting down and my rising up; You understand my thought afar off. You comprehend my path and my lying down, and are acquainted with all my ways.

PSALM 139:1-3

THE WORD SEARCHED in this beautiful psalm by King David is a mining term that means digging deep into the earth to find gold. David used it to describe God's grasp of his life because he realized that God's understanding of his heart was so deep that He dug into the very core of his soul. God knows each of us that way too.

We may feel that God has left us high and dry, but He hasn't. He is as near as our breath. We may be afraid that He doesn't care, but He cares so much that He is as attentive as a loving mother with her newborn child. We may believe that we're getting away with things because God isn't looking, but He knows every action we take and even every thought we think. Nothing escapes His notice!

We are completely, absolutely exposed in the sight of God. Like Adam and Eve in the Garden, we are naked before Him. However, unlike them in their unfallen state, we are often ashamed. God's intimate and complete knowledge of everything about us, though, is combined with grace, forgiveness, and love. He knows us, and He forgives us for being so selfish and making such foolish choices. He sees everything we do and perceives every thought, but He never turns away in disgust. A fresh grasp of the omniscience of God, then, helps us gain a new appreciation for His great grace.

How do you feel when you realize that God sees and knows everything about you?

How does a fresh grasp of His omniscience give you a new appreciation for His grace?

"There is tremendous relief in knowing that His love to me is utterly realistic, based at every point on prior knowledge of the worst about me, so that no discovery now can disillusion Him about me, in the way I am so often disillusioned about myself, and quench His determination to bless me."
—J. I. PACKER

EVERYWHERE

If I ascend into heaven, You are there; if I make my bed in hell, behold, You are there. If I take the wings of the morning, and dwell in the uttermost parts of the sea, even there Your hand shall lead me, and Your right hand shall hold me.

PSALM 139:8-10

THE ETERNAL NATURE OF GOD—past, present, and future—is clearly revealed by today's passage in Psalm 139. In beautiful and powerful poetic language, David explains that God is omnipresent. God is never bound by the limitations of time and space like those experienced by mere mortals.

We will never experience a moment or a place in our lives where God is not present in Spirit. When we are on the mountaintop of exhilaration, God is present in our joy. When we suffer in the valley of depression and isolate ourselves in the dark of despair, God is there as a light in our darkness. When we enjoy our greatest success, God rejoices with us. When our failures overwhelm our senses, He is there to bring equilibrium back to our upside-down world. When we are alone and indulge in the sin that besets us, God is there, too. God's presence brings either comfort or discomfort, depending on our actions and reactions to the pull of His ever-present Spirit.

When are you most aware of God's presence?

When you feel hopelessly distant from God, how will it affect you to remember that He is always with you?

"When you feel lonely, when you feel unwanted, when you feel sick and forgotten, remember you are precious to Him." —**MOTHER TERESA**

EVEN IN THE DARK

If I say, "Surely the darkness shall fall on me," even the night shall be light about me; indeed, the darkness shall not hide from You, but the night shines as the day; the darkness and the light are both alike to You. PSALM 139:11-12

DAVID EXPERIENCED TIMES of darkness when it seemed the light of hope would never shine again. He was attacked by enemies and betrayed by friends. He hid in the wilderness for years in fear for his life. But perhaps the darkness was worst in the hours of the night after he had committed adultery with Bathsheba and covered it up by having her husband, Uriah, killed (see 2 Samuel 11:1-17).

At some time in our lives, virtually all of us suffer periods of pitch-black spiritual darkness. We can't see, and we're sure nobody else can see either! We feel hopeless, and worse, we're afraid we'll always feel this way. In the depth of David's predicament, God gave him a fresh insight. David may not see any light, but God sees just as clearly in our darkness as He sees in the light. This realization gave David new hope. He didn't have to see light as long as he was convinced that the God of love and strength could see clearly.

When we are in the pit of darkness, without sight and without hope, we can be sure that God is never sightless. He sees us in the dark, and He sees a solution to our problem even when we can't see it. In that, we can be confident.

Describe a time when you felt in the dark spiritually and emotionally.

How does it affect you to realize that God sees clearly even when you can't see at all?

"There are seldom, if ever, any hopeless situations, but there are many people who lose hope in the face of some situations." —ZIG ZIGLAR

CRAFTED BY THE CREATOR

You formed my inward parts; You covered me in my mother's womb.

PSALM 139:13

WE'RE ALWAYS CHECKING ourselves out. We look in the mirror to see how we look, and if we're honest, most of us glance at our reflections in windows throughout the day. We compare our appearance with the models on fashion magazines and celebrities on the red carpet, and we have to face the fact again and again that we don't measure up! As Americans, we spend billions every year to change how we look, and most of us remain disheartened.

We need a new benchmark and new set of values, and David gives them to us in this beautiful poem. Almighty God, the One who is infinitely wise, kind, and strong, carefully crafted each of us in the womb. He used the building blocks of DNA, but the uniqueness of our individual appearance was in His hands. But it was not only our appearance. God crafted our personalities, our intellects, and our talents; and His creative work in each of us prepares us to fulfill the greatest goal life can offer: to be His man or His woman in the circumstances we face every day.

How do you feel about your appearance, intellect, and talents?

How would it change your sense of contentment and passion if you really believed that God crafted you?

"I want to help you grow as beautiful as God meant you to be when He thought of you first." —GEORGE MACDONALD

FEARFULLY AND WONDERFULLY MADE

I will praise You, for I am fearfully and wonderfully made; marvelous are Your works, and that my soul knows very well. PSALM 139:14

HUMILITY AND CONFIDENCE aren't opposites. They are compatible traits of someone who realizes he or she has been "fearfully and wonderfully made" by God. Everything we are—all of our abilities, our intellects, our talents, our skills, and our capabilities—have been hardwired into our DNA by Almighty God or shaped by the experiences He has orchestrated or allowed in our lives. Each of us, even the most self-doubting, is an amazing product created by the Master's hand. We need to notice how He has crafted us so we maximize our efforts to fit His design.

But take careful note: We are His design, not our own. Yes, we are incredible creatures, but we can't take credit. Even our discipline and desire to excel come from God's work in us. When we realize that God has made us who we are and we appreciate His creative genius, we more eagerly put our lives into His hands and say, "Lord, do whatever You want to do with me."

That's a prayer He's happy to answer.

Pride is ugly and destructive. Actually, most people who appear proud are only covering up their insecurities. The powerful blend of humility and confidence enables us to appreciate our strengths and use them with excellence, but we recognize that we didn't create those abilities. They are gifts from God. And that makes all the difference.

What are the strengths God has hardwired into you or developed in you through experiences?

What difference does it make to realize that God created you with your abilities and that they are gifts from Him to you?

"Man, made in the image of God, has a purpose to be in relationship to God, who is there. Man forgets his purpose and thus he forgets who he is and what life means." —FRANCIS A. SCHAEFFER

THINKING ABOUT ME?

How precious also are Your thoughts to me, O God! How great is the sum of them! If I should count them, they would be more in number than the sand; when I awake, I am still with You. PSALM 139:17-18

WHEN A GOOD FRIEND SAYS, "I've been thinking of you," we realize how much that person cares for us. When God says it, we're amazed we're that important to Him. David tells us that God doesn't have just a passing thought about us from time to time—His thoughts of us are as numerous as the grains of sand on the seashore! He's always thinking about us.

"Yeah," we might respond, "but *what's He thinking?*" Earlier in this psalm, David describes the awesome greatness of God and His complete knowledge of everything all the time. God knows literally every thought we have, which means He sees us at our best, and He sees us at our worst. Yet David says that God's thoughts are "precious" to him. How can that be? When we trust God with boldness and courage, God celebrates with us, and when we are selfish, God's grace and forgiveness shine through. His celebration of and grace for what we're thinking are precious thoughts by the One who knows everything—absolutely everything—about us.

How much do you think about God? He thinks about you all day every day, and His purposes for you are really good!

Does the fact that God constantly thinks about you encourage you or terrify you? Explain your answer.

What do you imagine that He's been thinking about you today?

"Too often we attempt to work for God to the limit of our competency, rather than to the limit of God's omnipotency." —HUDSON TAYLOR

AN INVITATION

Search me, O God, and know my heart; try me, and know my anxieties; and
see if there is any wicked way in me, and lead me in the way everlasting.

PSALM 139:23-24

PSALM 139 BEGINS with David's pronouncement that nothing in our lives escapes God's sight, and to be honest, the thought terrifies him! He wants to run away and hide, but he realizes there is nowhere he could go to get away from God's piercing vision. By the end of this poem, though, David's trust in God has been strengthened. He is convinced that God's blazing eyes are tempered by His amazing grace. Now, in the final lines, David actually invites God to search his heart, to show him any sin, and to change his life.

The transformation is remarkable—from wanting to run from God to inviting Him to look into every crevice and dark spot in David's heart. What could cause such a change? David became convinced that God loved him and wanted the best for him, and in fact, God had called him to be His partner in taking His message to the whole world! God's love and the honor of representing Him gave David a fresh desire for God to purify his life so that nothing would get in the way.

What are some attitudes and beliefs about God that make us want to stay away from Him?

Do you, like David, want to be sure that nothing gets in the way of your relationship with God? If so, pray these verses to God—and then listen.

"Anxiety is the natural result when our hopes are centered in anything short of God and His will for us." —BILLY GRAHAM

A WORK IN PROGRESS

Being confident of this very thing, that He who has begun a good work in you will complete it until the day of Jesus Christ. PHILIPPIANS 1:6 { MEMORY VERSE

THE MOMENT WE TRUST in Christ, some amazing transformations take place. All our sins are forgiven, we join God's family, we receive eternal life, and God's Spirit takes up residence inside us (to name just a few). These things are wonderful truths of our new life in Christ, but we've only begun to let those things sink deep into the crevices of our lives to change our motivations, thoughts, and habits. We are very much works in progress, and we'll remain unfinished until we see Jesus face-to-face.

As we consider this fact, two important principles emerge. First, we shouldn't expect perfection. We are on a long, long journey, and many of us have just learned to walk! We have much to learn, and we need to unpack the distortions, bad habits, and selfish attitudes we carry in our backpacks. If we think we should be perfect, we may deny that we are drifting off course from time to time, so we will fail to make corrections. Denial can lead to calamity.

And second, we aren't on this journey alone. God has committed Himself to be our guide all along the way. He is helping us unload some of the excess baggage we carry, and He gives us directions when we come to a crossroads. Sometimes we listen well, but sometimes we think we know the way without His help. We'll do a lot better if we pay attention to Him!

The trail is long, and we won't arrive at our destination in this life. Still, we're on the journey with Jesus for the greatest thrill of our lives.

How does it help you to know that you're a "work in progress"?

What do you need to do to walk more closely with God on the journey?

"There has never yet been a man in our history who led a life of ease whose name is worth remembering." —**THEODORE ROOSEVELT**

"A promise like that from a person would be impossible, but that promise from the God who cannot lie is exciting!" —**ZIG ZIGLAR**

A GIFT FROM GOD

Houses and riches are an inheritance from fathers, but a prudent wife is from the LORD. PROVERBS 19:14

IT'S SO EASY to take a spouse for granted. We are self-centered, and somehow we expect a wife to be like June Cleaver or a husband to be as attentive and wise as Ward. Unrealistic expectations always lead to deep disappointments. Instead of demanding more from our spouse, we need to cultivate a heart of thankfulness. Amazing things happen when we're thankful for the person who sits across the table from us!

People thrive on affirmation, and in fact, they often become what we say about them. If we say they are lazy and selfish, they often become even lazier and more self-absorbed, but if we focus on their good traits and express appreciation, fledgling positive character traits often blossom into great strengths!

One unkind word uttered when we're tired or distressed may not cause irreparable harm, but the absence of praise and the presence of constant criticism erode a relationship as surely as the Colorado River carved the Grand Canyon. When we see one another as gifts from God, we can take it up with Him when we're unhappy, but we can choose to speak words of affirmation and kindness to our spouse. He or she is a gift from God, and all of us treasure good gifts, don't we?

How would you describe the warmth/coldness factor in your marriage?

Make a list of the top five things you appreciate about your spouse, and share one of them today.

"Ruth is my soul mate and best friend, and I cannot imagine living a single day without her by my side." —BILLY GRAHAM

WEIGH YOUR WORDS

[Jesus said,] "I say to you that for every idle word men may speak, they will give account of it in the day of judgment. For by your words you will be justified, and by your words you will be condemned." MATTHEW 12:36-37

OUR WORDS HAVE THE POWER to heal or to destroy. Our choices in using them make a difference in people's lives, and God will judge those choices when we stand before Him to give an account of our lives. On that day, we can't say, "Oh, that's not what I meant," or "She didn't understand," or "I was just joking."

In this warning, Jesus tells us that even our "idle" words will pass through the fires of judgment. We can understand that really important statements will receive God's attention: defending a friend with courage, lovingly affirming our spouse at a critical moment of self-doubt, confronting the Little League coach for not playing a son enough, or lying to a parent. But even our most off-the-cuff remarks undergo God's scrutiny because they, too, have the power to heal or to destroy. A spontaneous word of praise can make someone's day, or a careless whisper of gossip can ruin a reputation.

The gravity of Jesus' statement makes us stop short and ask, "Whoa, this must be pretty important. What do I say that needs more attention?" What, indeed.

How have you seen seemingly insignificant remarks heal or destroy someone?

What do you need to do to speak more words of encouragement and avoid criticisms and condemnation—even in the most casual conversations?

"Words are the visible clothes that our invisible thoughts wear." —IKE REIGHARD

100X

He who received seed on the good ground is he who hears the word and understands it, who indeed bears fruit and produces: some a hundredfold, some sixty, some thirty. MATTHEW 13:23

JESUS TOLD A STORY using four types of soil to illustrate different responses to God (see Matthew 13:3-8, 18-23). A farmer scatters seed. Some of it falls on the road and is eaten by birds. Some falls on rocky soil. It sprouts up quickly but wilts in the hot sun because it doesn't have a good root system. Other seed falls among weeds and is choked out as it grows, but the last grains of seed fall on fertile soil where they grow, mature, and multiply tremendously.

In every community, church, and Christian group, we see these four responses to Christ. Some people hear God's truth; however, it doesn't seem to make the slightest dent. Others receive it gladly, but when difficulties surface, their joy quickly fades into despair. Many others grow for a while, then worries erode their faith and competing attractions of pleasure and possessions steal their hearts. But a few resist these temptations, grow strong in their faith, and touch the lives of tens or hundreds of others. Those whom God uses to mend broken families and guide wayward lives say there's nothing so thrilling or fulfilling in the world.

Each of us has the opportunity to choose the type of soil we want to be. Jesus' story explains the options, but He leaves the decision up to us.

What type of soil have you been for most of your Christian life? What are you now?

What are some changes you'd need to make to be a fourth-type-of-soil person?

"Far better it is to dare mighty things, to win glorious triumphs, even though checked by failure, than to rank with those poor spirits who neither enjoy much nor suffer much, because they live in the grey twilight that knows neither victory nor defeat." —THEODORE ROOSEVELT

KEEPING FOCUSED

Do not let your heart envy sinners, but be zealous for the fear of the LORD all the day. PROVERBS 23:17

COMPARISON CONSUMES OUR GAZES and steals our souls. When we look at what others have and what they have achieved, it's easy for us to see how we stack up. If we've got more and done more than others, we feel great about ourselves, but if we're coming up short, we get discouraged or we're driven to get ahead. Either way, we've lost our focus.

Ultimately, we live for an audience of One. God is the only One who is worthy of our affections and allegiance. When we compare ourselves with others, we quickly become consumed with pride or envy, and our passion for Christ quickly fades.

Solomon tells us that passion is a choice. He said, "Don't let your heart envy sinners." Envy doesn't just happen. It's the result of choosing to look, to compare, and to desire more than we have so we can look better than we do. To make the choice for godly passion, we need to value God's purposes more than getting ahead of others, and we need to care more about people's souls (including our own) than cars, clothes, and vacations.

As our hearts grasp the wonder, the majesty, and the mystery of knowing and following Christ, we realize that nothing else compares to Him. As long as we live in this world, the choice to focus on Him is never easy. But focus is a product of habit, and we can develop the habit of letting our minds and hearts soak up the riches of God instead of comparing the riches of this world.

What are some ways you can "not let your heart envy sinners"?

What about Christ is so valuable that it makes Him beyond compare?

"The price of greatness is responsibility." —WINSTON CHURCHILL

REFINING YOUR REPUTATION

The refining pot is for silver and the furnace for gold, and a man is valued by what others say of him. PROVERBS 27:21

OUR REPUTATIONS OCCASIONALLY may be unfairly tarnished when others spread gossip that's not true, but over time, the judgment of public opinion rings fairly true. That can be good news or bad news, depending on the opinion!

When precious metals endure the refining process, ore is heated to the melting point. At intervals, the dross, or sludge, is skimmed from the top, gradually leaving the purified metal. In the same way, the opinions of others are the fire in our lives to separate the noble from the selfish, the good from the bad. If we are wise, bad reports can be tremendously valuable—if we'll accept them and respond with changes. But if we take ourselves off the fire by excusing our actions and blaming someone else, we won't learn, and we won't benefit from the heat of criticism.

A good reputation takes time to earn, just as it takes time for the fire to heat ore and slowly purify gold and silver. We need to pay attention to others' opinions of us, but we should be careful not to weigh everyone's opinion equally. Place high value on the perceptions of wise people, but discount the backbiting gossip of angry people or those who flatter to win your approval.

Stay in the heat, learn hard lessons, and let God use the fires of others' opinions to purify your heart.

How do you respond to criticism?

Who are the people you trust to tell you the truth?

"To disregard what the world thinks of us is not only arrogant but utterly shameless." —CICERO

DON'T FOOL YOURSELF

Bear one another's burdens, and so fulfill the law of Christ. For if anyone thinks himself to be something, when he is nothing, he deceives himself. But let each one examine his own work, and then he will have rejoicing in himself alone, and not in another. For each one shall bear his own load. GALATIANS 6:2-5 { MEMORY VERSE

WHEN WE ARE INVOLVED in leading people or helping the disadvantaged, we can lose track of our motives. Controlling people is heady stuff. We feel powerful, and to be honest, we can feel indispensable. *Nobody can do it as well as I can*, we might tell ourselves. *What would they do without me?*

Paul reminds us not to fool ourselves. Humility is essential in leading and helping so that we don't let power go to our heads. Instead of being distracted by the abilities and positions of others, we need to stop and examine only our own work and our own hearts. The measuring stick, we soon learn, isn't that we know more than people below us in the organization or that we have more power than others and can tell them what to do. The measuring stick is Christ, who "emptied Himself" to serve (Philippians 2:7, NASB).

Comparison may be a natural thing everybody does, but people in leadership and in helping ministries need to avoid it at all costs because it feeds either insecurity or pride, not humility and trust in God. Ultimately, each of us will stand before Christ to give an account of our lives. On that day, He won't ask us if we were more powerful than others. He'll ask only if we did all we could to help, serve, and give, taking responsibility for our choices—all to "fulfill the law of Christ" to help others instead of wielding power for our own sake.

What roles do you have that can foster comparison with others?

What would it look like to humbly "fulfill the law of Christ" in each of these roles?

"It is one of the most beautiful compensations of life, that no man can sincerely try to help another without helping himself." —RALPH WALDO EMERSON

"Success is not measured by what you do compared to what others do; it is measured by what you do with the ability God gave you." —ZIG ZIGLAR

OUR SHIELD

Every word of God is pure; He is a shield to those who put their trust in Him.

PROVERBS 30:5

THOUGH RELATIVELY FEW of us have experienced war, all of us are under attack from a wide range of enemies. Envy, lust, and greed attack our hearts and tell us that God isn't enough to make us happy. Possessions, sex, and prestige, they insist, are more important than God's purposes. Friends and family turn against us, betray our trust, stab us in the back, or just walk away, leaving us alone and abandoned. Our culture shouts that no matter how much we have, it's never enough. And the enemy of our souls lies to us, telling us that God doesn't care, that He can't help us, and that we're on our own.

In the fight against all these enemies, God is our shield. He protects us by giving us insight from His Word so we can fight and win every battle. To be sure, warfare isn't clean and neat. Sometimes we get dirty, and occasionally we get hurt. But God's Word reminds us of His love and strength, and it gives us truth about God's purposes, our motives, and the destructive ways the world, our sinful flesh, and the devil are trying to bring us down.

When we fail to read God's Word and gain its wisdom, we are vulnerable, and attacks can devastate us. Read and study, grasp the truths of God, and trust Him in the midst of the battle.

What kind of attacks have you experienced lately?

How can the wisdom, insights, and truths from God's Word defend you?

"It's not what you know; it's what you use that makes a difference." —**ZIG ZIGLAR**

LIAR, LIAR

Do not add to His words, lest He rebuke you, and you be found a liar.

PROVERBS 30:6

MANY MODERN TRANSLATIONS of the Bible are over one thousand pages. Why in the world would we think of adding anything to it? But many of us do. All of us interpret the Scriptures through the grid of our culture and experience. We can't help it; it just happens. But our goal is to understand these truths the way the God-inspired authors intended their original audience to grasp them. For instance, Paul's harsh words to the believers in Galatia were prompted by their wavering faith and their tendency to go back to trusting in good works to save them from sin (see Galatians 3:2-5). His words spoke to a particular need in the lives of those people.

Today, we "add to His words" when we make them say what we want them to say instead of digging deep to get to the real meaning. That takes work, but it's well worth it. People who want to justify their extravagant lifestyles insist that God promises wealth to everybody who trusts Him. He does? That would be news to Jesus. And other people insist that if they just pray a certain way or hard enough, God will certainly answer their prayers. He will? He didn't answer Paul's prayer for healing, Job's request for answers, or even Jesus' petition to "let this cup pass from Me" (Matthew 26:39).

We like simple answers and answers that fit our lifestyles, but we need to go deeper to find the truth. Ultimately, God wants us to trust in Him no matter what difficulties we endure or joys we experience. When we insist on simple answers for life's most complex questions, and when those answers justify selfish behavior, we run great risk of being found to be liars.

What are some examples of simplistic answers to life's complex questions?

What are some ways you can dig deeper into God's Word?

"Some people believe in the 'Dalmatian theory' of the Bible. They believe the Bible is inspired in spots and that they are inspired to spot the spots." —W. A. CRISWELL

IT NEVER WITHERS

The grass withers, the flower fades, but the word of our God stands forever.

ISAIAH 40:8

A FEW PEOPLE THRIVE on change, but for most of us, change threatens us because it shakes the little sense of security we have. Our lives are full of stresses and expectations, and we try hard to stay one step ahead. We cherish the one restaurant we know will give us a great meal, the one vacation spot that always allows us to relax for a while, and the one friend who understands even when we're confused.

But there's another source of stability that's far more important: God's Word. Throughout the Bible, God tells us that everything around us can change—even heaven and earth can pass away (see Matthew 24:35)—but God's Word remains rock solid and dependable. What exactly does that mean, and how does it become a rock of stability in our lives?

The Bible doesn't tell us everything about every problem and opportunity, but it gives clear teaching about the nature of God and clear principles about life. From these, we realize we can trust God through any and every circumstance, and we find direction for handling open doors, closed doors, and no doors at all. Culture changes (do you remember bell-bottoms?), age, and mobility alter every aspect of our lives except one: the Word of God, which stands forever.

What are some things the Bible teaches about God's character that you can count on?

What are some principles it teaches about life that you can count on?

"The Bible fits man for life and prepares him for death." —DANIEL WEBSTER

GOOD ADVICE

Trust in the LORD with all your heart, and lean not on your own understanding.

PROVERBS 3:5

OUR IMMEDIATE AND NATURAL instinct is to trust what we can see, touch, and feel and to rely on our ability to figure out solutions to any problem. When the chips are down, we "lean" on our ability to analyze situations and figure out what to do next.

In fact, many of us become obsessed with figuring out what to do when times are tough. We call it "worry." We can't concentrate on the job in front of us because we're still thinking about the problem, situation, or comment that absorbs our minds. We can't sleep because we go over our fears and our plans again and again. We create scenarios and weigh options. We try to imagine others' responses, and our fears compound. Leaning on our own understanding may not sound like such a bad thing (after all, God gave us our minds), but hours, days, and weeks of endless analysis, confusion, and self-doubt can dominate our lives.

Our instinct, though, is flawed and limited. Another source of wisdom is far superior to our ability to figure things out. We are connected with the God of the universe, the One who knows all, sees all, and is powerfully able to accomplish anything He desires. The more we grasp this fundamental fact of the Christian faith, the more we will learn to overcome our instincts and trust in an unseen but all-seeing God.

In your experience, what are some differences between leaning on your own understanding and trusting in God?

What are some situations you face now in which you need to trust more in God? What will you trust Him to do?

"The longer I live the more faith I have in Providence, and the less faith in my interpretation of Providence." —JEREMIAH DAY

BETTER THAN SLICED BREAD

[Jesus] said, "It is written, 'Man shall not live by bread alone, but by every word that proceeds from the mouth of God.'" MATTHEW 4:4

JESUS COMPARED OUR NEED for physical nourishment with our need for spiritual nourishment. Both, He said, are essential for a healthy life. If we think about this parallel, the implications are quite sobering. Nightly news programs show the devastation caused by famine in remote corners of the world. Months or years of crop failures lead to forced migration and starvation. Images of gaunt figures shock us. In the spiritual world, we see starvation all around us, but we seldom identify the symptoms as a famine of God's Word. Broken families, depression, addiction, violence, crime, gangs, bitterness, racism, and a host of other problems are actually evidences of spiritual starvation.

On a physical level, few of us miss meals. We eat when we're hungry, but we also eat to prevent feelings of hunger. In our wealthy culture, eating is taken for granted, but many of us—even many of us who attend church every Sunday—are starving spiritually because we don't devour and digest God's Word. It's readily available. Most homes have copies of the Bible lying around, but we need to pick one up, chew on its truth, swallow its principles, and let its strength invigorate us to do what God wants us to do.

In what ways are physical eating and spiritual nourishment similar?

What do you need to do to nourish yourself more fully on God's Word?

"When I discipline myself to eat properly, live morally, exercise regularly, grow mentally and spiritually, and not to put drugs or alcohol in my body, I have given myself the freedom to be at my best, perform at my best, and reap all the rewards that go along with it." —ZIG ZIGLAR

CONVICTED TO CHANGE

Now it happened, when the king heard the words of the Book of the Law, that he tore his clothes. 2 KINGS 22:11

IN THE GENERATIONS after David and Solomon, God's people were in trouble. Some of their kings had followed God, but many had turned away from Him. They had formed alliances with unbelieving countries to save their necks, but God had allowed half the kingdom, Israel, to be overrun by the Assyrians. Now, a boy named Josiah became king of the other half, Judah (see 2 Kings 22:1-20).

Years of spiritual neglect had eroded the people's faith in God, and they had even lost the scroll of the Scriptures. One day, though, the high priest found the scroll. An attendant took it to Josiah and read it to him.

We can imagine the scene: The king sat on his throne listening to the words of God, which he had never heard before. The power and clarity of God's laws and promises instantly gripped his heart. He realized that all the problems they were experiencing occurred because their forefathers had not obeyed the words of the scroll. His sorrow was so strong that he tore his clothes in anguish.

Josiah wasn't just sorry, though. He took action. He renewed the covenant the people had made years ago with God, and he "cleaned house." He pulled down the altars to other gods the evil kings had erected; he kicked out false teachers, mediums, and spiritists; and he commanded that every idol in the land be thrown away.

When God convicts us of disobedience and selfishness, we need to follow Josiah's example. We need to let the Spirit touch us at the deepest level so that we feel genuine remorse, and then we need to take bold action to right wrongs and walk with God in truth and integrity.

When was the last time you felt truly convicted by God's Spirit about sin in your life? Describe your response.

What are some actions you need to take to "clean house" the way Josiah did?

"Greatness is a spiritual condition." —MATTHEW ARNOLD

CAUSE AND EFFECT

In all your ways acknowledge Him, and He shall direct your paths.

PROVERBS 3:6 { MEMORY VERSE

IT'S KIND OF AMAZING: We have a relationship with the most powerful, most loving, and wisest being in the universe, but we sometimes live our lives as though He doesn't exist. Because He's invisible, we forget He is always present in all of His majesty and kindness. We need reminders to "acknowledge Him."

We can acknowledge God in the good times by thanking Him for the loving, pleasant, and successful things we experience. We can acknowledge Him in times of loss by pouring out our hearts to the One who cares. We can acknowledge Him when we are lost or confused by asking Him for wisdom and then listening to the Spirit's nudging. And we can acknowledge Him when we are bored by asking Him to rekindle our sense of purpose.

In our relationships on earth, we often have to work through misunderstandings and misplaced expectations. That's true of our relationship with God, too, but we won't enjoy the love or work through problems with Him if we fail to first acknowledge He is there.

Like loved children, we instinctively trust those who have proven they are strong and wise. We ask questions, we listen, and we follow advice. God has proven Himself to us. When we acknowledge Him, we interact, we sense His Spirit's leading, and we follow His directions.

What are some reasons we fail to acknowledge God more often?

What would it mean in your life for you to acknowledge Him more?

"We all want progress, but if you're on the wrong road, progress means doing an about turn and walking back to the right road; in that case, the man who turns back soonest is the most progressive." —C. S. LEWIS

"Success is not a destination; it's a journey." —ZIG ZIGLAR

DON'T OUTSMART YOURSELF

Do not be wise in your own eyes; fear the LORD and depart from evil.

PROVERBS 3:7 { MEMORY VERSE

WE SEE IT ALL THE TIME: Federal agents arrest prominent businessmen for their part in corporate fraud, and the media broadcasts accounts of the shattered lives of celebrities who wrecked their lives with foolish decisions. When reporters interview these people, they reply, "It seemed like the right thing to do at the time. I didn't see anything wrong with it."

For them and for the rest of us, making decisions on our own can devastate us—and it ruins relationships with those we love. Over and over again in the Scriptures, God assures us that He will give us wisdom if we just ask for it.

Solomon knew a thing or two about dumb decisions. He had made plenty of them! In this brief ethical statement, he gives us two directives that can prevent us from depending on our own wisdom and making similar mistakes. First, he instructs us to "fear the LORD," which means to have the utmost respect and reverence for God. The bigger He appears in our hearts' perspective, the more we'll trust Him. Genuine reverence for God is an attitude of the heart that results in godly action. Second, Solomon told us to depart from evil. That advice should be a no-brainer, but all of us need to be reminded not to play with the fires of deception, greed, and pride.

Trusting in our own wisdom inevitably brings trouble, but we show true wisdom by respecting God and staying far away from evil.

What are some consequences you've experienced by trusting in your own wisdom instead of trusting in God?

What are some forms of evil that you need to stay away from today?

"Sooner or later we all sit down to a banquet of consequences."
—ROBERT LOUIS STEVENSON

SHIFTING LIFE'S PARADIGM

Evil men do not understand justice, but those who seek the LORD understand all.

PROVERBS 28:5

IN THE HEART OF EACH PERSON, God has instilled an innate sense of justice. At the core of our souls, our conscience tells us the difference between right and wrong. But when someone has pursued selfish ends long enough and hard enough, that sense of justice is clouded. Self-absorbed people experience a lot of disappointment and anger, and they often have a hair trigger when it comes to accusing God or anyone else who doesn't meet their demands. We often hear them say, "That's not fair!"

Our pursuit of God is a difficult climb. We experience wonderful moments when life is good, and at other times, we suffer through deep valleys of heartache. Much of the time, we march along life's trails with friends and family, enjoying everyday blessings and overcoming obstacles. On this journey, we develop wisdom, as well as the ability to see beneath the surface and grasp the fact that God knows exactly what He's doing, even when we don't. We "understand all," not by being clairvoyant, but by trusting that God is both good and great and that He is active in our lives all day every day.

Wise people realize that in this life some things aren't fair, and they can live with that fact because they know that in the next life, a righteous Judge will make all things right.

What are some things that cause people to say, "Life's not fair"?

What's the connection between trusting God and acquiring wisdom?

"A faith that has not been tested cannot be trusted." —ADRIAN ROGERS

FROM THE ROOT TO THE FRUIT

Honor the LORD with your possessions, and with the firstfruits of all your increase. PROVERBS 3:9

THE WAY WE HANDLE our possessions speaks volumes about the content of our hearts. There's nothing wrong with having nice things, but there's something terribly wrong about the greed to have more and more. The first step in honoring God with everything we own is to realize that, in fact, God owns it all—we're just borrowing it for a short while.

We bring a smile to God's face when we express thanks for what we have instead of complaining because we don't have the latest version of a toy we want. We give God joy when we take care of what He has loaned us instead of trashing things. And we make God's heart glad when we use our possessions to help others who are less fortunate.

In agricultural communities, the "firstfruits" are the first crops of the harvest. As a statement to God and a reminder to ourselves, we don't spend the first part of any increase (raise, bonus, or gift) on ourselves. We take it to God and give it to Him.

Full hearts and open hands—they are the marks of someone who truly loves God and uses possessions to please Him.

As you think about your desire for things and your use of them, what brings a smile to God's face, and what makes Him frown?

What is one thing you can do today to honor God with your possessions?

"Plant a kernel of wheat and you reap a pint; plant a pint, and you reap a bushel. Always the law works to give you back more than you give." —**ANTHONY NORVELL**

GREAT IS THY FAITHFULNESS

Every good gift and every perfect gift is from above, and comes down from the
Father of lights, with whom there is no variation or shadow of turning.

JAMES 1:17

IN THE WONDERFUL and popular old hymn "Great Is Thy Faithfulness,"
Thomas Chisholm wrote, "O God my Father, / There is no shadow of turning
with Thee; / Thou changest not, Thy compassions they fail not; / As Thou hast
been Thou forever wilt be."

Theologians tell us that God is immutable—His nature never changes.
For many of us, our eyes glaze over when someone quotes old hymns and
theologians, but this truth is essential to our emotional stability and spiritual growth. People are fickle. We change our minds about every conceivable
thing—sometimes several times in a few minutes. If we are indecisive too
often, people around us wonder if they can count on us. The same conclusion
would be true of God if His decisions and nature changed, but they don't.

When everything else in our lives is out of control, God is the rock-solid
foundation we can stand on. When the future looks like a thick fog bank, God
is the lighthouse. We may fear that a spouse or parent or best friend or boss
will waver, but we never have to wonder if God's love, strength, and purpose
for us will change. They won't.

Our faith is based on many things: the evidence of God's creative hand
in nature; His love and power described in the Bible; the life, death, and
resurrection of Christ; and the miracle of changed lives around us. In the
ultimate sense, though, our faith rests on the truth that we can count on
God's faithfulness. At the bottom of all the muck of struggles and confusion, we find a solid rock.

Why is it important to our faith that God never changes?

What are you counting on Him for today?

"I have held many things in my hands and I have lost them all, but whatever I
have placed in God's hands, that I still possess." —MARTIN LUTHER

THE FAMILY NAME

A good name is to be chosen rather than great riches, loving favor rather than silver and gold. PROVERBS 22:1

IN EVERY AGE and in every culture, a person's name has been important. Whether names signify characteristics of the person or the family or if they have been passed down from one generation to another, the mention of a name can stir praise or shame.

For those of us who follow Christ, our names carry double meaning. As our character is tested and shaped and we prove to be trustworthy, the mention of our names will bring smiles to people's faces. But as believers, our reputation doesn't stop with "Jones" or "Smith" or "Kosnowski." We are children of the King, with a royal heritage and noble lineage. The God of the universe calls us His own. He created us, and He bought us back from slavery to sin.

Nothing—absolutely nothing—is more important than our names as God's beloved children. Riches will end, fame will fade, and possessions will rust and rot, but the "loving favor" of God will last for eternity.

What names do we call ourselves, especially when we've done something we're not proud of? Those angry declarations may express our emotions at the moment, but they aren't the truth about who we are in the eyes of God—and that's the most important truth of all.

How well are you earning a good reputation and a good name among your peers?

What names do you call yourself when you've failed? What's the real truth about your identity?

"Paint the picture of your life with godly decisions and you will never be ashamed to attach your signature to the portrait you create." —IKE REIGHARD

EXALTED IN ALL THE EARTH

Be still, and know that I am God; I will be exalted among the nations, I will be exalted in the earth! PSALM 46:10

THE PSALMIST WAS HAVING a really bad day! Everything around him was out of control. His problems were so severe that it seemed the mountains were being thrown into the sea and an earthquake was shaking the earth! His political world was turned upside down: The nations raged, and he felt threatened on every side (see Psalm 46:1-3, 6). We don't know how much of this was actual and how much was metaphorical, but either way, he was in big trouble.

In the midst of all the turmoil, God spoke to him and said calmly, "Be still, and know that I am God." The Lord didn't run around trying to fix everything, and He didn't direct the psalmist to work like crazy to make everything right. Work might come later, but for now, he needed God's perspective. And the only way to get it was to stop, look, listen, and remember the goodness and greatness of Almighty God. When the time was right, God's grace and strength would be evident in nature and on the political scene, and He would reign where chaos had existed.

Modern society produces tremendous stress. Expectations are sky-high, and opportunities quickly morph into demands for more things, better opportunities, and higher achievements. Some of our stresses come from outside, but we create many others. Whatever the source, God stands in the midst of our chaotic lives. When everything seems to be coming unglued, He whispers, "Stop. Be still. Listen to Me, and be sure that I can do anything that needs to be done."

Will we listen?

Describe a time when you felt like your life was coming unglued.

How does it help to stop, be still, and focus on God in times of chaos?

"I am profitably engaged in reading the Bible. Take all of this book upon reason that you can, and the balance by faith, and you will live and die a better man."
—ABRAHAM LINCOLN

PLAIN AND SIMPLE

This is the testimony: that God has given us eternal life, and this life is in His Son. He who has the Son has life; he who does not have the Son of God does not have life. 1 JOHN 5:11-12 { MEMORY VERSE

SOME PEOPLE BELIEVE it is prideful to think they can be sure of their salvation. They think only God knows if people are saved, because no one is ever completely free from sin in this life. Many of these people see the Christian life as a classroom, and they think God grades on a curve. If they've done enough right and avoided enough sins, maybe, just maybe, they'll score high enough to pass.

John, though, gives us a completely different perspective. The issue isn't having more deeds on the good side of the scale than on the bad side. The central, singular point of salvation is this: Do we have the Son? Salvation is a gift. We can't earn it. In fact, we acknowledge our complete inability to do enough things right to twist God's arm to let us into heaven. Instead, we stand before Him with empty hands and open hearts, trusting that Christ's sacrifice paid for our sins completely and ushered us into God's family. In faith, we turn from our own efforts and embrace Jesus, God's Son.

John's message is plain and simple, but it threatens those who want to prove themselves to God and others by giving enough, serving enough, and attending church enough to earn acceptance. The focal point of faith, John tells us, is Christ. He is all we have and all we need. Then, out of full hearts, we give, serve, and attend church because we're already accepted, not because we're trying to become accepted. It makes a huge difference!

How can someone know that he or she "has the Son"?

Do you? How does your grasp of the simplicity and humility of your faith in Christ affect your attitude and actions?

"All self effort is but sinking sand, Christ alone is the rock of our salvation."
—H. A. IRONSIDE

"Christianity is not a religion; it is a relationship with a person—Jesus Christ."
—ZIG ZIGLAR

SHARING THE GOOD NEWS

It is written: "How beautiful are the feet of those who preach the gospel of peace, who bring glad tidings of good things!" ROMANS 10:15

TODAY, WE USE E-MAIL and cell phones to communicate with people in the next room or on the other side of the world. In ancient times, however, messages were carried the old-fashioned way: by couriers. They braved rugged terrain, blistering heat, and threats of thieves to take news, good or bad, across the land. Our communication tools are computers and phones; their tools were the sandals on their feet.

In his letter to the Romans, Paul uses a quote from Isaiah 52:7, when messengers brought news to exiles in Babylon that they were now freed from captivity. After seventy years of torture and humiliation, the captives were free! In the same way, we who take the message of Christ's forgiveness to others bring great news of stunning freedom. In this case, it's not freedom from political oppression, but freedom from sin and death.

Think of the best news you've ever heard, and remember the utter thrill of hearing it for the first time. We have the wonderful role of taking the best news ever told to people who desperately need to hear it. In the ancient world, thankful, thrilled people would say to those who brought good news, "Your feet are beautiful!" When we take the news of Christ's forgiveness to guilt-ridden people, our feet are beautiful too.

What's the best news you've ever received?

What are some things you need to do to make your feet beautiful to lost and oppressed people around you?

"This generation of Christians is responsible for this generation of souls on the earth!" —KEITH GREEN

REACHING OUT IN LOVE

We love Him because He first loved us. If someone says, "I love God," and hates his brother, he is a liar; for he who does not love his brother whom he has seen, how can he love God whom he has not seen? And this commandment we have from Him: that he who loves God must love his brother also.

1 JOHN 4:19-21

SOME PEOPLE ANNOY US. They interrupt us when we're trying to concentrate, ignore us when we need their help, or give us unwanted advice. Sometimes, the best we can do is to tolerate them.

Tolerating people, however, isn't loving them, and God has set a high standard for us in relationships—especially in the family of God. Our love for people, though, doesn't come from self-effort. God has imparted genuine, unconditional love to us, and He gives us an example of what love looks like. He is the prime mover, the One who initiated love toward us when we were completely unlovable. He showered us with grace, forgiveness, and affection, and we respond warmly by calling Him "Abba, Father" (see Romans 8:15, NLT).

The love we show others indicates our level of love for God. If we fail to love horizontally, we can assume there's a problem in our vertical relationship with God. We won't reach out in love until God has first reached into our hearts to enable us to love Him.

We love those around us by pursuing what's best for them. When we're listening, we're fully present in the moment. When we're caring, we give everything we've got because we're aware that God gave His all to us. The more we experience the transforming love of God, the more His love spills out of us toward those around us.

Who are the people and what are the situations when the best you can do is to tolerate them?

How can you experience God's love more deeply? What difference will it make?

"I am doing 'better than good' because I love the unlovable and give hope to the helpless, friendship to the friendless, and encouragement to the discouraged."
—ZIG ZIGLAR

MORE THAN WE THINK

To Him who is able to do exceedingly abundantly above all that we ask or think, according to the power that works in us, to Him be glory.

EPHESIANS 3:20-21 { MEMORY VERSE

OUR GOD, AS THE SONG SAYS, is an awesome God. There is nothing—literally nothing—that is impossible for Him. As we look through the annals of Scripture, we see God doing many amazing things. He directed Noah to build a boat and then sent a worldwide flood to judge the earth. He promised Abraham descendants as numerous as the stars in the sky, and He produced the first child of that promise from an aged couple far past their prime. God directed Gideon to get rid of almost all his men before they went into battle against overwhelming odds. He sent fire from heaven to burn up the sacrifice and moat to reveal Himself to Elijah and rebuke the prophets of Baal.

The Gospels give us volumes of miracles. Jesus healed the sick, raised the dead, cleansed lepers, and changed hearts over and over again. Wherever He went, miracles followed Him.

But what about now, and what about you and me? Does God still work in the same way? God is still in the business of revealing His love and power. Sometimes He works physical miracles, but more often, He works the miracle of redemption in individuals' hearts and the miracle of restoration in broken relationships. God's power and purpose haven't changed. He still can—and will—do far more than we can ask or think.

What amazing things have you seen that can be attributed to God?

What are you trusting Him to do in your life now?

"Abraham Maslow observed that 'the story of the human race is men and women selling themselves short.' The story of too many Christians is selling God short."
—IKE REIGHARD

"If a man can take moldy bread and make penicillin, imagine what God can do with you." —ZIG ZIGLAR

WHEN LIFE OVERWHELMS YOU

Immediately Jesus spoke to them, saying, "Be of good cheer! It is I; do not be afraid." MATTHEW 14:27

WE DON'T GET INTO TROUBLE only because we've made stupid mistakes. Sometimes, God allows difficulties in our lives so He can remind us of how much we need Him. One day, Jesus told His men to take a boat across the lake while He went up the mountain to pray. Late at night, the men still hadn't reached the shore, and a storm blew up. Several of them were experienced fishermen who had been in countless storms, but this time, they knew they were in big trouble! They thought they'd drown.

In the middle of the raging waves and howling wind, they could faintly see a figure *walking on the water* toward them. The fear of drowning suddenly paled next to the fear of being visited by a ghost. But it wasn't a ghost. It was Jesus! Jesus, the flesh-and-blood Son of God approached them. He must have had a smile on His face when He told them, "Be of good cheer, guys! It's Me. There's no need to be afraid."

From time to time, we feel overwhelmed by storms in our lives too. Sometimes they occur because we've made dumb mistakes and we're experiencing the consequences, but sometimes they occur because we've followed God's leading. Either way, Jesus reminds us that storms aren't an obstacle to Him at all. He will provide for us, and His presence will cheer us up.

What are some storms you've experienced in the past few years?

How will it help you next time (or this time) to know that Jesus is never overwhelmed by storms?

"The center of God's will is our only safety." —BETSIE TEN BOOM

THE WELL OF THE HEART

Not what goes into the mouth defiles a man; but what comes out of the mouth, this defiles a man. MATTHEW 15:11

IN JESUS' DAY, people were more particular about foods than a conference of dieters! They had rules about what you could eat and what you couldn't eat, and they had rules about the rules. They were convinced that the food people ate could bless them or ruin them, but Jesus turned their thinking upside down. He told them that what goes into their mouths isn't as important as what comes out of them. Our words reveal the content of our hearts, and our words have the power to create or to destroy, to heal or to hurt.

Most of us think very little about our communication, even with those we love the most. We've developed habits of saying the same things in the same ways to the same people, and these habits seem to work well enough. But do they? We need to be more intentional about the words we say to one another. Healing messages say, "I love you," "I'm proud of you," and "You're really good at that!" Critical words cut like a knife. And sarcasm is the same knife with a pearl handle. Silence, too, can be just as deadly because a person's self-doubt often fills the emptiness.

Words reveal what's in our hearts. If what spills out is too often negative, biting, caustic, or sarcastic, we need to ask God to fill the well with faith, hope, and love so that positive words come out by the bucketful.

Think of the conversations you've had in the past day. How would you describe the content of your words?

What changes do you need to make in your communication, especially with those you love?

"What comes out of your mouth is determined by what goes into your mind."
—ZIG ZIGLAR

FROM HERO TO ZERO

[Jesus] turned and said to Peter, "Get behind Me, Satan! You are an offense to Me, for you are not mindful of the things of God, but the things of men."

MATTHEW 16:23

YOU'VE GOT TO LOVE PETER. In one of the most significant moments in Jesus' life, He had asked His followers if they knew who He really was. Peter spoke up and said, "You are the Christ, the Son of the living God" (Matthew 16:16). Very good, Pete.

But only a moment later, Jesus explained that His role as the Christ was to suffer at the hands of religious leaders and be put to death. When Jesus spoke those words, Peter interrupted, "No way that's going to happen to You!" (see Matthew 16:22). So Jesus put him in his place.

The ways of God are sometimes very different from what we can imagine. In fact, they can be the polar opposite of what we think is good and right and fair. For Jesus, the Father's path led Him to betrayal and the Cross, and then to a glorious resurrection. In the same way, God may lead us through dark times in our lives before we come out into the light. If we fight against Him, we earn His correction, but if we trust that He will eventually lead us into the light, we can walk with Him even in the darkest moments of our lives.

Arguing with Him may be natural, but it's counterproductive. Just ask Peter.

Have you ever said, "No way!" to God about a path where He was leading you?

What are some situations in your life today in which you need to trust God to lead you out of darkness into light?

"God's will is what every one of us would choose if we had all of God's facts."
—IKE REIGHARD

THE FAITH OF A CHILD

Jesus called a little child to Him, set him in the midst of [the disciples], and said, "Assuredly, I say to you, unless you are converted and become as little children, you will by no means enter the kingdom of heaven." MATTHEW 18:2-3

IN JESUS' DAY, children were not the epicenter of family life. To the surprise of everyone gathered around Him one day, Jesus called a child to come over and sit with Him. He pointed to the little child and said to the adults, "You need to become like this little guy."

Jesus wasn't suggesting that adults should act like immature kids. No, the message is about faith, not age. Children have a simple faith. They believe because someone in authority tells them something is true. They don't over-analyze, and they don't get bogged down in all the what-ifs. They take things at face value, which is how Jesus wants us to take Him.

Children also gladly receive gifts without second-guessing or feeling guilty. At Christmas, many adults carefully unwrap presents to save the wrapping paper, but kids tear into them with reckless abandon! In the same way, Jesus wants us to receive the gifts He gives us (forgiveness, adoption into God's family, promises, truth, and so forth) with unfettered gratefulness.

Immaturity isn't something to aspire to, but childlike faith is a valuable commodity in God's Kingdom. We can be so complicated, full of questions and doubts and excuses for not believing. But we can begin where the disciples began that day, listening, watching, and marveling at the lesson Jesus taught, and we can ask Him to produce that childlike faith in us, too.

Describe a childlike faith. Is it attractive to you? Why or why not?

Take some time to ask God to give you that kind of faith in Him.

"God sends no one away empty except those who are full of themselves."
—D. L. MOODY

A FATE WORSE THAN DEATH

Whoever causes one of these little ones who believe in Me to sin, it would be better for him if a millstone were hung around his neck, and he were drowned in the depth of the sea. MATTHEW 18:6

WHEREVER HE WENT, Jesus was the champion of outcasts and the oppressed. Yes, we know that "God is love" and that Jesus was tender and kind, but His love made Him fierce in defense of the helpless. The Gospels contain some of the most dramatic verbal battles in literature, and almost without exception, Jesus fought against the powerful and the proud to protect the powerless and the poor.

We often focus on Jesus' promises to give us an abundant life, peace, and joy, but He delivered stern warnings, too. To make Himself crystal clear, He said that those who mislead, wound, or take advantage of helpless people—in this case, children—would suffer God's righteous, fierce justice. In comparison to God's punishment, it would be better if abusers were drowned in the ocean!

Does this warning have anything to do with us? Yes, whenever we find ourselves in a position of power, we need to heed Christ's warning. When we relate to children (our own or others'), poor people, displaced people, employees who serve under us, or anyone else over whom we exercise authority, that relationship is a sacred trust. We report directly to God for our attitudes and behavior, and He isn't thrilled if we abuse those under us, ignore them, use them for selfish gain, make jokes at their expense, or take them for granted.

Jesus didn't mince words. He made Himself very clear. Will we listen?

Who are the people in your life who are "little ones"?

What are some specific things you need to change to value them more highly?

"If Christ lives in us, controlling our personalities, we will leave glorious marks on the lives we touch. Not because of our lovely characters, but because of His."
—EUGENIA PRICE

BELIEVE

[Jesus said,] "Whatever things you ask in prayer, believing, you will receive."

MATTHEW 21:22

TOO OFTEN, we divorce prayer from its source of power. If we see prayer as an activity to perform and check off our list of spiritual deeds for the day, we miss the heart, substance, and opportunity it offers. Jesus reminds us that prayer is connecting with the God of the universe, the One who spoke the stars into existence, and the One who orchestrates all of history. His power is matchless, and His love without limits.

Christ's promise that we will receive anything we ask for comes with a condition: We must believe. A torrent of words—even eloquent or flowery ones—doesn't please God, and intense emotions don't necessarily move His hand. But faith—even small, fledgling faith in God—makes Him smile and connects us to His heart and His purposes.

"Believing prayer" is characterized by a genuine commitment to God's desires. We long for God to be honored, not us. We want Him to touch lives, not for us to be in control. To know what God wants, we search the Scriptures to find out what's on His heart and how He wants to work in people's lives, and we listen to the Spirit's whisper as we sit silently with open hearts.

This kind of prayer never demands that God act a certain way. Instead, believing prayer acknowledges our inadequacies and limitations and focuses on God's greatness and goodness to direct both the prayer and His answer.

How would you define and describe "believing prayer"?

What are some steps you can take today to develop a habit of praying this way?

"Satan trembles when he sees the weakest saint upon his knees." —WILLIAM COWPER

MOUNTAIN-MOVING FAITH

Jesus said to them, . . . "Assuredly, I say to you, if you have faith as a mustard seed, you will say to this mountain, 'Move from here to there,' and it will move; and nothing will be impossible for you." MATTHEW 17:20 { MEMORY VERSE

JESUS WAS THE MASTER of the metaphor. He often used common items to illustrate important spiritual principles, and the one He uses here is one of the most powerful and beloved. In a farming culture, people were very familiar with all kinds of seeds. The smallest one used in a family garden was a mustard seed, but in time, it grew into one of the largest garden plants—up to ten feet tall. Like a mustard seed, our faith may start small, but God causes it to grow tall and strong.

How large can it grow? Large enough to "move a mountain." Jesus used this metaphor to mean a mountain of problems, so the implication is that if we believe God, He will move a mountain of difficulties and bless us. He doesn't require that we have mountain-sized faith at the beginning—just enough to get started. As our faith grows, we trust God for more and bigger things. Before long, we see Him "move mountains" in our lives and in the lives of those we love.

We marvel at people who have great faith. They seem to be able to trust God when the rest of us shrink back in doubt. Jesus' explanation, though, gives us hope because all of us can start where we are, even if we have only the smallest seed of faith. God will water it, weed it, and fertilize it, and before long, our faith will grow strong.

Do you have faith at least the size of a mustard seed today? Explain your answer.

What are some mountains of difficulty that need to be moved in your life?

"Faith is different from proof: The latter is human; the former is a gift from God."
—BLAISE PASCAL

*"Faith is your reaction to God's ability." —***ZIG ZIGLAR**

GOD OF THE LIVING

Concerning the resurrection of the dead, have you not read what was spoken to you by God, saying, "I am the God of Abraham, the God of Isaac, and the God of Jacob"? God is not the God of the dead, but of the living.

MATTHEW 22:31-32

PEOPLE HAVE ALWAYS been fascinated with death. The mysteries of what happens once we have taken our last breath on earth have always been intriguing. We want to know what happens when someone breathes his or her last, and we want some assurance that death is not the end. Jesus gave us a strong promise when He corrected the assumptions of those who thought death was the end. He promised resurrection and life, and in fact, He said that believers who have died are alive—right now!

Christ's resurrection from the dead is the most hopeful signal ever given to mankind. Death isn't the end, and life conquers the grave. God doesn't reign over cemeteries, tombs, and church floors. He reigns over those who are alive—in this life and in the one to come.

This promise gives us confidence that we can face death with a strong sense of hope. At the moment our human spirit leaves us, we enter the presence of God, the angels, and all the believers who have gone before us. And there, we'll be more alive than we've ever been.

> Why is it important to you that God is the God of the living and not of the dead?
>
> What do you look forward to in the next life?

> "The resurrection is not merely important to the historic Christian faith; without it, there would be no Christianity. It is the singular doctrine that elevates Christianity above all other world religions." —ADRIAN ROGERS

THE NAME OF THE LORD

[Jesus said,] "I say to you, you shall see Me no more till you say, 'Blessed is He who comes in the name of the LORD!'" MATTHEW 23:39

FOR OVER THREE YEARS, Jesus had taught on hillsides and in private homes, He had argued with religious leaders to show people a new way to live, and He had healed countless sick and crippled people. He longed for people to grasp the truth of God's grace and experience real life, but many— far too many—had said no to Him. As He approached Jerusalem during His last week on earth, His heart broke for the people. Their stubbornness and hard hearts would prove devastating to them, and He knew it. He cried out in sadness, and He told them they would miss out on the greatest things in life: knowing and following Him.

Jesus promised to come back. In His first time on earth, He came with a warm heart and a message of grace. When He comes again, however, He will come as the powerful, avenging Judge.

When Jesus rode into Jerusalem on a donkey the week before He was killed, the crowd shouted, "Hosanna to the Son of David! 'Blessed is He who comes in the name of the LORD!'" (Matthew 21:9). And they celebrated. When He comes back, people will say the same words, but on that day, He will complete the transformation He began so many years before. On that future day, human history will culminate in a cataclysmic shift, and Christ will rule on earth.

Jesus gives all of us a choice: to acknowledge Him as our Savior now and celebrate, or acknowledge Him as Judge when He comes back. Which choice have you made? Which choice have your friends and family made?

How do you think Jesus felt when people rejected Him and His message that last week?

Are you celebrating Him as Savior, or are you waiting for Him as the Judge? Explain your answer.

"Who can deny that Jesus of Nazareth, the Incarnate Son of the Most High God, is the Eternal Glory of the Jewish race?" **—BENJAMIN DISRAELI**

WHEN WILL THE END COME?

[Jesus said,] "He who endures to the end shall be saved. And this gospel of the kingdom will be preached in all the world as a witness to all the nations, and then the end will come." MATTHEW 24:13-14

FOR MANY OF US, history seems to be endless cycles of prosperity and famine, peace and war. Our history courses in college bored us to death with facts, dates, and obscure biographies of people we'd never heard of and never planned to mention again. The events of today blend in with the past, and though news anchors try to make every day sound unique, the news quickly fades in our memories. But Jesus announced that a day will come when history as we know it will come to an abrupt conclusion. On that particular day, everything will change. That's the promise; that's the threat.

Some believers become preoccupied with figuring out every detail of the "end times." The Scriptures give us just enough of a glimpse into the future to tantalize us, but not enough to provide complete answers. Even Jesus said He didn't know the time the end would occur (see Matthew 24:36)!

If we can't know the details for sure, what difference does His prediction make? It should cause us to live each moment of every day with the certainty that what we do today matters. Our choices, attitudes, and relationships shape today, but they also determine the eternal destinies of the people around us. We may not have the details on the end of the world, but we have the truth about the One who has paid the price to forgive sins and give eternal life. If Jesus returns tomorrow, we're ready, and if He delays, we have the opportunity to take more people with us.

Do you often think about "the end," when Jesus returns? Why or why not?

How would a stronger grasp of this future reality affect your choices today?

"Go, send, or disobey." —JOHN PIPER

GOOD WORK

The labor of the righteous leads to life, the wages of the wicked to sin.

PROVERBS 10:16

FOR ALL OF US, finding a good "fit" in our work has multiple benefits. When our responsibilities each day match our skills, personality, experience, and passions, incredible things can happen. That's especially true for Christians who see their work as an opportunity to honor God. As Solomon said, this kind of work leads to life!

Can work really be a source of God's blessing? Yes. If we find the right fit and work to honor God, He unleashes His power in us and through us to accomplish great things and impact many people. In his insightful book *The Call*, Os Guinness defines our spiritual calling as "the truth that God calls us to himself so decisively that everything we are, everything we do, and everything we have is invested with a special devotion, dynamism, and direction lived out as a response to his summons and service."*

At work, we can labor each day with integrity and enthusiasm because we know that what we do—and how we do it—really counts. Fulfillment at work spills over to our time with our families. Instead of being angry or drained when we walk through the door at the end of the day, we can be excited about what God is doing, and our joy can spread to our spouses and children. In the community, we can be known as people who treat others fairly and who have earned respect. In all areas of life, we can sense God's purpose and presence and delight in following Him.

How much does your work give life, and how much does it rob you of life?

What do you need to do to align your work with God's purposes and presence?

"We are what we repeatedly do. Excellence, then, is not an act, but a habit."
—ARISTOTLE

---

* Os Guinness, *The Call: Finding and Fulfilling the Central Purpose of Your Life* (Nashville: W Publishing, 1998), 29.

WALK WITH THE WISE

He who walks with wise men will be wise, but the companion of fools will be destroyed. PROVERBS 13:20

WE SEE IT ALL THE TIME: Teenagers join the "wrong crowd," and they make dumb choices they never would have made before. Sometimes these choices are minor annoyances for their parents, but sometimes they're fatal. The choice of friends isn't important just for teenagers, though. It's crucial for all of us.

Why are some of us attracted to "fools"? In many cases, we're attracted to them because they seem to live exciting lives. They take risks; they laugh loudly, play loudly, and sing loudly. This life looks like fun, and the truth is, it *is* fun—for a while. Many of us are wired to enjoy taking risks, and fools take more risks than others. The rush of adrenaline can be addictive.

On the other hand, "wise people" sometimes have a bad reputation. Actually, we often mistakenly believe *boring, stiff, religious,* and *self-righteous* are words that describe wisdom, and that doesn't make wisdom attractive at all! True wisdom, though, is the ability to really live, to squeeze every drop of meaning out of life, and to look to God to give us the greatest adventure life has to offer. Unfortunately, there are a lot more stiff, self-righteous people out there than there are those who are truly wise and live exciting, Christ-honoring lives.

Can you find a wise friend or two? Yes, they're out there, but you may have to look hard to find them. Can you be one? That's your challenge.

Why do you think fools can be so attractive to so many people?

How would you describe a really wise person?

"Your best friend is the one who brings out your highest and best, never your lowest and least." —IKE REIGHARD

THE LEAST OF THESE

The King will answer and say to them, "Assuredly, I say to you, inasmuch as you did it to one of the least of these My brethren, you did it to Me."

MATTHEW 25:40

IN THE DAYS before He was to be killed, Jesus had some very intense conversations with people. Every word counted, and every message had the power to change lives. During those days, Jesus argued with religious leaders and He spent time with His closest followers. He talked about having soft hearts toward God, and He predicted a tragic future for those who turned their backs on God.

Outward appearance, Jesus explained, can be a sham. God cares far more about the content of our hearts and the expression of our hearts in loving actions. One of the clearest windows on the condition of our hearts, Jesus said, is how we treat "the least of these" around us.

Who are these people? They are the ones most of us ignore. We move to the suburbs to get away from them. If they *do* get in our way, we pass by as quickly as possible. Avoiding them, though, isn't what pleases Jesus. He values those of us who see needs and take steps to meet them. The needs of nice, clean people? Yes, but also the needs of those who are dirty, who are outcasts, and who can't give anything in return. We show our devotion to Christ when we feed the hungry, give a drink to those who are thirsty, invite strangers to our homes, clothe those who wear rags, and visit the sick and the prisoners.

Who are some needy people you see every day? Do you need to leave a cocoon of safety and peace to be with them?

What is one new habit you can develop to care for needy people?

"Small things done with great love can change the world." —MOTHER TERESA

LIKE NEON SIGNS

Let your light so shine before men, that they may see your good works and glorify your Father in heaven. MATTHEW 5:16 { MEMORY VERSE

WHEN WE DRIVE down a city street at night, we see hundreds of lit-up signs advertising company products and services. Some are incredibly bright, and some barely flicker. Some are big and bold, and some are more subdued. Every one of them, though, advertises something.

In the same way, every person is like a neon sign shining in the darkness, and every one of us communicates a message to anyone who notices. Jesus tells us that we have the opportunity to design our life's sign and determine how it shines for people to see. And in fact, our choices about the design make a tremendous difference for today and for all eternity because He has chosen us to "advertise" the grace, mercy, kindness, and purposes of our Heavenly Father!

All of us made choices long ago that have shaped our lives and the signs we've designed, but God gives us the opportunity to make a new design if we need to. By His grace, we can trust Him to transform our hearts so that far more of His love shines through. Some of us need to do some major design work; some need to screw in a fresh bulb or two. All of us need to take a few minutes to reflect on what we've been advertising and what we want on our signs.

Describe what your sign has looked like for the last couple of months.

What changes need to happen so that your sign points people to the grace and truth of your Father in heaven?

"Every sin is the distortion of an energy breathed into us—an energy which, if not thus distorted, would have blossomed into one of those holy acts whereof 'God did it' and 'I did it' are both true descriptions." —C. S. LEWIS

"Man was designed for accomplishment, engineered for success, and endowed with the seeds of greatness." —ZIG ZIGLAR

LOVE GOD AND FORGIVE OTHERS

If you forgive men their trespasses, your heavenly Father will also forgive you.

MATTHEW 6:14

GOD'S FORGIVENESS of our sins isn't conditional. Christ has paid the price already, so our forgiveness is already purchased. But the legal fact that the penalty for our sins has been paid doesn't assure us that we'll feel forgiven. Our *experience* of forgiveness depends on our willingness to *express* forgiveness to those who have hurt us.

We live in the real world, and we all get hurt by people from time to time. Sometimes, it's a small cut, but sometimes people leave us with gaping wounds. Anger is a normal response to injustice and hurt, but if anger isn't resolved, it soon turns into resentment and bitterness—which sour our attitudes and poison every relationship.

Bitterness is one of the chief causes of emotional stress and stress-related illnesses. We relive painful events over and over, and we rehearse ways we will get revenge. We can't sleep, and we can't eat. Our relationship with God becomes shallow and empty. Our lives are consumed with the hurt inflicted on us, but quite often, the person who hurt us isn't even aware of our daily emotional pain, and he or she might not even care.

The only remedy to break this pattern of bitterness is to forgive the one who hurt us. No, it won't be easy. We'll have to go to the well of God's love and forgiveness and drink deeply so that we have plenty to pour out to others. The choice to forgive, though, opens the floodgates of God's presence and power. We just have to give up our bitterness first.

What are some consequences of bitterness in people's lives?

Is there someone you need to forgive? Start the process now.

"If we would read the secret history of our enemies, we would find in each man's life sorrow and suffering enough to disarm all hostility."
—HENRY WADSWORTH LONGFELLOW

THE PARADOX OF LIFE

[Jesus said,] "Whoever desires to save his life will lose it, but whoever loses his life for My sake and the gospel's will save it." MARK 8:35

DIE TO LIVE. It's the ultimate paradox of life. All of us want the most out of life. We want our lives to count for something, and we want to feel that we're living life to the max each day at home and at work. Most of us grab onto our lives and hold on as tightly as we can in our quest to live fully, but Jesus offers a different way. Instead of grabbing on, we need to let go. Instead of clinging to our rights, we need to give them up. Instead of demanding our way, we must abdicate the throne to One who knows far more than we do.

The paradox principle can be illustrated this way: If you hold sand in both hands, you have to squeeze the sand to keep it in place. The harder you squeeze, though, the more sand shifts and drops from your hands. And while you're holding that sand, you can't take a gift of gold that someone wants to give you. You've "saved" the sand by clinging to it, but you've missed out on a far greater thrill.

The question each of us must answer is this: Is the life Christ offers more valuable than the life I can make on my own? If not, then we need to grasp all we can while we can. But if the abundant life Jesus offers is richer, deeper, and more thrilling than any other, we can let go of what we have to receive what we really want. And we make that evaluation a hundred times a day.

Describe the paradox principle.

Is Christ's offer worth more than what you can achieve on your own? Why or why not?

"He is no fool who gives what he cannot keep to gain that which he cannot lose." —JIM ELLIOT

TRUE RELIGION

Pure and undefiled religion before God and the Father is this: to visit orphans and widows in their trouble, and to keep oneself unspotted from the world.

JAMES 1:27

WE LIVE IN AN ENTERTAINMENT CULTURE, but the Christian life isn't a spectator sport. We live in an age of instant news coverage and blogs on all kinds of topics, but the Spirit of Christ in us isn't content with analysis. When Christ's grace and truth penetrate our hearts, we're compelled to take action. We notice people in need, and we jump to help them. We hear of people who have an opportunity to touch lives, and we call to offer assistance. No, we can't just sit around any longer. We want to get our hands dirty and make a difference.

Jesus warned us not to practice our faith in front of an audience to win applause (see Matthew 6:1-6). Instead, He told us to give, pray, and serve in secret, where only God knows what we're doing. James had the same idea. He said that we could tell if we truly possess a "pure and undefiled religion" if we are willing to go to the down-and-out, the ones who are usually forgotten, and meet their needs. In the first century in Palestine, the forgotten people were widows and orphans. Today, these people certainly are on the list, but so are the thousands of homeless people in our cities and the tens of thousands of prisoners in our jails. What are we doing to touch their lives? What will we do today?

But James adds the insight that true faith surfaces in another choice we make: to stay away from sinful attitudes, words, and actions. The real thing, then, is a choice to live for Christ in inward lives of purity and outward expressions of helping the unfortunate. Both are essential.

Who is the best example you know of someone who lives a true faith?

What steps do you need to take today to have true faith?

"Sympathy is no substitute for action." —DAVID LIVINGSTONE

ROOTS OF BITTERNESS

Pursue peace with all people, and holiness, without which no one will see the Lord: looking carefully lest anyone fall short of the grace of God; lest any root of bitterness springing up cause trouble, and by this many become defiled.

HEBREWS 12:14-15

CERTAIN KINDS OF ROOTS can be dug up, dried, ground, and mixed with oil to make dyes to color clothes. And as any housewife could tell us, a dye misused causes a terrible stain. Bitterness is like a misused dye—it colors how we look at life, and it stains every relationship. The writer to the Hebrews encourages us to pursue peace in every relationship and to be careful so that a "root of bitterness" won't cause problems.

People who are bitter feel they have every right to their feelings and perspectives. After all, somebody did them wrong! They *feel like* victims because they *are* victims. God doesn't promise protection from every hurt we experience, but He doesn't want our anger and hurt to fester into bitterness and ruin every aspect of our lives. The author of Hebrews accurately observed that when someone is bitter, "many become defiled"—not just the bitter person, but everyone else near that person. The stains of the dye permeate every thread in the fabric.

Bitter people look for fights. They may say they don't like them, but they actually thrive on the adrenaline produced by intense disagreements. Instead, God wants us to stop this process before it starts: to pursue peace with all people. When they hurt us, we are to forgive them quickly. We need to watch out so that patterns of recrimination don't steal our joy, sap our energy, and ruin our ability to represent Christ.

Bitterness is serious business. It's a cancer that can't be tolerated, or it'll kill us. And it's contagious.

What does it mean to pursue peace with someone you disagree with?

How can you overcome bitterness?

"You can alter your life by altering your attitude." —WILLIAM JAMES

CHANGE YOUR WORLD

[Jesus said,] "You shall receive power when the Holy Spirit has come upon you; and you shall be witnesses to Me in Jerusalem, and in all Judea and Samaria, and to the end of the earth." ACTS 1:8

JUST BEFORE JESUS ascended into a cloud, He had some final words for His followers: a promise and a directive. In a few days, He told them, a monumental moment would occur. He had told them about it a few weeks before, and now it was going to be a reality. The Holy Spirit was going to enter each of them and take up residence there! No longer would God be at arm's length. Now He would live inside them.

The Holy Spirit is called the Comforter, but He also could be called the Generator because He supplies power for believers to follow Christ's directions and change the world. Jesus told those first disciples that they would represent Him as His ambassadors, first in Jerusalem; then in the surrounding areas; and, finally, to the remotest corners of the globe.

Jesus gives us the same promise and directive today. If we have trusted in Christ, His Spirit now lives inside us to comfort us, guide us, and give us power to do what God wants us to do. And what, exactly, does He want us to do? He has given us the incredible honor of representing Him in our families and neighborhoods, in our workplaces, and at school. He has given us the power to pray, to give, and to reach the world for Christ.

Are you ready to change your world?

What does the Holy Spirit want to do in you and through you?

What are some ways you can represent Christ to people around you today?

"The Great Commission is not an option to be considered, it is a command to be obeyed." —HUDSON TAYLOR

FINISH THE WORK

[Jesus said,] "I have glorified You on the earth. I have finished the work which You have given Me to do." JOHN 17:4

AT THE END OF HIS LIFE, Jesus could say to the Father, "I've finished what I came to do." Does that mean that there weren't more sick people to heal, more sermons to be preached, and more disciples to train? Does it mean that every person He cared for had heard His message and responded? Were there no more unchecked boxes on Jesus' to-do list? Jesus was crystal clear about why He came, and He was certain He had completed His task.

Jesus came to set up the Kingdom of God on earth. To fulfill that vision, He needed to accomplish two goals: to provide direct access to God through forgiveness of sins and to leave behind some people who could carry the message to the rest of the world. On the night He was betrayed, Jesus knew that the next day's events would fulfill the first goal, and as He looked around while He prayed, He looked into the faces of the people who would be filled with the Holy Spirit and take the gospel to the ends of the earth. His mission was complete.

Can we make the same claim? At the end of each day, week, month, and year and at the end of our lives, can we pray confidently, "Father, I've done what You wanted me to do"? Is that even possible? Yes, it is, and it gives immeasurable satisfaction to our lives. First, we have to align our priorities with God's, and then we need to carry out our tasks in a way that honors Him. When we encounter difficulties (Jesus certainly faced more than His fair share), we keep trusting God to lead us and use us.

How would you know if you have completed the work God gave you to do each day?

What would have to change in your walk with God for this to happen?

"If a commission by an earthly king is considered an honor, how can a commission by a Heavenly King be considered a sacrifice?" —**DAVID LIVINGSTONE**

NO GREATER COMMANDMENT

Jesus [said], "The first of all the commandments is: 'Hear, O Israel, the LORD our God, the LORD is one. And you shall love the LORD your God with all your heart, with all your soul, with all your mind, and with all your strength.' This is the first commandment." MARK 12:29-30 { MEMORY VERSE

GOD DOESN'T WANT MUCH—just everything we have. He doesn't expect much—just every ounce of passion, heart, and love we can muster. He doesn't demand much—just that we put Him first every minute of every day. And He has every reason to expect this of us because He created us to function best when we are fully devoted to Him.

Ancient Greek philosophers stressed the virtue of balance: "Moderation in all things." In most areas of our lives, that advice rings true. We need balance in our diets, exercise, sleep, work habits, spending, investments, and most other aspects of life. But in our relationship with God, balance is never extolled. Radical, abject, complete devotion is the only acceptable response to the God of the universe, who stooped to rescue us from sin and death. He deserves nothing less than our whole hearts.

The Old Testament contains hundreds of commands dealing with every aspect of existence, but to the religious leaders of the first century, that list wasn't good enough. They added hundreds more to define exactly what God (or they) expected of people. With the proliferation of commands as the background, someone asked Jesus, "Which one is most important?" Without hesitation, He replied, "The one that says, 'Love God with everything you've got.'" When we do that, each part of our lives comes into alignment—or drops away because it's no longer important. When we fail to put God first, everything seems equally important, and we spend all our energies trying to please people, proving ourselves, or hiding from risks. God's first commandment demands complete devotion, and it makes perfect sense. It's the way He created us to live.

What would it mean for you to love God with all your heart?

What changes would you need to make?

"The true follower of Christ will not ask, 'If I embrace this truth, what will it cost me?' Rather he will say, 'This is the truth. God help me to walk in it, let come what may!'" —A. W. TOZER

"Realistically, we can be happier and more enthusiastic about everything we do, provided we are doing it for Jesus." —ZIG ZIGLAR

YOUR NEIGHBOR

[Jesus said,] "And the second, like it, is this: 'You shall love your neighbor as your-self.' There is no other commandment greater than these." MARK 12:31

JESUS HAD JUST IDENTIFIED the "greatest commandment" in the Scrip-tures, the single, most important directive God has given us: Love God with everything you've got. Now He adds an addendum to that directive. When we love God with all our hearts, it affects our human relationships too. The sec-ond command also focuses on the power of love: "You shall love your neigh-bor as yourself."

"As yourself." Jesus could have said, "Love people a lot" or "Love people the way you love your pets," but He said that our love for others should com-pare favorably to the attention we give to our own needs. When we're hungry, we find something in the refrigerator. When we're sleepy, we go to bed (or at least, we *should* go to bed). We don't spend a lot of time wondering if we have this need or that one. If it's obvious, we just meet it. Our love for others should have the same reflexive quality: When we see their needs, we simply meet those needs.

Too often, we get wrapped up in our own little worlds, and we're con-sumed with our own needs without even noticing the needs of those around us. Or we're so exhausted at the end of each day that we can't imagine giving out to anyone else, especially to demanding kids or a spouse who is at least as tired as we are.

We have to break this cycle, back up, regroup, and bring some sanity to our lives so we'll have the perspective, energy, and compassion for the people we see each day, and especially those who live under the same roof with us. Then we can love them like we love ourselves.

Describe what it means to love someone the way you love yourself.

What are some practical things you can do to have more energy to devote to loving others?

"The highest and best way to love others is to apply the SALT Principle:
*   **S**ee others as Jesus sees them.*
*   **A**ccept others as Jesus accepts them.*
*   **L**ove others as Jesus loves them.*
*   **T**ouch others as Jesus touches them."*
—IKE REIGHARD

LISTEN CAREFULLY

Your ears shall hear a word behind you, saying, "This is the way, walk in it,"
whenever you turn to the right hand or whenever you turn to the left.

ISAIAH 30:21

MANY STUDENTS DRIVE their parents crazy by listening to music while they study. "Oh, it doesn't distract me at all," the kids claim. "It's just background noise. I really don't even hear it."

In the same way, we can tune out the Holy Spirit's whispers and become oblivious to His communication with us. The people of Israel had grown tired of God's repeated pleas to turn to Him, and they complained, "Don't tell us anymore!" (see Isaiah 30:10-11). But God didn't quit. He persisted in speaking to them to show them areas that needed repentance. We may tune Him out, but He never tunes us out.

The Spirit speaks "a word behind" us, gently nudging us in a direction and reminding us of a truth from God's Word. He never shouts, and He never demands. He always lets us make our own choices, even if those choices lead to pain and heartache.

For many of us, however, the whisper of the Spirit is drowned out by the noise of our culture. A hectic pace, demands at work and home, to-do lists, and the stress of living modern life create a buzz that makes it difficult to hear the Spirit. When we realize what we're missing, we make adjustments. We carve out time to be alone and to be quiet, to read and to reflect, and to stop everything so we can really listen. And we invite the Holy Spirit to whisper once again His directions to us. If we practice enough, listening becomes a way of life.

If you aren't listening enough to the Spirit, what are you missing?

What can you do today to carve out time to listen?

"Never try to explain God until you have obeyed Him. The only bit of God we understand is the bit we have obeyed." —OSWALD CHAMBERS

BEING A NORTH STAR

Those who are wise shall shine like the brightness of the firmament, and those who turn many to righteousness like the stars forever and ever.

DANIEL 12:3

FOR CENTURIES, mariners used the North Star to determine their course on the seas. Whenever they got lost, they could make course corrections based on that fixed point in the sky, and in clear weather conditions, it kept them on the right track night after night.

Wise people serve as signposts in the same way. Rigorous faith in a good, powerful, and all-knowing God makes them excellent examples to others in their families, at work, at church, and in their neighborhoods. Like a well-lit path or the unmistakable sentinel in the night sky, those whose lives are characterized by steadfast faith show others the way to live.

We don't become signposts and stars in a flash. We gain wisdom from the powerful combination of studying God's Word, being sensitive to God's Spirit, and spending time with people who are truly wise. These efforts require an investment of time, energy, and emotion. Is it worth it? For a while, it may not seem so. The early stages of spiritual discovery often bring more questions than answers, but if we are persistent, the pieces begin to come together.

Are you willing to pay the price to become a signpost and a star to guide others around you?

Do you want to be the kind of wise person who has a profound influence on others? Why or why not?

Are you willing to pay the price? Explain your answer.

"To see His star is good, but to see His face is better." —D. L. MOODY

IN GOD'S RIGHT HAND

*Fear not, for I am with you; be not dismayed, for I am your God. I will
strengthen you, yes, I will help you, I will uphold you with My righteous right
hand.* ISAIAH 41:10

AT PARTICULAR MOMENTS in our lives, all of us face bewildering circumstances. Counselors tell us that the most common problems in marriages are
money, sex, in-laws, and children. To that list, we can add an array of work-related stresses and personal difficulties. From time to time, we say, to no one
in particular, "I just don't know what to do!"

We often turn to family and friends for help, but God invites us to "go to
the top" to get His assistance. In this verse, God explains that we don't have to
wade through a phone tree to make a connection with Him. He doesn't e-mail
us a link we can go to for the answer to our problems or send out a technician
to fix them. He has promised His support—in person!

What an amazing promise! The God of the universe reminds us of the
contract He made, first with Moses—"I will be your God, and you will be my
people" (Jeremiah 7:23, NLT)—and it applies to us, too. We belong to Him,
and He has committed Himself to strengthen, lead, support, and uphold us.
To make His point completely clear, God finishes with a flourish. He doesn't
keep us at arm's length as He helps us; He holds us close and secure in His
right hand. It doesn't get any more personal than that.

Since God is invisible, what does this promise really mean?

**What are some recent or current situations in your life in which you need
God's personal help? Ask Him for it now.**

"The only thing we have to fear is fear itself." —**FRANKLIN ROOSEVELT**

CHANGING YOUR PARADIGM

"My thoughts are not your thoughts, nor are your ways My ways," says the LORD. *"For as the heavens are higher than the earth, so are My ways higher than your ways, and My thoughts than your thoughts."* ISAIAH 55:8-9

ONE OF THE MOST IMPORTANT TRUTHS we can learn in our journey of faith is that God is a lot smarter than we are! We spend much of each day figuring out difficult situations and solving problems, and we're pretty good at it too. We get paid for our ability to analyze things accurately, and we receive praise at home and at work for being "the answer man" or "the answer woman."

Sooner or later, though, God leads us into some dark alleys where we feel utterly, completely lost. A compliant child becomes rebellious, and everything we do makes him or her only more defiant. We feel that we're losing a son or daughter. Cancer rears its ugly head in our own bodies or in the bodies of those we love. We go through cycles of treatment and a roller coaster ride of emotions. We face problems we can't seem to solve with our in-laws, in our marriages, with money, with our bosses, or with unemployment. We may enter the pit of depression for seemingly no reason at all.

At those moments, we instinctively shake our fists at God and ask why. But few answers come. Sooner or later, we realize that, after all, we aren't God. We can't figure out what He's doing because we don't have His infinite wisdom and complete knowledge. At that moment, all we can do is bow and say, "Lord, You know far more than I do, and Your ways are far higher than mine." And then, we can rest in Him again.

What are some of the dangers of thinking we know more than God?

What are some situations right now in which you need to trust that God's insights and paths are far higher than yours?

"The last human freedom you and I possess is the ability to choose our attitude in any given set of circumstances." —VIKTOR FRANKL

NEVER LOSE HEART

[Jesus] spoke a parable to them, that men always ought to pray and not lose heart. LUKE 18:1

PEOPLE WHO READ the Bible fairly regularly notice some statements that are regularly repeated: "Fear not," "Wait on the Lord," and "Don't lose heart." Why does God give us these messages so often? Because it's so easy to give in to fear, to become impatient with God's timing, and to give up and quit because following God seems too hard.

Jesus told a story to address the problem of unanswered prayer—or at least, confusing delays in God's answers to our prayers. A widow went to a judge to get an answer to a legal dispute, but he ignored her. She wouldn't quit. She kept going back again and again. Finally, the exhausted and exasperated judge gave her an answer. Jesus must have had a smile on His face when He compared our loving, compassionate Father with the stubborn, neglectful judge in the story. "Surely," Jesus explained, "we can trust the Father to answer us if we plead with Him night and day" (see Luke 18:7).

How long have you prayed for a particular person or about a specific situation? Delays may occur for many reasons. God may be preparing the situation or the person, or He may be preparing us to receive what we've asked for. Or He may be working in our hearts to show us that we can trust Him even when He says no to our persistent request. In any case, we can be sure that eventually, we'll receive an answer from God, and with that assurance, we won't lose heart.

In the past, when have you been tempted to lose heart because God's answer was delayed?

What is a situation right now in which you are waiting for God's answer?

"Life is a grindstone. But whether it grinds us down or polishes us up depends on us."
—THOMAS L. HOLDCROFT

REJOICE!

Rejoice in the Lord always. Again I will say, rejoice! PHILIPPIANS 4:4 ⟨ MEMORY VERSE

REJOICING is both a response and a choice. In response to the goodness and greatness of God, we praise God and thank Him for His gifts to us. But whether or not we feel like it, and whether or not we see any reason for it, Paul tells us to rejoice always. Praise and thanks during difficult times rivet our minds on God's truth and stimulate trust in Him, even when we don't know what He's doing.

Paul certainly had opportunities to practice rejoicing always. In Acts, Luke records the phenomenal ways God used Paul to take the message of Christ to the known world. In every city, people responded to the gospel and trusted Christ. But also in every city, opposition rose up to try to stop Paul. In his letter to the Philippians, he describes how others were taking advantage of his being in prison to "steal his thunder" and take his platform (see Philippians 1:15-18). That didn't matter to Paul. He rejoiced because the message was getting out, even if the messengers had selfish motives. And Paul describes how God had been faithful when he enjoyed plenty and when he barely had enough to eat (see Philippians 4:11-13). Either way, God had proven Himself to be good, kind, and gracious to him.

Can we, like Paul, focus our attention on God's character and trust Him in every situation? Sometimes, we rejoice and our hearts almost burst with gratitude, but at other times, we make gut-level choices to thank Him during painful seasons of life. In every situation and every relationship, through good times and bad, when we have plenty and when we have barely enough, we choose to rejoice. It's a choice that pleases God and reinforces our faith.

How would it help you to make the choice to rejoice even when you don't feel like it?

What are some situations right now that require that choice?

"If there is hope in the future, then there is power in the present." —JOHN MAXWELL

"Encouragement is the fuel on which hope runs." —ZIG ZIGLAR

BEFORE WE LOVED HIM

God demonstrates His own love toward us, in that while we were still sinners,
Christ died for us. ROMANS 5:8

MOST OF OUR HUMAN RELATIONSHIPS are based on mutual attraction and benefits. We enjoy our friends because they make us feel good, we were attracted to our spouses because we felt more alive with them, and we work at our jobs because we receive satisfaction and a salary. When times get tough, we hang in there for a while, but if things don't improve, we're tempted to bail out.

Because family relationships involve more commitment, we stick it out through thick and thin, but even then, strains and disagreements erode our affections. God's love for us, however, is different—radically different. He doesn't demand compliance to rules or certain behaviors to win His love. He gives it liberally, freely, and without conditions. Paul says that God lavishes His love on us (see Ephesians 1:7-8, NIV)! We don't deserve such good treatment from God. That's why it's called grace.

God doesn't love us because we're worthy of His affection; He loves us in spite of our rebellion, apathy, and selfishness. We have nothing to offer to win His approval, but He loves us anyway. And He didn't wait for us to respond to shower us with love. Paul tells us that God loved us "while we were still sinners." God's love, though, isn't syrupy sentimentality. It's bold, active affection that moves toward us to win our hearts. The depth of this love is demonstrated by how much and how selflessly it gives, and Christ's death on the cross is the ultimate gift.

Do we ever wonder if God really cares? When we doubt, we can look at the Cross.

Describe the most selfless love you've ever seen.

Thank God for His unconditional, radical love for you.

"If Jesus Christ be God and died for me, then no sacrifice can be too great for me
to make for Him." —C. T. STUDD

GOD CARES

Humble yourselves under the mighty hand of God, that He may exalt you in due time, casting all your care upon Him, for He cares for you.

1 PETER 5:6-7 { MEMORY VERSE

COUNTLESS STORIES in the Scriptures show us God's care for people. In Genesis, He created a world of plants, animals, seasons, and water to provide for us so we could live. He freed His people from slavery in Egypt and then gave them food to eat every day on the journey to the Promised Land. He gave them instructions so they could live the best life possible, and He forgave and restored them when they got off track. In the New Testament, Jesus' interactions with people show us God's love up close. He touched lepers, forgave adulterers, healed the sick, raised the dead, and was infinitely patient with followers, who were painfully slow to grasp His character and His mission.

If God's care is unmistakable, why do we have difficulty trusting Him when we're in need? Peter gives us a clue. At least one factor, he explains, is our pride, which says, "I don't need God. I can do it all by myself." Pride pushes God away and blocks the channel of His love and power to meet our needs.

We long to experience God's presence and care, but some of us long even more to appear self-sufficient. The first step—the most important step—to experiencing God's care is to humbly admit our need for Him. Without this honesty, we go it alone, and we miss the wonder of seeing Him work in and through us in the most difficult moments in our lives.

What are some reasons people insist on trusting themselves instead of turning to God for help?

Do you need to experience God's presence and care in your life today? Humble yourself and trust Him to provide for you.

"When we trust God, He trusts us and blesses us over and over." —ZIG ZIGLAR

LAUS DEO

Praise the LORD! Praise, O servants of the LORD, praise the name of the LORD! Blessed be the name of the LORD from this time forth and forever-more! From the rising of the sun to its going down the LORD's name is to be praised. The LORD is high above all nations, His glory above the heavens.

PSALM 113:1-4

WHAT DO YOU PRAISE? Most of us praise our favorite sports team, a great restaurant, a great band, successful companies, or the courage of a hero we admire.

When we praise these things, what do we do? We shine a light on their most positive attributes, calling attention to them so that others will think highly of these things too.

How do we feel when we praise something or someone? We are emotion-ally engaged, excited about others' knowing what we know and feeling what we feel.

But we utter genuine praise only when our hearts are connected to the thing we're praising. Otherwise, it's just empty chatter.

In this beautiful psalm, sung each year at the beginning of the Jewish Passover meal, the psalmist is certainly emotionally engaged! He calls on everyone to join him, and he wants us all to praise God all day, for all time, and in all places. He wants the world to know that God is wonderful, mighty, and gracious.

On one side of the capstone of the Washington Monument, 555 feet high, a plaque reads *Laus Deo* ("Praise to God"). The builders wanted to be sure that God received the credit for their work and their nation, so they engraved these Latin words permanently at the top. You and I have the same opportu-nity every day to give God credit for all He has given us, including our ability to work and care and help others.

What or whom do you praise most often? Does God seem as wonderful as that person or thing? Why or why not?

What are some ways praise can become more central to your daily life?

"It is the duty of all nations to acknowledge the providence of Almighty God and to obey His will." —**GEORGE WASHINGTON**

THE GOD FOR ALL NATIONS

Praise the LORD, all you Gentiles! Laud Him, all you peoples! For His merciful kindness is great toward us, and the truth of the LORD endures forever. Praise the LORD! PSALM 117:1-2

ETHNOCENTRIC. It's a pleasant-sounding word, but it's full of arrogance. When we think we are the only nation or race God blesses, we badly misunderstand the breadth and depth of the grace of God. Sure, He loves us with an undying love, but He loves everyone else on the planet just as passionately. He has no favorites.

The Israelites had been given a mandate to take the message of God's love to every nation, but they got wrapped up in their role as God's chosen people. God chose them so they could bless others, not so they could remain in a "holy huddle." On those few occasions when they did reach out to touch other cultures, God richly blessed them. When they withdrew into pride and exclusivity, God withdrew His hand of blessing.

Our nation has gone through spasms of being incredibly inclusive, welcoming people of every land to join our melting pot, but also of being terribly exclusive, banning immigrants and treating those who came as second-class citizens. Christians need to realize that God's grace transcends national boundaries, race, and culture, just as they needed to do so at other points in our history. God loves people from all over the globe, whether they've immigrated to America or live in the remotest deserts of foreign lands. Our primary task as believers is to break down the walls and love them into God's Kingdom.

To what extent are you ethnocentric? (What would your children or best friends say about your level of ethnocentrism?)

What are some ways you can break down walls and love people from other races and cultures into the Kingdom?

"God governs in the affairs of men. And if a sparrow cannot fall to the ground without His notice, is it probable that an empire can rise without His aid?"
—BENJAMIN FRANKLIN

LIBERTY FOR ALL

So shall I keep Your law continually, forever and ever. And I will walk at liberty, for I seek Your precepts. PSALM 119:44-45

PARADOXICALLY, we don't experience true liberty by throwing off all restrictions. We enjoy genuine freedom only in the context of laws. When the laws of a nation are just, reasonable, and good, its citizens know what is expected of them—in traffic, in business, in the community, in the home. And as long as they live within those laws, they prosper.

Spiritual life works the same way, but it sometimes requires maturity to value God's laws and experience freedom. Young believers get a taste of grace, and they sometimes think it doesn't matter what they do; the sky's the limit! But sooner or later, they face the painful consequences of breaking God's laws, and they learn to value the restrictions.

God's Word records hundreds of laws to guide us, protect us, and provide the most rewarding life possible. They aren't given to us to steal our fun and make our lives miserable. Quite the opposite. As we live by them "continually, forever and ever," we experience freedom from fear, relief from guilt, richer relationships with people, and a closer relationship with the One who wants us to thrive by following His loving guidance.

Our prisons are full of people who feel bitter, guilty, angry, and oppressed because they didn't follow the laws of the land. Similarly, our homes and neighborhoods contain people who suffer the consequences of lying, stealing, adultery, jealousy, laziness, and all other forms of selfishness.

The happiest people in the world are those who follow laws—God's and man's—and enjoy the liberty obedience gives them.

What are some evidences in your life and your family of the loss of freedom for breaking God's or man's laws?

Has the Holy Spirit tapped you on the shoulder to tell you that you need to follow a specific law? If so, what will you do about it?

"With a good conscience our only sure reward, with history the final judge of our deeds, let us go forth to lead the land we love, asking His blessing and His help but knowing that here on earth, God's work must truly be our own."
—JOHN F. KENNEDY

EXTRAVAGANT GOODNESS

Oh, that men would give thanks to the LORD for His goodness, and for His wonderful works to the children of men! Let them exalt Him also in the assembly of the people, and praise Him in the company of the elders.

PSALM 107:31-32

WHEN THE BIBLE SAYS that God is good, it means that all of God's intentions toward us are for our benefit, and His actions are designed to accomplish those intentions. But do we believe it? Do we really believe that God is good, not in some cosmic sense, but in a real-life, tangible way so that our belief makes a difference in our lives today?

We sometimes limit the scope of what we call "good," to the detriment of wisdom and spiritual vitality. We think of all the "good things" of life— ice cream, camping, dinner with friends, our team winning the championship—and it's easy for us to confine "good" to only those events that are pleasant. But God's goodness isn't confined in any way. He intends for each of us to grow strong in our faith, and He orchestrates circumstances to test us, stretch us, and cause us to realize how much we depend on Him. His "goodness" isn't measured only by pleasant times (though He gives those in abundance). Instead, He is more like a great coach who knows how to get the best out of his players, pushing some, encouraging all, and testing each one to his or her limits.

If, at our insistence, God's goodness were shown only in the narrow, limited giving of pleasant experiences, we would remain spiritual infants. But God insists on growing us up. Unfortunately, we all have to go through "adolescence," when we struggle to believe that the authority in our lives (God in this case) is wise and good. If we stay with it and gain real wisdom, though, we'll learn to see God's extravagant goodness in every situation we encounter. He's a great coach!

How have you thought of God's goodness up to this point in your life?

How does it help you to think of God as a coach whose task is to test you and stretch you so that you learn to depend on Him?

"To the same Divine Author of every good and perfect gift [James 1:17] we are indebted for all those privileges and advantages, religious as well as civil, which are so richly enjoyed in this favored land." —JAMES MADISON

THE PURSUIT OF HAPPINESS

Our mouth was filled with laughter, and our tongue with singing. Then they said among the nations, "The LORD has done great things for them." The LORD has done great things for us, and we are glad. PSALM 126:2-3

MOST OF US CAN'T IMAGINE being exiled for many years, struggling to find hope amid the despair, and then finally coming home again. Prisoners in Nazi concentration camps who were freed by the Allies certainly experienced this roller coaster of emotions, and political prisoners in any land can relate too. When this psalm was written, the nation of Israel had been in captivity. Many had been killed, many were tortured, and many died of starvation and hopelessness. When the survivors were set free and nearing home, they were overcome with relief, joy, and thankfulness. They were so happy that they couldn't stop laughing!

In America, all of us (except for Native Americans) are wanderers or descendants of wanderers who found a new home. Some of us and many of our ancestors escaped famine, abject poverty, political or religious oppression, slavery, or threats of death but found new hope in a free land! Many immigrants who came through Ellis Island tell of the same kind of joy and hope that the Israelites felt when they returned home.

In a spiritual sense, all of us who know Christ were once "strangers" in despair, living in a foreign land of hopelessness and certain death. But God has rescued us, freed us, and brought us into the land of His forgiveness, love, peace, and strength.

Release from political captivity isn't very common, but those who experience it laugh with joy. Release from spiritual captivity is a far more common experience. We need to be gripped by its reality so we marvel at our freedom and sing with gladness.

Think about the prison of sin and spiritual death. How would you describe your release from that prison?

Tell God how grateful you are for His setting you free and bringing you home.

"Religion and good morals are the only solid foundation of public liberty and happiness." —SAMUEL ADAMS

ABOUT HIS BUSINESS

[Jesus said,] "The Spirit of the LORD is upon Me, because He has anointed Me to preach the gospel to the poor; He has sent Me to heal the brokenhearted, to proclaim liberty to the captives and recovery of sight to the blind, to set at liberty those who are oppressed." LUKE 4:18

IT WAS ONE OF THOSE MOMENTS that you'd give anything to have witnessed in person. It was an announcement that people had longed to hear for countless generations, but it was such good news that many in the room that day refused to believe it. In one of His first acts in His ministry, Jesus walked into a synagogue and picked up the scroll of Scripture to read. He unrolled it and read Isaiah's prophecy of the Messiah's role to comfort, heal, free, and restore wounded and oppressed people (see Isaiah 61:1-2). The people listening had heard this passage read dozens of times before, but today would be different.

Jesus finished reading, handed the scroll back to the attendant, looked out at the faces looking back at Him, and said, "I am that person. That was written about Me. I'm here to do all those things in people's lives, and if you believe, they'll happen in your life" (see Luke 4:21).

Someone in the audience questioned how Jesus could possibly be the promised Messiah, and after some back and forth dialogue, the people were angry with Jesus. In fact, they were so angry that they wanted to kill Him! Ironic, isn't it? They threatened to take the life of the One who came to give life, to hurt the One who came to heal. Why did they respond this way? Because now the long-awaited promise had arrived, and now they had to choose to believe or to doubt. Many chose to doubt because believing required too much of them.

Jesus was about His Father's business that day. Some believed; some doubted. He's still about His Father's business today. Do you believe?

Why do you think the people were filled with wrath and wanted to kill Jesus?

How do you think you would have responded that day?

"If God calls you to be a missionary, don't stoop to be a king."
—CHARLES HADDON SPURGEON

AN ATTITUDE OF GRATITUDE

You are already full! You are already rich! You have reigned as kings without us—and indeed I could wish you did reign, that we also might reign with you!

1 CORINTHIANS 4:8

COMPARISON KILLS a thankful heart. Far too often, we look around at what others have, and discouragement creeps into our thoughts. Gradually (or not so gradually), discontent takes over, and complaints spill out of our mouths. Comparison convinces us that whatever we have isn't enough. Raises, bonuses, and windfalls of any kind satisfy only for a moment, and we quickly revert back to demanding more and more. Chasing the dream sounds exciting, but it can lead to a hardened heart.

Instead, Paul reminds the believers in Corinth that God had already poured out His riches of grace on them. They had gone from condemned prisoners to beloved children of the King! They had been spiritual paupers, and now they were rich beyond measure in God's blessings. They had been lost and impotent, wandering through life without hope, but now they "reigned as kings"!

Each of us looks in a mirror every day, either the mirror of earthly success and approval, which tells us we never have enough, or the mirror of God's grace and truth, which says we're already rich. Which one do you believe?

How are you affected (attitude, desires, demands, actions) by comparison?

How would it change your life if you looked more often in the mirror of God's grace and truth, which says you're already rich?

*"The more gratitude you express, the more you will experience to have gratitude for." —*ZIG ZIGLAR

RICHER THAN YOU THINK

My God shall supply all your need according to His riches in glory by Christ Jesus. PHILIPPIANS 4:19 { MEMORY VERSE

PAUL'S PROMISE that God would meet every need comes in response to the Philippians' generosity to give to God's work. Times were tough in the first-century mission field, and Paul often had very few supporters. He really appreciated the ones who stood behind him! The Philippians had sent him a wonderful gift. Paul describes it as a "sweet-smelling aroma, an acceptable sacrifice, well pleasing to God" (Philippians 4:18). Was it an aromatic candle? No, I don't think so. Whatever it was, the gift was as sweet to Paul as a bouquet of fresh flowers.

The gift, though, had cost the Philippians a lot. As a perceptive leader, Paul understood that some of them might be wondering, "Hmmm. If we gave money we needed to live on, what's going to happen to us?" Paul answered by telling them that God wouldn't forget their generosity. He would meet their needs in a way that revealed His direct involvement in their lives and His pleasure in their generous hearts.

The promise isn't that God will meet every desire or every want. It is that God will meet every need—especially those needs created when we have given over and above what we can afford to support God's work in the world. In an affluent culture like ours, most of us have few real needs. We enjoy the latest technology, we want a nicer car, and we expect a better vacation than last year. Maybe we should give so much to God that He has to meet real needs in our lives. That would be an adventure!

When have you given the most to the Lord's work? How did you feel about it?

What is God prompting you to do now in your giving?

"God's work done in God's way will never lack God's supply." —HUDSON TAYLOR

"I can testify that the Lord is as good as His Word. If we trust, believe, and bring our tithes into the storehouse, He will pour out His blessings of all kinds, including personal, family, and business." —ZIG ZIGLAR

GREATER THAN THESE

[Jesus said,] "Most assuredly, I say to you, he who believes in Me, the works that I do he will do also; and greater works than these he will do, because I go to My Father." JOHN 14:12

"GREATER THAN THE WORKS Jesus did? You've got to be kidding!" That's the way most of us respond when we read Jesus' words, but we're missing the point. We're thinking about healing the sick, giving sight to the blind, walking on water, and raising people from the dead. Jesus wasn't saying that we'd do more of those things than He did. Those aren't the primary reasons He came, anyway.

What was the primary "work" He did? He took the gospel to people. Jesus came to communicate the incredibly good news of God's forgiveness, love, and acceptance to a lost and dying world.

Where did He do it? During His brief life on earth, Jesus was confined to a very small patch of ground, just a few miles from one town to the next in the backwater country of Palestine.

When Jesus went to the Father, He sent the Holy Spirit to live inside each believer. Today, there are estimated to be a billion Christians worldwide. With the Spirit's direction and life-changing power, God uses us to take the gospel to far more people throughout the world than Jesus met in tiny Palestine. That's the point Jesus was making.

The question for all of us is, Are we doing our part? Are we actively engaged in telling friends and neighbors about Christ, praying for missionaries, giving to fund mission efforts, and going to see what God is doing throughout the world? If we are, then we're doing "greater works" than He did because, collectively, we're going to more people to tell them about Him.

Are you doing your part? Explain your answer.

What is one thing you can do in the next few days that will help you do your part more effectively? When will you do it?

"Pray for great things, expect great things, work for great things, but above all, pray." —R. A. TORREY

ALIGNED TO ACHIEVE

Whatever we ask we receive from Him, because we keep His commandments and do those things that are pleasing in His sight. 1 JOHN 3:22

AS BELIEVERS, we know that success in life isn't quantum physics or rocket science. If we follow Christ's directions, He promises to make our lives richer and more rewarding than we can imagine. If we obey His commands, our hearts will be aligned with His heart and He will delight in answering our prayers.

But do we know what He demands of us? And do we even care? The answers to these questions may not be simple. Somehow, many of us have divorced the biblical truth we've learned from our daily lives. If we're pressed to remember, we can think of some commands God has given us. *Let's see now, don't murder, don't lie, and don't commit adultery.* But many of us don't let God's commands to love and forgive others infuse our daily relationships at home and at work. We leave our church services and go right back to harboring resentments, withholding affection, and blaming people who fail to measure up to our standards.

First, then, we need a refresher course on what God commands us to be and do in every relationship and in every situation. Once we know His instructions, we then need to remember that our choices touch His heart. He is the infinite, Almighty God, but our attitudes and actions bring a smile or a frown to His face. If we know Him at all, we want to make Him smile.

Every command God gives us is for our own good and to expand His Kingdom through us to show His love to others. Our obedience is important. People's lives depend on it.

What are some commands God has for you today?

Does making God smile motivate you to obey Him? Why or why not?

"When you have great desires for heavenly things, when your desires are such as God approves of, when you want what God wants, then you will have what you like." —CHARLES HADDON SPURGEON

OLD AND NEW

Put off, concerning your former conduct, the old man which grows corrupt according to the deceitful lusts, and be renewed in the spirit of your mind, and . . . put on the new man which was created according to God, in true righteousness and holiness. EPHESIANS 4:22-24

IN SOME WAYS, being a Christian makes life more complicated. Instead of having one nature (selfish and sinful though it is), we have two. When we become believers, incredibly wonderful and dramatic things happen. God forgives us for all our sins, we become children of God, and we have eternal life, to name just a few. But our old sinful nature doesn't evaporate. It's still there, whispering to us that God doesn't care; that we're foolish for following Him; and that, after all, there's nothing wrong with being selfish. Paul tells us that not only is our old selfish nature still there—it's getting worse!

Paul uses the metaphor of getting dressed to help us understand how to live by our new nature. It's as simple as putting on clean clothes. First, we recognize that our old clothes are dirty, and we take steps to take them off. When the Spirit of God shines His light on our pride, arrogance, indifference, or other sins, we say, "Yes, Lord. I see them too." We confess our sin, and we lay that behavior aside like a dirty shirt.

We then grab a clean shirt—new behavior that honors God and blesses people—and put it on. During this process, we let God's Word sink deep into our minds to refresh us and renew us. Without His truth, we wander around in dirty clothes, not knowing why people think we stink!

Don't be surprised when you recognize sinful attitudes and actions in your life. They are part of your old nature, which will be with you until you see Jesus face-to-face. But do something about them. Change clothes!

What are some dirty clothes you've worn lately? When did you realize they were dirty?

What are some clean clothes you need to put on today?

"Let my heart be broken with the things that break God's heart." —**BOB PIERCE**

TREASURES FROM THE DARK

I will give you the treasures of darkness and hidden riches of secret places, that you may know that I, the Lord, who call you by your name, am the God of Israel. ISAIAH 45:3

THE THOUGHT OF FINDING A TREASURE has thrilled people from the beginning of time. Ancient cultures told myths about it, and today, millions watch as lottery numbers are posted each day. Some treasures require years of search and sacrifice. Mel Fisher searched for the *Atocha*, a Spanish galleon, for seventeen years before he found the treasure, worth about four hundred million dollars, off the Florida Keys. And some people are instant millionaires from buying a one-dollar sweepstakes ticket.

In the book of Isaiah, God describes a completely different kind of treasure, but one that is worth more than all the gold, silver, and jewels in the world. In the most difficult and most excruciating moments of our lives, God wants us to find a treasure. When times are good, we roll along with only a superficial pursuit of God, but in our pain, we cry out to Him from the deepest recesses of our souls. We desperately need to know Him, His heart, and His purpose for us right then. In that cry for help, God reveals Himself to us so that we grasp more of His character. We may not know why something happened, but that matters less if we know we can trust the One who holds all things in His hands.

In our darkest moments, we develop intimacy with God. We're convinced that He is almighty and beyond comprehension, but more than ever, we're convinced that we can trust Him completely. That's true treasure.

We never manufacture times of darkness so that we can find this treasure, but when these times occur, we can have confidence that God will meet us there.

What are some times of darkness you've experienced?

In what ways is knowing God more deeply and intimately true treasure to you?

"Watch where God puts you into darkness, and when you are there, keep your mouth shut. . . . When you are in the dark, listen, and God will give you a very precious message for someone else when you get into the light."
—OSWALD CHAMBERS

"Adversity is God's way of preparing me to help other people." —IKE REIGHARD

THE ISSUES OF LIFE

Keep your heart with all diligence, for out of it spring the issues of life.

PROVERBS 4:23

THEOLOGIANS SAY that, in the Bible, the word *heart* means "the seat of reflection," where we analyze every motive, every relationship, and every action in our lives. The heart, then, is like a lens that enables us to look at life either clearly or with distortions. This lens is so important that Solomon encourages us to protect it at all costs because our perceptions affect every aspect of our lives.

What's in our hearts? Even for the most mature believers, we'd have to say it's a mixed bag. We want to have pure motives, but if we're honest, we admit that some of our attitudes are pretty selfish. We want to have impeccable integrity, but we realize we've exaggerated the truth more than once to make ourselves look a little better. The first step in keeping our hearts, then, is to be honest about what we find when we look inside.

We have the choice to let our hearts drift along or to focus them on God's truth, God's purposes, and God's ways. To keep our hearts with all diligence means that we long to honor God in all we do, and we treasure love and integrity as we deal with people. We can fill our hearts with these treasures, or we can leave them dry and empty. The choice is ours, but our decisions each day about our hearts will make all the difference in our relationships, our work, our directions in life, our peace of mind, our strength of spirit, and our sense of fulfillment.

Take a snapshot. What's the condition of your heart right now?

What are some ways you can fill your heart with faith, hope, and love, and then protect it?

"What lies behind us and what lies before us are tiny matters compared to what lies within us." —RALPH WALDO EMERSON

ASK: ALWAYS SEEK KNOWLEDGE

[Jesus said,] "Ask, and it will be given to you; seek, and you will find; knock, and it will be opened to you." MATTHEW 7:7 { MEMORY VERSE

SOME OF US READ a verse like this, and we assume that the Christian life should be like a cruise—where we're waited on hand and foot without a care in the world. When circumstances turn out to be *not quite that way*, we're disappointed. But our walk of faith is much more like a challenging hike. We have to prepare for it, and there are many unexpected twists and turns. Parts of it are exhilarating, and other parts require tenacity to keep going.

What, then, does Christ's invitation mean? It doesn't mean He'll make life as easy as a cruise; instead, He promises to equip us for the long hike. How? By giving us the knowledge and wisdom we need to take the next step at each point on the journey. All along the way we ASK; we always seek knowledge from God and about God. We ASK in order to take advantage of opportunities and to overcome obstacles. We ASK when we love life or when we feel like quitting, when we enjoy popularity or when we're alone. In every situation and at every moment, Christ invites us to tap into His heart and His wisdom. His plan isn't to make life as easy as a cruise, but to give us direction, encouragement, and the desire to enjoy walking with Him.

> **When you pray, what do you most often ask for?**
>
> **Take some time now to ask God for knowledge and wisdom for today's hike.**

> *"Decision is the spark that ignites action. Until a decision is made, nothing happens."* —**WILLARD PETERSON**
>
> *"Far too many people have no idea of what they can do because all they have been told is what they can't do. They don't know what they want because they don't know what is available to them."* —**ZIG ZIGLAR**

THE SECRET OF PERSEVERANCE

Those who wait on the LORD shall renew their strength; they shall mount up with wings like eagles, they shall run and not be weary, they shall walk and not faint. ISAIAH 40:31

WAITING IS SUCH A DRAG. Most of us hate waiting with a passion! When we get in any line (at a red light, at the grocery-store checkout, at a ticket window, or anywhere else), we first scan the available lines to see which one might move fastest, and after we make our choice, we watch the people who got in the other lines when we got in ours. If any of them move faster, we boil!

Waiting is an essential part of God's plan for our lives, but it's not just killing time. When we "wait on the LORD," our focus is on Him, His goals, and His path for us. We wait expectantly, not impatiently, because we are increasingly convinced that God is up to something—something good—that we haven't experienced before. We rivet our hearts on God's character, and we are sure that waiting on Him to act will be worth every second.

The secret of perseverance isn't to grit our teeth as time passes. The secret is to focus. We wait expectantly, trusting that a good, wise, all-knowing God will accomplish His gracious purposes in His good time. We trust that while we wait He's preparing the situation, other people, or us for something special.

Describe a time when you had to wait on God.

What difference did it make (or will it make next time) for you to focus your heart on God's character and trust His purposes while waiting?

"The life of faith is not a life of mounting up with wings, but a life of walking and not fainting. . . . Faith never knows where it is being led, but it loves and knows the One who is leading." —OSWALD CHAMBERS

RUN YOUR OWN RACE

Do you not know that those who run in a race all run, but one receives the prize?
Run in such a way that you may obtain it. 1 CORINTHIANS 9:24

WHEN WE CONSTANTLY MEASURE OURSELVES by the successes and failures of others, we run the risk of losing our identity. When we feel insecure, we try to copy those who look successful and we criticize those who mess up. Our goal is to be—and stay—one up on everybody else. Of course, this way of living forces us to be on guard all the time. We can't afford to let anybody look better than we do. We live in fear that somebody will find out that we aren't as "put together" as we want them to think, and our relationships suffer. We smile on the outside, but we're worried sick. Some of us have lived this way so long that we don't even realize there's another way to live.

When we meet Jesus face-to-face, He's not going to ask us if we were as successful as somebody else. He's going to ask only whether we did what He asked us to do in the way that He wanted us to do it. Each of us has our own race to run, and we need to devote our energies to running that race—and only that race—as well as we possibly can.

When you realize you're comparing yourself to others, either positively or negatively, remember that you are responsible to run your own race, not someone else's. Running your own race is doing the best you can every chance you get with what you have for a purpose that outlives you.

What are some ways that "comparison kills"?

How would it help you to focus on running your own race?

"Winners evaluate themselves in a positive manner and look for their strengths as they work to overcome weaknesses." —ZIG ZIGLAR

WHEN MUCH IS GIVEN

[Jesus said,] "To whom much is given, from him much will be required; and to whom much has been committed, of him they will ask the more."

LUKE 12:48

WE CAN ONLY SPECULATE how Jesus' statement about "much" sounded to poor, dusty shepherds and farmers in His day and what it must sound like to people in parts of the world today who are barely surviving. Most of us are, by historic and current standards of living, the wealthiest people the world has ever seen. No, we don't have the wealth of Bill Gates or Warren Buffett, but we are fabulously rich.

We can look at our balance sheet in one of two ways: We can compare our net worth with those who have much more and feel inferior, hurt, and a little angry that things haven't worked out as well as we had hoped. Or we can watch the news of drought, famine, floods, and genocidal wars and breathe a deep sigh of relief, realizing we have it made!

There will come a day when we stand before Christ to give an account of all He has entrusted to us. On that day, He won't ask how our balance sheet compared with anyone else's. He'll ask, "What did you do with all I entrusted to you?"

Responsibility prods us to take action, but guilt makes a lousy motivator. A far better push comes from actually investing our resources in the causes God cares about and seeing lives changed. Making a difference in others' lives is a thrill! We want to give more, and God knows we have plenty to give.

Where do you see yourself on the scale of "haves" versus "have-nots"?

What would motivate you to invest more of your resources in God's work?

"Success is doing the very best I can every chance I get with what I have for a purpose that is bigger than I am and that will outlive me." —IKE REIGHARD

GOD'S WILL FOR EVERY MOMENT

Rejoice always, pray without ceasing, in everything give thanks; for this is the will of God in Christ Jesus for you. 1 THESSALONIANS 5:16-18

SOME OF US are more emotional than others. We ride a roller coaster of highs and lows in our hopes and expectations. When we're up, we're on top of the world, but when we're down, we're a step away from being suicidal! Other people are more consistent in their emotional composition, but they miss out on the thrill of experiencing true joy. Whatever our personality and emotional makeup, however, God's will for all of us is to focus our hearts so completely on Him that we constantly and consistently rejoice, pray, and thank Him. To experience true joy, some of us need to avoid letting our emotions rule our lives, but others need to add a little spunk to their emotions.

The moods of most people around us each day are heavily influenced—if not completely dictated—by the circumstances of life. Christians, though, are different. The grace of God and His mercy, love, and strength can dominate our minds and hearts so completely that circumstances don't dominate us. Even when life seems totally unfair, we focus on God's kindness and forgiveness and we find genuine contentment. Instead of focusing on our problems and trying to fix them ourselves, we turn to God, casting all our cares on Him (see 1 Peter 5:7), and we remember to pray for others who need God's help.

In every situation, good or bad, we give thanks—not for the problems we face, but for God's presence with us in the midst of those problems and for the hope that God will use them somehow to accomplish good things.

God's will isn't too complicated. First and foremost, it's looking to Him and letting His character fill our minds and our hearts every moment of every day.

Rate yourself on a scale of zero (zip) to ten (doing great, thank you!) in focusing on God during difficult times in your life.

What are some situations you face today in which you need to rejoice, pray, and give thanks? What difference will it make?

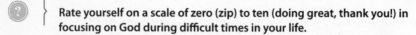

"The Bible does say, 'Pray without ceasing,' but I don't see where it says you have to stop working in order to pray. As a matter of fact, I believe that anybody who can walk and chew gum at the same time can work and pray at the same time."
—ZIG ZIGLAR

GOLDEN RULE

Whatever you want men to do to you, do also to them, for this is the Law and the Prophets. MATTHEW 7:12

EVERY MAJOR RELIGION has its own version of the Golden Rule. Does this fact minimize its importance? Not at all. It shows that God has put it in the hearts of people everywhere to realize this foundational principle of life: If we want to be treated with respect and love, we need to treat others that way first.

The principle seems so simple, but we see it violated every day. All of us long to be accepted—it's the first and foremost desire of every human heart—but we make a sport of behaviors that tear down, rip apart, crush, ignore, and ridicule people around us. Most of us don't actually abuse others. We're too sophisticated for that. Instead, we use gossip, sarcasm, and silence to insert the knife when people don't suspect anything. If we're caught, we say, "Hey, I was just kidding!"

Living by the Golden Rule involves a series of conscious choices to initiate kindness, respect, honor, words of affirmation, and patience to proclaim to someone, "You matter to me!" If we make radical acceptance of others a central value in our lives, amazing things will happen. First, some of the people who know us best will need to recover from shock, but after a short while, they'll realize they don't have to protect themselves from us anymore, and they'll relax. Then, slowly but surely, they'll begin to give back the acceptance they've received from us. That's how it works. It's not all that hard, really.

Who is the person you know who most lives by the Golden Rule?

What can you do today to take steps to implement it for yourself? Be specific.

"Man must cease attributing his problems to his environment, and learn again to exercise his will—his personal responsibility in the realm of faith and morals."
—ALBERT SCHWEITZER

ETERNAL PATIENCE

The Lord is not slack concerning His promise, as some count slackness, but is longsuffering toward us, not willing that any should perish but that all should come to repentance. 2 PETER 3:9

WHEN WE READ about Christ's coming back to earth, the power and majesty of the scene boggles our minds. We envision Him on a cloud with trumpets blaring and believers, dead and alive, defying gravity to join Him in the air. We imagine Him returning to earth as the Warrior who slays His enemies, and we can see Him taking the throne in Jerusalem to rule on earth. During Christ's thousand-year rule, amazing things will happen. Nature will be turned upside down—the lion will lie down with the lamb.

"Come on back!" we plead. However, we may be ready, but others aren't. One of the reasons Christ postpones His return is to give more people an opportunity to respond to the message of grace. We care about the lost people we know in our families and neighborhoods, but God longs for every heart around the world to turn to Him. He is saying, "Not yet. I'm not ready to come because there are still more people who haven't heard, and more who haven't trusted in Me. Not now. Not yet. But it won't be long."

When Christ returns, wrongs will be made right, and God's faithful people will be honored. Our hearts long for God's justice and grace to rule throughout the world, but God has a higher priority. He delays judgment for sinners and honor for saints so that more lost people can be found. The delay we endure is a small price to pay for an eternity of forgiveness, peace, and joy for even one more person. And we suspect it'll be a lot more than one who responds.

Do you long for Christ's return? Why or why not?

From your perspective, is the delay reasonable and fair?

"When you turn to God, you discover He has been facing you all the time."
—ZIG ZIGLAR

HAVING THE WISDOM TO ASK FOR WISDOM

If any of you lacks wisdom, let him ask of God, who gives to all liberally and without reproach, and it will be given to him. JAMES 1:5 { MEMORY VERSE

CORPORATIONS HIRE CONSULTANTS for any and all management needs, and executive coaches assist leaders to take steps forward in their personal lives and careers. In the business world, we readily recognize the need for outside assistance. We want feedback, we want the infusion of new ideas, and we want accountability. These are exactly what God promises if we'll just ask Him for them.

Why is it that God and the Scriptures are the last places some of us look for wisdom? When a problem comes along, we read books, call friends, and scour the Internet for articles related to our need. We expect this approach from those who don't know Christ, but Christians have the greatest resource the universe has ever known: God Himself.

Certainly, we can learn a lot from seminars and books, from marriage and family workshops, and from fitness experts. But our first, most important, and most powerful source of wisdom is God. He is just waiting for us to turn (finally) to Him, to express our need, to search the Scriptures to find out what He has already said about an issue, and to invite His Spirit to guide us.

When we hire a consultant, we receive a promise for services to be rendered. God's promise is that He will pour out His wisdom "liberally" when we ask, and "without reproach," that is, without condemning us for getting into trouble in the first place. Can it get any better than that?

How is God's promise to give us wisdom like and unlike hiring a consultant or coach?

How do you need God's wisdom to guide you today? Ask Him for it.

"Wisdom is the right use of knowledge. To know is not to be wise. Many men know a great deal, and are all the greater fools for it. There is no fool so great as a knowing fool. But to know how to use knowledge is to have wisdom."
—**CHARLES HADDON SPURGEON**

"God sees everything at once and knows what you are called to do. Our part is not to play God, but to trust God—to believe that our single, solitary life can make a difference."—**ZIG ZIGLAR**

THE LAW OF RECIPROCITY

The generous soul will be made rich, and he who waters will also be watered himself. PROVERBS 11:25

THERE ARE PLENTY OF TIMES when life confuses us, but God has orchestrated the world so that many things are amazingly predictable. The laws of nature include cycles of weather and rhythms of planting and harvest. In human relationships, too, we find easily identifiable principles at work. One of these principles is the law of reciprocity: People get back what they give out.

The book of Proverbs contains a number of examples of this law. Anger expressed results in angry replies, and kindness offered is rewarded with kindness received. The way we handle our resources, too, produces reciprocal responses. Here and in other passages in the Old and New Testaments, we find the remarkable principle that generosity will be rewarded in kind. To make the point crystal clear, Solomon, in the verse above, says the same thing in two different ways.

To guard against a selfish, mechanistic approach, Solomon includes the small but crucial element: "*The generous soul* will be made rich." God wants his people to be generous at the deepest level of their hearts, caring for people and His Kingdom instead of looking for a great return on an investment. A great return is promised, but only for those who give with willing, gracious, full hearts of thankfulness. Those who give generously and gladly don't care as much about the promise of return. They are far more interested in using their resources to make a difference. If the return takes a while, they aren't flustered, and if God takes them through a time of difficulty, they accept, like Job, both blessing and adversity.

The law of reciprocity is a principle God instituted to bless us, but He's more interested in the attitude of our hearts than the numbers on a check.

Why is it important for our hearts to be right when we give generously?

How is the law of reciprocity working out for you? Any changes needed?

"Goodness is the only investment that never fails." —HENRY DAVID THOREAU

TAKE A REALLY GOOD LOOK

Jesus stooped down and wrote on the ground with His finger, as though He did not hear. So when they continued asking Him, He raised Himself up and said to them, "He who is without sin among you, let him throw a stone at her first."

JOHN 8:6-7

THE MOMENT WAS FULL of equal parts drama and comedy. A woman had been caught in the act of adultery, and the crowd wanted Jesus to condemn her. They had stones in hand, ready to execute the death sentence. They glared at Jesus to see what He would do, and suddenly, He stooped to the ground and began doodling in the dirt! What in the world was He doing?

They were confused and outraged, but the ones in the front near Jesus were the first to notice what He was writing in the dirt. Nudges and whispers made their way through the crowd as men probably saw something they never expected to see that day: their own sins written in plain sight on the ground. But the men wouldn't quit. They still wanted to see the woman die for her sins. Then Jesus stood up, looked at the men, and said, "Sure, stone her, but let the one without sin throw the first stone."

In our lives, we often want people who sin against us to pay for what they've done. We hold stones of condemnation and gossip in our hands, and we can't wait to let them sail! Sometimes, though, Jesus writes in the dirt of our souls, "Do you remember when you were so selfish? It's no different from what that person did to you. Now, do you still want to blast away to get revenge?"

When we take a good look inside ourselves, we realize that we're guilty too. So maybe we should put our rocks down and walk away.

Is there anyone you'd like to stone today?

What would Jesus write in the dirt if you stood in front of Him? How would you respond?

"Some people find fault like there is a reward for it." —ZIG ZIGLAR

A FRIEND OF SINNERS

The Son of Man has come eating and drinking, and you say, "Look, a glutton and a winebibber, a friend of tax collectors and sinners!" LUKE 7:34

JESUS NEVER FORGOT the reason He came. After a few years of ministry, He could have closed ranks, gathered His followers, and lived a comfortable life as a respected rabbi, but He kept taking risks to reach out to sinners—and He caught a lot of flak for it.

The religious establishment ridiculed Jesus because He spent so much time with "unclean" people, sick people, and people with questionable reputations. Associating with them, they were certain, couldn't possibly be God's will. If those people straightened out their lives and did all the right things, maybe then they would be acceptable. Before that, though, the riffraff were off-limits.

How do addicts, adulterers, agnostics, and homeless people feel when they walk through the doors of our churches? How do they feel when they sit next to us at church or stand next to us at the coffee shop? Do we look down our noses at them, judging them as inferior? Even those furthest from God didn't feel rejected by Jesus. They delighted in His presence, not because He lowered His standards of righteousness, but because He raised His standard of authentic love for them.

Who are the "tax collectors and sinners" in your neighborhood with whom few people want to spend time? Who are the outcasts at work, or maybe in your family? Jesus proved to be the friend of such people. You can too.

Who are the "tax collectors and sinners" in your world?

How do they feel around you? How do you want them to feel?

"While dining with sinners, Jesus was dreaming of their becoming saints."
—IKE REIGHARD

A FRESH LOOK AT DYING

The righteous perishes, and no man takes it to heart; merciful men are taken away, while no one considers that the righteous is taken away from evil. He shall enter into peace; they shall rest in their beds, each one walking in his uprightness. ISAIAH 57:1-2

WE GRIEVE AT FUNERALS because we miss the person we love, and rightly so. The person's death may bring a sense of relief if he or she suffered from a debilitating illness for many years. But escape from physical pain is only part of the relief believers experience when they walk through life's portals into the presence of Christ. They also escape the presence of evil.

Fish probably aren't aware they're wet, and we probably aren't aware of the impact of evil on our lives because we've never been completely separated from it. As believers, we've said no to sin a million times, and we've tasted the delights of knowing God, but in this life, the smell of sin has always remained.

At the moment our spirits depart our bodies, though, an amazing thing happens. All evidences of evil—bitterness, greed, jealousy, hatred, sickness, aging, and so forth—vanish as we enter God's presence. There, we "enter into peace," perfect peace that we've never known before, with rest and with activity that fulfills us like nothing we've ever enjoyed before.

Knowing that this delight awaits us gives us patience and perspective today.

What do you think it will be like to escape the presence of evil?

How does this perspective give you strength and hope for today?

"I am ready to meet God face to face tonight and look into those eyes of infinite holiness, for all my sins are covered by the atoning blood." —R. A. TORREY

HOLDING ON TO THE HAND OF GOD

I was so foolish and ignorant; I was like a beast before You. Nevertheless I am continually with You; You hold me by my right hand. You will guide me with Your counsel, and afterward receive me to glory. PSALM 73:22-24

THE PSALMIST ASAPH was so angry he couldn't see straight! He felt that he had been given a bum deal: Evil people were flourishing, but he had followed God and was struggling. It wasn't fair! He lashed out at God, and he sulked in self-pity. He doesn't tell us exactly what he said to God, but we can be sure that it wasn't pretty because he described himself as "a beast."

In one of the most poignant and beautiful passages in the Bible, we find that when Asaph was at his worst, God was at His best. Asaph ranted and raved at God, but God continued to be loving, patient, and kind toward him. In fact, God kept holding his hand like a loving mother firmly and patiently holds the hand of a toddler in a tantrum.

God gave Asaph the assurance that He would lead him down the right path, and at the end of that season or the end of life itself, God would gladly receive him in love.

When we are at our worst, we often imagine that God is fiercely resentful or that He turns His back on us in disgust. We may have experienced those responses from our parents, siblings, spouses, or other people, but God's response is quite different. Even when we are beasts, He stays near, patiently loving us, reassuring us, and holding our hands. What a statement of His grace!

When you are at your worst, how have you imagined God responding to you?

What difference does it (will it) make to realize that He is patient, loving, kind, and near when you are angry with Him?

"I pray God I may be given the wisdom and the providence to do my duty in the true spirit of this great people." —WOODROW WILSON

SIGNED, SEALED, AND DELIVERED

He who establishes us with you in Christ and has anointed us is God, who also has sealed us and given us the Spirit in our hearts as a guarantee.

2 CORINTHIANS 1:21-22

A SURVEY OF CHURCH ATTENDERS shows that half of them don't know if they'll go to heaven when they die. They live in the ethereal world of hope and fear, wondering if they've done enough, if God is good enough, and if all they've heard about God is really true. People, though, don't have to live with fear and doubt.

Look at the words Paul uses to describe the certainty of our relationship with Christ. He said that God "establishes" us in His grace and forgiveness like an unshakable building on a strong foundation. He explained that God "sealed" us. In the Roman world, this was a very significant analogy. The authority of Rome was unquestioned. When a Roman governor put his seal on something, it signified ownership and security. Nothing could break the Roman seal, and nothing, Paul infers, can break God's seal of ownership and security in our lives.

But that's not all. Paul finishes with a flourish by telling us that the Holy Spirit's presence in our hearts is a guarantee that we'll live with God for eternity. True believers sense His presence, if not continually, at least enough to be convinced that we belong to Him.

Can people be sure of their eternal destiny? According to Paul, the answer is a resounding yes!

Before you read this passage, how sure were you that you were heaven bound?

And now? Explain your answer.

"You don't have to worry about tomorrow because God is already there."
—ZIG ZIGLAR

ABIGAIL'S GIFT

David said to Abigail: "Blessed is the LORD God of Israel, who sent you this day to meet me! And blessed is your advice and blessed are you, because you have kept me this day from coming to bloodshed and from avenging myself with my own hand." 1 SAMUEL 25:32-33

ABIGAIL WAS MARRIED to a first-class jerk. King David's men had been fighting a war for a long time, and when they arrived near Nabal and Abigail's home, they were hungry. The men asked for something to eat, but Nabal wasn't gracious. In fact, he didn't even meet the minimum standard of propriety to provide for strangers. He coldly dismissed the men, who soon reported the rebuke to David (see 1 Samuel 25:3-13).

David had shown remarkable restraint when King Saul treated him badly, but restraint went out the window this time! David and his men headed to Nabal's house with only one thing on their minds: revenge. Abigail, though, heard they were coming and realized the encounter would bring bloodshed that ultimately might harm David's reputation. She loaded up some donkeys with food and intercepted David before he reached the house. When she gave him the food, she also humbly gave David advice to avoid his killing her husband (see 1 Samuel 25:24-31).

David grasped Abigail's wisdom. After David and his men left with the food, God stepped in. Nabal dropped over dead after a banquet. David sent for Abigail, and the two of them were married.

When we're in a difficult situation or relationship, we may want to resolve the problem ourselves. We need, though, to trust God and act wisely. Abigail didn't kill her husband, and when David wanted to kill him, she stepped between them. God rewarded her integrity and wisdom, and He'll reward ours, too. When we want to take things into our own hands, we need to stop, trust God, and know that sooner or later our time is coming.

How would you have acted if you had been Abigail? if you had been David?

What are some situations you face in which you are tempted to take things into your own hands instead of trusting God?

"The solution to a problem I had wrestled with for three solid months came to me when I completely forgot about my needs and became engrossed in finding a way to meet the needs of others." —ZIG ZIGLAR

TRUE CONFESSION

If you confess with your mouth the Lord Jesus and believe in your heart that God has raised Him from the dead, you will be saved. ROMANS 10:9 { MEMORY VERSE

MANY PEOPLE ARE TERRIBLY CONFUSED about what it means to become a Christian. They can't fathom the startling concept of grace: God's unmerited favor toward sinners like us. They cling to the false notion that God is a stern teacher and the hope that He grades on a curve!

Others among us dive into the Bible and come up with a million requirements for being a child of God or evidences that our faith is real. Perhaps we say that we can't know we're Christians unless we tithe, go to church every Sunday, read the Bible thirty minutes each day (or is it an hour?), pray a certain way, and on and on. Of course, those things are important to help us grow in our faith, but they don't earn us a place in heaven. We do them because we *want* to, not because we *have* to.

Paul made it clear and simple: Two fundamental truths are essential to salvation. First, we must agree that the Jesus who walked the earth is also the God of the universe. The term *Lord* refers to Yahweh of the Old Testament, the God who met with Moses and led him and the children of Israel out of slavery in Egypt to the Promised Land. Jesus wasn't just a good man who died a martyr's death. He was Almighty God who came as the Lamb of God to take away the sins of the world. To pay for the sins of others, He had to be sinless Himself—God in the flesh.

Second, we must grasp the truth that the Lord of life rose physically from the dead after He was crucified. Actually, if we believe Jesus was God in the flesh, then the Resurrection isn't a difficult proposition to accept.

These two truths form the bedrock of our faith, connect us with the grace of God (versus self-effort), and motivate us to please God all day every day.

What are the different effects of self-effort to earn God's acceptance and faith in Christ?

How would you explain to others your belief in these two truths?

"To be like Christ is to be a Christian." —WILLIAM PENN

"It's exciting to know that an all-knowing, all-loving God, the Creator of the universe, who knows even when a sparrow falls, loved me so much before I was born that He came to earth to lay down His own life that I might live." —ZIG ZIGLAR

HE IS RISEN!

[The angel said,] "He is not here; for He is risen, as He said. Come, see the place where the Lord lay. And go quickly and tell His disciples that He is risen from the dead, and indeed He is going before you into Galilee; there you will see Him. Behold, I have told you." MATTHEW 28:6-7

FROM FRIDAY AFTERNOON, when Joseph of Arimathea took Jesus down from the cross and put Him in a tomb, until early Sunday morning, Christ's followers were devastated. Their hopes and dreams had been shattered by the cruel execution of the One they loved. Now, on Sunday morning, the men were still unable to make sense of what had happened, and they didn't move from their homes. A few faithful women, though, wanted to show their love for Jesus one more time by going to the tomb with spices to put on His body (see Luke 24:1).

Their walk to the cemetery must have been long and silent. What was left to be said? Their tears had spoken volumes over the last three days. But as they approached the tomb, they saw that the stone had been rolled away, and an angel, glowing like lightning, sat on the stone! His message thrilled and amazed them. "He's not here," the angel reported as he pointed to the empty tomb. "He's alive!"

The women probably wanted to pinch themselves. During those terrible days, their emotions had been dealt a severe blow and were stretched to the breaking point. Now, an angel was talking to them! It was, in a literal sense, incredible, but they believed him, and they rushed off to tell the rest of Jesus' followers.

The angel promised that they would see Jesus again, and indeed, they did only an hour or so later. The promise to all of us is that we'll see Him too. The message the angel spoke that morning is music to our ears, as well.

What do you think that moment was like when the angel spoke to the women?

What is the significance in your life that Jesus has risen from the dead?

"The entire plan for the future has its key in the resurrection." —BILLY GRAHAM

A FOUNTAIN OF FORGIVENESS

If we confess our sins, He is faithful and just to forgive us our sins and to cleanse us from all unrighteousness. 1 JOHN 1:9 { MEMORY VERSE

NO ONE IN HIS OR HER RIGHT MIND would live with an open sore if a tube of medicine would heal the hurt. In the same way, God has given us the incredible promise to heal the wounds of our guilt. His promise to forgive is ready and waiting for us to claim it. Will we?

For some of us, the gift of forgiveness seems too good to be true. We're convinced that our sin is too bad or that we've been doing it too long for it to be within the scope of God's cleansing. And besides, we're convinced we'll probably do it again, so what's the use?

God's promise is not to forgive us once and then leave us alone. His forgiveness is comprehensive, covering all our sins. None of them surprise Him. He's omniscient, and He knew each one before He created the world! He forgives with His eyes wide open.

John tells us that God is "faithful and just" to forgive us. He is faithful to fulfill His promise, and forgiveness is an act of justice because Christ has already paid the price on the cross. Our confession doesn't make us forgiven, but it taps into the limitless well of forgiveness provided to us by Christ's sacrifice.

If we grasp the scope of this promise, we won't hesitate to respond to the Spirit's tap on the shoulder to tell us an attitude or action is sin. We'll say, "Yes, Lord. I agree with You. Thank You for the forgiveness You promised!"

Do you access God's promise of forgiveness most of the time, some of the time, or very seldom? Explain your answer.

As you read today's paragraphs, did the Spirit tap you on the shoulder to remind you of a sin you need forgiveness for? If He did, thank Him now for His grace and forgiveness.

"In the end, it is important to remember that we cannot become what we need to be by remaining what we are." —MAX DE PREE

"The phrase, 'God said it, I believe it, and that settles it' is partially true. My friend, if God said it, that settles it, whether you believe it or not." —ZIG ZIGLAR

STONE-COLD TRUTHS

God spoke all these words, saying: "I am the LORD your God, who brought you out of the land of Egypt, out of the house of bondage. You shall have no other gods before Me." EXODUS 20:1-3

THROUGHOUT HUMAN HISTORY, God has used many different ways to communicate with us. On different occasions, He has spoken to people through voices, dreams, calamities, a cataclysmic flood, our consciences, the written Word, a flaming bush that didn't burn, and becoming one of us for a brief time. One of the most dramatic moments of God's desire to connect with us was when He carved stone tablets and gave them to Moses. On these tablets, also known as the Ten Commandments, God gave clear, powerful directions to enable us to relate to Him (the first four commands) and to one another (the last six).

As a preamble to the first command, God reminds the people of Israel of their recent history. Shortly before this moment, God had freed them from slavery in Egypt. He miraculously rescued them when the Egyptian army had them pinned against the sea, and He provided food for them every day in the wilderness. Without doubt, God had proven His greatness and grace to them. Nothing could compare to His majesty and His loving-kindness. With that in mind, the first commandment says clearly, "Keep Me at the top."

It's easy for us to think that we don't have any problem with idolatry and competing gods in our lives, but let's take a closer look. All around us, people put success, money, pleasure, and power in the center of their lives. And if we're honest, these things threaten to crowd God out of the center of our own lives too. We may not bow before a golden calf, but our minds can easily be preoccupied with gaining more than we have now. Keeping God in the center is a decision and a process.

What are some things that threaten to crowd God out of the center of your life?

What do you gain and lose by having Him in the center?

"Our main business is not to see what lies dimly at a distance, but to do what lies clearly at hand." —THOMAS CARLYLE

REAL REST

[God said,] "Remember the Sabbath day, to keep it holy. Six days you shall labor and do all your work, but the seventh day is the Sabbath of the LORD your God. In it you shall do no work." EXODUS 20:8-10

GOD DIDN'T GIVE US the Sabbath to make us weird. He gave it to us because He made us with the need for rest. We function best when we take a day off each week to rest our minds and bodies, recalibrate our priorities, and refocus on God.

Many of us don't know how to rest. We're geared up 24/7 to accomplish as much as we possibly can while at work and to play hard in the evenings and on weekends. We experience what some call "hurry sickness," rushing around so much that we make ourselves (and others) physically and emotionally sick. Some of us wear stress as a badge of honor. We take pride in our packed schedules, but we don't realize the damage we're inflicting on ourselves. One man had a revelation: "My pride about always being busy was sick. Gradually, I became more driven, but I also became more isolated and more demanding of people around me. Being in a hurry all the time generated a tremendous amount of anger, and I never gave myself time to decompress."

The Sabbath, however, isn't just a day off for us to do nothing. It should be filled with things that refresh us: time to worship God; invest in our family relationships; read a good book; enjoy a hobby; and yes, kick off our shoes and relax. A lifestyle of being always on the go is addictive, and any addiction is hard to overcome. It takes focused attention, discipline, courage, and the encouragement of others who are on the same path.

Do you see any "hurry sickness" in your life?

What are some specific things you can do to make a Sabbath rest meaningful?

"If a man cannot earn a living working six days a week, what would make him think he could make it if he works seven days a week?" —TRUETT CATHY

THE GIFT OF HONOR

[God said,] "Honor your father and your mother, that your days may be long upon the land which the LORD your God is giving you." EXODUS 20:12

MANY OF US COME to a startling conclusion about our parents. In our teens, we believe they are one card short of a full deck, but when we are a bit older, we realize they are really wonderful people—flawed, but wonderful. Families are the glue of any society, and our relationships with our parents are important from birth to death. There's never a time when we cease to be our parents' child, and the need to honor them never ends.

Some people read the words of this verse and understandably grit their teeth and mutter, "Never!" They've been deeply wounded by their parents, and they've spent their lives recovering from the hurts they've endured. Whether our parents have been the best on earth or the worst from hell, God gave us a directive to honor them. That doesn't mean we approve of all their behavior or we excuse the wounds they've inflicted on us. It means we speak words of appreciation and not complaint to them . . . and any time we mention them to others. A lady who was severely abused by her father followed this pattern and learned to say, "At least he played a part in bringing me into this world. I'm thankful to him for that."

Speaking words of affirmation to and about our parents has dramatically positive effects. God promises that our obedience in this area results in long life. This promise isn't repeated for any other command, so we're wise to pay attention! How does that work? Learning to treat our parents with respect and honor takes a lot of pressure off one of our most important relationships. If we can relate to them in a positive way, we probably relate to everyone else in our lives with love, respect, and thankfulness. When stress goes down, life expectancy goes up. That's God's promise.

Make a list of things you appreciate about your parents, even if you were abused or abandoned.

How might honoring your parents have a multiplied impact on the rest of your life?

"Nothing is more honorable than a grateful heart." —LUCIUS ANNAEUS SENECA

SANCTITY OF LIFE

[God said,] "You shall not murder." EXODUS 20:13

MOST OF US haven't killed anybody, so we can check this one off the Top Ten list. But is that all this commandment means? Jesus gave us two important insights about this issue. First, He instructed us to "love the LORD your God with all your heart . . . and . . . your neighbor as yourself" (Matthew 22:37-39). All the rest of the commands throughout the Bible, He explained, are wrapped into these two commands. Our goal, then, is not simply to avoid the crime of first-degree murder. If we respond to God's gracious invitation to know Him and experience His grace, we'll love even our enemies instead of wanting to kill them.

Jesus' second insight is that in God's eyes hating people is the same as murder (see Matthew 5:21-22). God looks at our intention, and when we harbor bitterness and the desire for revenge, we are far from the heart of God.

Throughout the Scriptures and in human history, we see that God is incredibly patient with people who are slow to respond, and He forgives those—people like us—who fall short of loving Him and others with their whole hearts. The more we experience His forgiveness, the more we'll forgive those who inflame our passion for revenge. But we won't just wash our hands of them and stand back. We'll care for them and wish the best for them. We'll treasure family and friends, overlooking many of their shortcomings; forgiving others; and at all times, treating them the way we long to be treated.

Murder? No, God wants us to be far removed from even the thought of it. Love is His ethic, His purpose, and His example for us to follow.

What do you think Jesus meant when He said that hatred is like murder?

Is there any animosity in your heart that needs to be replaced with God's love? If so, how can that happen?

"Wicked men obey from fear: good men, from love." —ARISTOTLE

MORE PRECIOUS THAN GOLD

[God said,] "You shall not commit adultery." EXODUS 20:14

LIKE THE PREVIOUS COMMANDMENT, God's prohibition against adultery means far more than meets the eye. More than simply avoiding premarital or extramarital sex, God wants us to treasure our spouses and not allow anything to erode the delight we can experience in marriage.

In marriage, friction is inevitable, but in our culture, the pace of life and the countless distractions seem to magnify minor moments of friction into roaring fires of resentment. When we are dissatisfied, our minds drift, and our eyes stay too long on a photo in a magazine, the shape of a coworker's body, or the images on an Internet site. Before long, the unthinkable becomes possible, and we gradually slide toward tremendous pain.

It's not enough to acknowledge the stresses of our culture on our marriage. That's a good starting point, but we need to make a significant investment in the life and strength of our most important human relationship. We need to spend time and other resources to build trust, have fun, and win back the heart of one who may be drifting. Relationships don't remain static. They either move forward or backward. Make sure you are investing your energies and passions in creating the best marriage on the planet!

What are some factors that cause a couple's delight in each other to erode?

If you are married or dating, what is one thing you can do today to express genuine affection to the person you love?

"There are some things, like faithfulness in marriage, that are black and white issues." —ZIG ZIGLAR

KEEP YOUR MITTS OFF!

[God said,] "You shall not steal." EXODUS 20:15

LIKE THE COMMAND AGAINST MURDER, this one goes beyond the prohibition of criminal activity and focuses on our heart attitudes. An insatiable thirst for more, no matter the means we use to get it, shows that our hearts are focused on things rather than on God. That, the Bible says clearly, is idolatry. Stealing to get more may be an extreme example, but the jealousy that our yearning for more creates is a more common ailment. And jealousy ruins hearts and relationships.

If we trace jealousy back to its root, we find a gnawing lack of trust in God's goodness. Instead of being thankful for all He has given us, we compare our possessions and pleasures with those our friends enjoy, too often find that we don't measure up, and do whatever it takes to get what we don't have. But even when we have more than others around us, we still aren't satisfied for very long because we look at the lives of the rich and famous and feel that nagging discontent again.

A window into our souls is the ratio of thankful thoughts to musings about the things we want but don't have. If that ratio is tilted the wrong way, the sheer weight of our thoughts tips us over into jealousy, envy, and discontent. Thankfulness, though, is a choice, not just a feeling. We are wise to do whatever it takes to rivet our minds on the goodness of God and the riches, both material and nonmaterial, He has given us.

What's the ratio of thankfulness to the desire for more in your thought life?

Take some time now to make a list of things you are thankful for.

*"When we do more than we are paid to do, eventually we will be paid more for what we do." —*ZIG ZIGLAR

TELL THE TRUTH

[God said,] "You shall not bear false witness against your neighbor."

EXODUS 20:16

THE COMMAND TO AVOID BEARING FALSE WITNESS sounds like a script from a John Grisham novel. It certainly means to speak "the whole truth and nothing but the truth" under oath in court, but God wants us to be honest both in and out of the courtroom.

We break this commandment when we exaggerate the truth to impress our friends or coworkers, and we break it when we gossip in order to ruin others' reputations. When we gossip, we may be speaking the truth but we speak with selfish motives. And quite often, the devious thrill of gossiping pushes us over the edge so that we make sure we amplify any perceived wrong the person has done, and we conveniently forget the better traits of his or her character. Of course, we also transgress this command when we outright lie to cover a sin we've committed.

There are many reasons to tell the truth and to tell it with humility and grace. We follow the pattern of Christ, who embodied both truth and grace. When we are committed to the truth, we don't have to look over our shoulders all the time to see whether we're going to get caught. The truth may be painful at times, but it shows that we trust God with reality instead of trying to create our own version of it. And eventually—probably in this life but certainly in the one to come—we will have to face the consequences of our deceptions. These are good reasons to speak the truth all the time.

> What are some benefits and consequences of "white" lies?
>
> How can you take steps to speak the truth instead of exaggerating or deceiving?

> *"A lie can travel halfway around the world while the truth is putting on its shoes."*
> —MARK TWAIN

I WANT YOURS!

[God said,] "You shall not covet your neighbor's house; you shall not covet your neighbor's wife, nor his male servant, nor his female servant, nor his ox, nor his donkey, nor anything that is your neighbor's." EXODUS 20:17

THE PREVIOUS FIVE COMMANDMENTS deal with behavior; this one focuses directly on our motives. Author Steve Farrar observes that most people in our culture suffer from the sickness of "affluenza." He's right. Modern advertising is pervasive. It invades our eyes and ears all day every day, and we welcome it! The avalanche of messages convinces us that if we don't have this product or that service we should be the most discontented people who ever lived. And most of these commercials present beautiful people who are thrilled because they've bought new things!

One of the most devastating yet subtle effects of advertising today is that it creates the illusion of an ideal life that is easily attainable by acquisitions. Our expectations for more soon turn to demands, and we resent those who have what we believe we rightly deserve. There's nothing wrong with noticing that others have things we don't have, but we cross the line when we resent them and demand those things for ourselves.

Parents have a God-given privilege of teaching and modeling for their children to value the things of God more than material possessions. Whining should never be rewarded. In fact, some parents tell their kids, "Whatever you whine for, you automatically don't get." That solves a lot of problems! And some parents also demonstrate thankfulness for all God has given them and the joy of giving to others. That's the solution to coveting—a solution all of us can apply.

How would you describe the symptoms of "affluenza"?

What are some specific ways you can overcome the marketing promise of an ideal life?

"If standard of living is your major objective, quality of life almost never improves; but if quality of life is your number one objective, your standard of living almost always improves." —ZIG ZIGLAR

A HEART-TO-HEART TALK

[The Lord said,] "[Elijah] will turn the hearts of the fathers to the children, and the hearts of the children to their fathers, lest I come and strike the earth with a curse." MALACHI 4:6

TODAY, STUDIES SHOW that 40 percent of children grow up without a father in the home, and another 40 percent have dads who are physically present but emotionally absent. This absence of a father's love and guidance devastates children as much as the plagues devastated Pharaoh and the Egyptians.

In this verse, God promises to send the prophet Elijah back to earth before the final cataclysm of history. The prophet's role won't be geopolitical. Instead, he'll focus his attention on fathers and their kids. Today, broken marriages, misplaced priorities, addictions, and run-of-the-mill selfishness have ruined countless relationships between fathers and their kids. Many of them want to make changes, but bitterness hardens their hearts and prevents progress. Each one insists, "I'm right, and you're wrong" or "I'm hurt, and it's all your fault." Is there hope to break this deadlock?

Forgiveness is the one and only solution to bitterness, and if one side won't take initiative, the other can. First, we go to God with the realization of our own sinfulness and our need for His forgiveness. Then, out of full hearts, we choose to forgive those who hurt us. No, it's not easy, but it's the only way to restore the most cherished relationships in our lives.

How have you seen bitterness destroy families?

Is there anyone in your family you need to forgive? First, experience God's forgiveness, and then choose to forgive those who hurt you.

"The true secret of giving advice is after you have honestly given it to be perfectly indifferent whether it is taken or not, and never persist in trying to set people right." —HANNAH WHITALL SMITH

WHAT TO DO WHEN YOU'RE WEAK

Watch and pray, lest you enter into temptation. The spirit indeed is willing, but the flesh is weak. MATTHEW 26:41

WE CAN LEARN a thing or two from our friends in Alcoholics Anonymous. They are ruthlessly honest about their weaknesses, which led to tragic consequences because they gave in again and again to the temptation to drink. For years, they denied they had a problem, or if they were confronted with it, they said, "Oh, it's no big deal." But it *was* a big deal. Now, honesty about their weaknesses is the foundation for recovery, growth, and strength.

Most of us don't want to admit we're weak in any way. We try to project that we have it all together, but our bravado makes us vulnerable to temptation in our sexual appetites, ethics, preoccupation with material possessions, neglect of God, or a dozen other areas of life.

Jesus told His followers (and us) to avoid temptation by doing two things when weak. First, watch for trouble. We need to be good students of our hearts and our behavior so that we see temptation before it springs its trap. We don't have to be geniuses to notice these things. We can tell when we're thinking more about those things, when they seem more attractive, and when the consequences seem to escape our thoughts. And we can notice the situations (stress, tiredness, conflict, and so forth) that seem to trigger the desire to escape.

Second, Jesus reminded His followers to connect with God when weak. At those difficult moments, we may think that prayer is the last thing we want to do, but Jesus said it should be high on the list.

When you feel weak, watch and pray.

When you're weak, what temptations do you need to watch for?

When you're weak, do you want to connect with God? Why or why not?

"If the Holy Spirit guides us, he will do it according to the Scriptures and never contrary to them." —GEORGE MÜLLER

KEEPING TRACK OF TIME

See ... that you walk circumspectly, not as fools but as wise, redeeming the time, because the days are evil. EPHESIANS 5:15-16

PEOPLE WASTE TIME in two very different ways. We usually associate the term with people who procrastinate and don't do the things they're responsible for. "Stop wasting time and get to work!" we tell them. But another, more insidious form is probably more common, yet not as obvious: investing time and energy in the wrong pursuits. We waste time heading down a path of selfish goals with the aim of getting to the top and running over anyone who gets in our way. We waste time by worrying too much about what others think of us, reliving past conversations because we're afraid we said the wrong thing, or projecting our fears into the future. And we waste time when we measure our lives by the fullness of our schedules instead of the richness of our relationships.

Paul reminds us that every minute counts. We are in a cosmic but invisible struggle between the forces of good and evil. Time is one of our greatest resources in this fight. It allows us to connect with our Commander and to carry out His directions. Far too often, though, we don't think of time this way. We just do the same things we've been doing without a moment's analysis.

The goal isn't to be busy. We redeem the time by seeing every moment as a gift from God to be used to honor Him, to work and live with an eternal purpose in mind, and to have a positive impact on those He loves—which is everybody we see every day.

What are the most common ways you see people wasting time?

How would it change your life to realize that every moment is a gift from God to be redeemed and used to honor Him?

"I find the doing of the will of God leaves me no time for disputing about His plans."
—GEORGE MACDONALD

NO CONDEMNATION

There is therefore now no condemnation to those who are in Christ Jesus, who do not walk according to the flesh, but according to the Spirit. ROMANS 8:1 { MEMORY VERSE

WE TEND TO MAKE ONE of two mistakes as we think about our sins: We are either too sensitive to them or not sensitive enough. For some reason, some of us aren't grieved when our selfishness hurts others and pushes God away. We need the Holy Spirit's light to shine on the damage our sins cause so that we become more sensitive to them.

In this verse, however, Paul is addressing the opposite problem: people who feel oppressive guilt and shame because of their sins. Real guilt focuses on specific sins. God uses real guilt to remind us that we're forgiven. False guilt, though, consumes our minds and hearts with a generalized, foreboding self-condemnation: *I'm a terrible person, and I'll never be any better.*

In one of the most glowing statements of fact in the Bible, Paul tells us that believers never have to fear God's condemnation again. It's over. Done. Gone. Now, God's arms are open wide, and He pours out His love for His children—even those who are reluctant to believe He loves them. Real guilt is completely forgiven, and false guilt is washed away by the marvelous truth of God's unconditional acceptance.

If you struggle with false guilt—the nagging, oppressive sense of shame that you're too bad for God to love you—this is great news! Let the power and beauty of God's forgiveness sink deep into your heart. It may take a while for the truth to completely uproot all the doubts and shame, but it'll happen. Count on it.

Describe the cause and impact of false guilt in the lives of sensitive people.

How does the truth in this verse address false guilt?

"I have never found any way to undo what Christ has done." —BEN HADEN

"I know His promises are true, that He has given me eternal life, and I will spend eternity with Him. It's comforting beyond belief to know that you never have to put a question mark after anything to which God has put a period." —ZIG ZIGLAR

LIFE'S BIGGEST TEST

I urge you to reaffirm your love to him. For to this end I also wrote, that I might put you to the test, whether you are obedient in all things.

2 CORINTHIANS 2:8-9

BAD THINGS WERE GOING ON in the church in Corinth—really bad things. Sexual sin was rampant, and Paul intended to put an end to it. He wrote a scathing letter instructing the church to discipline a man who had committed a particularly heinous sexual sin. Paul told them to kick him out of the church. A few months later, a report came back that the church had done what he told them to do, and the man had repented! Church leaders, though, weren't sure what to do. Should they keep him out or invite him back into the fold?

Paul's stern demeanor dissolved with the news of the repentant heart. Now, he begged them to accept the man back with open hearts. Forgive him, restore him, and accept him as their brother again. But Paul also gave them a new insight about his intentions: His directive to discipline the sinning brother was a test for the church as much as it was a test for the man. He knew that it would be easier for them to excuse him and act as if his sin were no big deal rather than to blast him and refuse to love him if he repented. But they passed the test.

Dealing with others' sins is always a test for us. Will we be firm enough to require change in these people, and will we forgive them if they admit they were wrong? Handling sin is life's biggest test for churches—and for families.

> How did your family handle significant sins like addictions, abuse, and rebellion (if they were present in your family)?
>
> Describe the purpose and process of dealing with others' sins.

> *"If you are not living in the will of God, you are uncomfortable in the Word of God."*
> —ZIG ZIGLAR

DOORS OF OPPORTUNITY

Jesse said to his son David, "Take now for your brothers an ephah of this dried grain and these ten loaves, and run to your brothers at the camp. And carry these ten cheeses to the captain of their thousand, and see how your brothers fare, and bring back news of them." 1 SAMUEL 17:17-18

WHEN WE THINK OF DAVID, we remember his killing the giant Goliath, honoring his friendship with Jonathan, running from Saul, and uniting the kingdom. We also remember some of his less stellar moments, such as committing adultery and murder. But we often forget how it all got started. David's childhood was not a happy one. Because he was the youngest, David was often overlooked by his parents, who gave preference to his older brothers. Today, we might recommend that David get into therapy, but God had another way to build confidence in the young man.

David's brothers were soldiers in Saul's army, fighting the Philistines. David's dad told him to take some special food to his brothers and their captain and to bring back news about his beloved sons. When he arrived at the camp, David saw that the entire army cowered in fear of the Philistine giant. David took the opportunity to offer his services to Saul (in spite of the taunts of his brothers) and won one of the greatest victories of personal bravery in military history.

The door of opportunity, though, swung open in an unlikely way. Though David had often been forgotten at home, God used the circumstances to open a wide door of opportunity for David to excel. David didn't wallow in self-pity. He marched through the door of opportunity. His life and the lives of all Israel were radically changed that day.

How did God use a painful situation as an open door for David?

Is there a difficult circumstance in your life that God might use to open a door for you?

"Great doors of opportunity swing on the tiny hinges of obedience."
—IKE REIGHARD

GOD'S HANDIWORK

The heavens declare the glory of God; and the firmament shows His handiwork.

PSALM 19:1

ONE OF THE MOST HELPFUL and spiritually uplifting activities we can do is notice nature. Even a casual glance at the stars or a garden shows us the vast scale of God's creation and the incredible complexity of every creature. To measure distances in space, scientists use the distance light travels in a year. Light travels at 186,000 miles per second, or about 6 trillion miles a year, so we call that distance a *light-year*. At that amazing speed, light from the sun takes over 8 minutes to reach the earth. The nearest star in the galaxy is Alpha Centauri, 4.3 light-years away, so that the light astronomers see when they look at it left Alpha Centauri 4.3 years earlier.

The earth is an amazing phenomenon, with several distinct characteristics necessary for life that, as far as we know, don't exist in this combination anywhere else in the universe. And as biologists analyze the intricacies of DNA, they find complexity and predictability beyond anything they imagined.

Weather systems, landforms, ocean currents and other large-scale features amaze us. Hurricanes, tornadoes, volcanoes, and earthquakes disrupt our lives and reveal how fragile we can be. And on a much smaller, less violent scale, we delight in the beauty of a single flower or the movements of a lizard grabbing its next meal.

Noticing God's creative work takes only a moment, but we need to take it a step further and reflect on the implications of what we see. If Creation is so vast, God is greater still, and if His handiwork is so amazingly intricate, we can be sure that He knows every detail of our lives, too. Noticing nature results in deeper trust.

Do you take time to delight in nature and notice God's handiwork? Why or why not?

What does nature teach you about God?

"God writes the gospel not in the Bible alone, but on trees and flowers and clouds and stars." —MARTIN LUTHER

ABIDE IN ME

[Jesus said,] "I am the vine, you are the branches. He who abides in Me, and I in him, bears much fruit; for without Me you can do nothing." JOHN 15:5

IN THIS BEAUTIFUL METAPHOR, Jesus illustrated the integral relationship we have with Him. We don't have to own a vineyard to understand His analogy. We've seen enough ads for fine wines to get the point. Bunches of fine, healthy grapes grow only if the branch is vitally connected to the vine. Jesus describes that connection as *abiding*, which means "to be completely at home."

When we are completely at home with a roommate or spouse, we aren't on edge. We relax, we communicate, and we get things done with minimal friction. In that environment, we share common goals, and we work together to reach those goals. In the same way, our relationship with Jesus can be so completely "at home" that we communicate often and easily, sharing a common purpose to honor the Father in everything we do. We have rich, deep conversations, and we genuinely enjoy each other.

In a strong, intimate relationship with Christ, His power, peace, and purpose flow into us and through us, and His Spirit works wonders to transform us and change others we touch—those are healthy bunches of spiritual grapes.

In the same way that a branch can't produce grapes unless nourishment flows from the vine into it, we can't produce anything apart from a vibrant relationship with Christ. When Jesus said, "You can do nothing," He didn't mean we can't brush our teeth or perform any other task without His help. Plenty of people do all kinds of things without Christ. He means that we can't do anything *of eternal significance* apart from His direction and power.

How can a person tell if he or she has this kind of vital connection with Christ?

What does it (or would it) mean for you to genuinely abide in Him?

"There is no justification without sanctification, no forgiveness without renewal of life, no real faith from which the fruits of new obedience do not grow."
—MARTIN LUTHER

A CROWNING ACHIEVEMENT

Blessed is the man who endures temptation; for when he has been approved, he will receive the crown of life which the Lord has promised to those who love Him.

JAMES 1:12

WE GIVE AWARDS in every field of business, academics, and government, and we give them for every conceivable achievement. Imagine giving a top award at a big banquet to the person who endured and conquered temptation most effectively! That, James tells us, is the award God gives, and it includes the "crown of life" as a symbol of the person's dedication to God.

How do we endure temptation? First, we have to recognize it. Far too often, we glamorize sin, excuse it, laugh at it, and let it become a normal part of our lives. White lies, sexual jokes, gossip, a critical attitude, and many other behaviors are part of life for most people—including many Christians. We won't resist the temptation to sin if we don't realize it's destructive.

When we recognize the temptation, we need to get as far away from it as possible. Change the channel, delete the song, filter the site, close our mouths, or walk away. Nature, though, abhors a vacuum, so we need to replace the temptation with something good and wholesome and honoring to God and the people in our lives. Read inspiring books, listen to uplifting songs and talks, hang out with people who build others up instead of tearing them down, speak words of hope and affirmation.

Nobody said these things are easy. Resisting and enduring temptation takes focused attention and energy, and it requires tenacity to keep resisting when the temptation rises again out of nowhere. But God generously rewards, with the crown of life, those who hang in there—what a reward!

What are the most common temptations you face each day?

What are some ways you can recognize them, resist them, replace them, and endure?

"Character cannot be developed in ease and quiet. Only through experience of trial and suffering can the soul be strengthened, vision cleared, ambition inspired and success achieved." —HELEN KELLER

WHAT JESUS IS

*Of Him you are in Christ Jesus, who became for us wisdom from God—
and righteousness and sanctification and redemption.*

1 CORINTHIANS 1:30

THE BELIEVERS IN CORINTH were, sad to say, much like wealthy people throughout history: They were proud of their possessions and positions, and they looked down on those who didn't have as much. Paul, though, put them in their place. He wrote that God has a very different standard operating procedure. God uses the weak to shame the mighty, the foolish to shame the supposedly wise, and the common to shame the noble (see 1 Corinthians 1:27). Does that sound harsh? No, it reflects God's attitude and actions when Jesus stepped out of the glory of heaven to enter a broken, sin-stained world to give His life for us. For our sake, He became seemingly weak and foolish, and He died like a common criminal.

Jesus, though, didn't stand on a hilltop and make pronouncements about the wisdom of God. He *became* God's wisdom in flesh and blood. In the Old Testament, people looked to prophets to tell them about God's character, but Jesus personally embodied all the truth and grace we need to know. Do we want to grasp God's fiery righteousness? Jesus demonstrated the holiness of God by never sinning and by standing up for truth in the face of fierce opposition. Do we want to know what it means to be sanctified? Jesus was set apart to fulfill the Father's mission. He's the only person who was born to die, not born to live. Do we want to get a handle on redemption? We need only look at the Cross to see the sinless Son of God dying in our place to purchase forgiveness, peace, and eternal life. In Jesus, wisdom isn't just a concept—it's a Person.

Why is it important to you that wisdom is a Person?

Tell Christ how much you appreciate all He has done for you.

"Do you need help today? Lift up your hands to the Lord in supplication and in expectation, and soon you will lift up your hands in jubilation and celebration."
—WARREN W. WIERSBE

ALL THINGS

I can do all things through Christ who strengthens me.

PHILIPPIANS 4:13 } MEMORY VERSE

THIS IS ONE of the most frequently quoted—and most often misunderstood—verses in the Bible. Many people see it as a blank check on God's account that they can cash whenever they want His help to accomplish anything they want to do. Sorry, but that's not Paul's point at all.

The "all things" in this verse refers to his previous comments about contentment. Paul had explained that he had found the secret of being content in any and every situation, whether he was enjoying wealth, pleasure, and plenty or had very little of the world's riches and comfort (see Philippians 4:11-12). The secret, Paul relates, is to focus on Christ and be delighted in Him above all else.

But Paul was a realist. He knew that finding contentment in difficult times is hard. In those times, he needed Christ to give him perspective and strength to keep his heart focused on Him. Only then could he be truly content, at peace instead of gritting his teeth with each passing minute. Paul, though, was supremely confident that Christ would, in fact, give him the resources he needed to respond well to every situation.

We need to take a long, hard look at our hearts to see what disrupts our sense of contentment. Then, we can turn to Christ for wisdom to get His perspective and strength to endure difficulties with grace and gratitude. The world and our friends and family members want to know if our faith is genuine. If we complain when we experience a small bump in our comfortable road, they have reason to wonder. If, however, our contentment and joy are unshaken when we experience loss, they can see that our hope in Christ is the real deal.

How can you prepare your heart so that you continue to experience contentment during difficult times?

Describe how Christ can give you wisdom and strength during those times.

"You never test the resources of God until you attempt the impossible." —F. B. MEYER

"The Savior I love and worship is an every day, every need Lord who knows my needs and supplies them even before I ask." —ZIG ZIGLAR

I CAN ONLY IMAGINE

*It is written: "Eye has not seen, nor ear heard, nor have entered into the heart
of man the things which God has prepared for those who love Him."*

1 CORINTHIANS 2:9

SOME OF US SIT in church week after week singing the songs and listening to
the sermons, but in our hearts, we secretly doubt that all the promises about
heaven really apply to us. *Yeah, they sound great,* we tell ourselves, *but they're
for the rest of the people sitting here, not me.* The overwhelming reality of our
sinfulness makes us feel as if we're beyond God's grace and that heaven is only
a pipe dream.

The wonderful, optimistic promise Paul quoted was written—don't miss
this—to the Corinthian believers. They were the most prideful, blatantly selfish, brazenly sexual, least mature believers in the world, but Paul's faith in the
transforming grace and power of God extended even—maybe especially—to
them. The promise of eternal life applied to them!

What are some things God has prepared for us in eternity? Too often,
we think of heaven as a place where people wear robes and play harps or
sit through endless church services. Those images don't sound very inviting!
Instead, an accurate picture of heaven is one of adventure, variety, and creativity. God promises us new bodies that are like Jesus' resurrected body (see
1 Corinthians 15:42-49; 2 Corinthians 5:1-3, NLT). Will we levitate and pass
through solids? We'll see.

Jesus said He was leaving earth "to prepare a place" for us (John 14:2). We
don't know exactly what heaven looks like, but we do know that we will rule
with Him over the new heaven and new earth.

What can you imagine that God has prepared for you in heaven?

What do you look forward to most?

*"If we really understood Heaven, we would be most unhappy and unsatisfied with
life on earth. We would rebel against our earthly limitations. If we saw Heaven, we
could not bear this earth. That's why Heaven is forever: we cannot bear to leave it
after we get there."* —C. L. ALLEN

A VERY BIG QUESTION

Do you not know that you are the temple of God and that the Spirit of God dwells in you? 1 CORINTHIANS 3:16

ONE OF THE MOST ASTOUNDING TRUTHS of the Christian life is that the moment we trust in Christ as our Savior, His Spirit takes up residence in our bodies. Yes, that's right, *inside* us. Paul relates this insight immediately after explaining that a day is coming when all our actions and attitudes will pass through the fire to be graded by Christ (see 1 Corinthians 3:12-15). What's the connection between being a temple of the Holy Spirit and this report card?

God doesn't ask us to love the unlovely, live with courageous faith, and forgive our enemies *on our own*. He knows we can't do it by ourselves, so He gives us His Spirit to guide and empower us to do His will. The Spirit uses the truth of Scripture, His gentle nudge, circumstances, and the wisdom of mature friends to guide us, and He transforms our hearts to care more about Him and others than about our selfish interests.

The Spirit provides supernatural resources to equip us, but Paul's question also implies that we live under the watchful eye of the One who lives inside us. Nothing—literally nothing—escapes His notice. We obey Christ, then, for many different reasons: the promise of rewards, the Spirit's resources to enable and empower us, and the reminder that we live under His all-seeing eyes. Together, they form a powerful motivational punch to keep us pursuing God and His purposes.

On a scale of zero (not at all) to ten (all day every day), how much are you aware of the Spirit's presence in you?

Does the fact that He lives inside you motivate you? Explain your answer.

"It is gloriously exciting to know that we can stay connected to the source of all power and authority just by opening our hearts and our minds to Him."
—ZIG ZIGLAR

DON'T KID YOURSELF

Be doers of the word, and not hearers only, deceiving yourselves.

JAMES 1:22

JUST AS SITTING IN A GARAGE doesn't make us a car, sitting in a church doesn't make us real Christians. But when we experience a genuine regeneration through Christ, it changes everything we are, everything we do, and everywhere we go.

How many times do we sit through a church service, only to forget all but one or two points when someone at lunch asks, "What was the message about today?" Many of us don't absorb what we hear because we haven't made a previous commitment to act on what we will hear. The commitment to obey sharpens our minds and galvanizes our wills to put the truth into action.

In Christ's day, the religious leaders taught about God, His laws, and His ways, but they failed to live by the basic tenet of loving God with all their hearts and their neighbors as themselves. They were satisfied—in fact, they were proud—of words without actions and platitudes without commitments. They deceived themselves, believing that words were enough.

The decision to absorb truth so that it transforms our behavior is made before we walk through the church door or put in the CD of the talk. We resolve to be disciples, men and women who represent the heart and message of Christ each and every day. To fulfill that commitment, we know we need all the help we can get, so we listen intently, take notes, talk to friends about specific applications, and make plans to make a difference. That's how we become "doers of the word, and not hearers only."

Are you a doer or only a hearer? Explain your answer.

Have you made the decision to represent Christ? How does (or will) that decision change how you listen to truth?

"The last temptation is the greatest treason: to do the right deed for the wrong reason." —T. S. ELIOT

USELESS RELIGION

If anyone among you thinks he is religious, and does not bridle his tongue but deceives his own heart, this one's religion is useless. JAMES 1:26

WE'VE KNOWN SINCE CHILDHOOD that the thighbone is connected to the knee bone, and James tells us that the heart is connected to the tongue. In fact, James has quite a lot to say about our speech. He reminds us that we can use it to bless or to curse, to heal or to destroy. Though the tongue is small, it has the capacity to do big things.

Our language and tone of voice reflect the content of our hearts. If our hearts are in alignment with Christ's love and purposes, our tongues communicate warmth, forgiveness, acceptance, and wisdom. If our hearts aren't aligned with God's mission, however, we may claim to be following Christ, but we are deceiving ourselves. Our speech, then, is an accurate measuring device that shows the true content of our hearts.

Useless religion is a powerful term. Religion promises to put us in touch with God, enable us to experience His presence, and change our lives. The inability to control our tongues shows that God hasn't actually touched our hearts, transformation hasn't taken place, and the grand promises haven't become true for us.

This sobering assessment may be painful, but it can be the beginning of a new day! The realization that our hearts are still hard can bring us to a point where we cry out for God to work deeply, powerfully, and specifically in our lives. A fearless and searching inventory of our tongues and our hearts may be heart wrenching, but not nearly as painful as finding out later that our religion has been useless.

What does your speech in the past twenty-four hours indicate about the content of your heart?

What changes need to be made so that your religion isn't useless?

"There is no blessing until we look deep down in our own soul and see our spiritual life as it really is." —ALAN REDPATH

THE TRUMPET'S SOUND

If the trumpet makes an uncertain sound, who will prepare for battle?

1 CORINTHIANS 14:8

PAUL ENCOURAGED the Corinthians to use clear language in communicating truth to one another, and one of the analogies he used was the sound of a trumpet. In that day and up into the twentieth century, military commanders communicated orders to their troops with distinct trumpet sounds. It was important for the trumpeter to blow strong, long, and clearly so every soldier would know whether to advance or retreat, to stand and fight, or to move to the left or right.

The trumpeter, though, was a man with hopes and fears like any other. He was positioned near the commander, and he heard the officers discuss the options and consequences on the battlefield. If he heard that they all might be slaughtered, his lips could pucker when he tried to blow the horn and he would make "an uncertain sound." The soldiers in the line weren't fools. They could distinguish a confident trumpet sound from a warbled one, and they surmised that the uncertain sound might indicate greater danger. Naturally, the uncertain sound caused them to look for a way out!

In the same way, unclear language as we talk about Christ causes people around us to look for a way out too! We don't have to be theologians to talk about Christ, but we need to focus on the basics of the faith—especially when we're talking to unbelievers or those who are new in their faith. We may want to impress people with our vast knowledge of eschatological metaphysics, but we'd best leave that to the seminarians.

Focus on Christ and the changes He has made in your life. Blow your trumpet loud, clear, and strong, and everybody will benefit.

How do you feel and respond when someone talks unclearly about spiritual things?

What spiritual topics can you talk about easily and clearly?

"Attitude, to me, is more important than facts. It is more important than the past, the education, the money, than circumstances, than failure, than successes, than what other people think or say or do. It is more important than appearance, giftedness or skill. It will make or break a company . . . a church . . . a home. The remarkable thing is we have a choice every day regarding the attitude we will embrace for that day. I am convinced that life is 10% what happens to me and 90% how I react to it. And so it is with you. . . . We are in charge of our attitudes."
—CHARLES SWINDOLL

KNOW WHAT YOU'VE GOT

Let your conduct be without covetousness; be content with such things as you have. For He Himself has said, "I will never leave you nor forsake you."

HEBREWS 13:5

WANTING WHAT OTHERS HAVE comes from either insecurity or greed. When we feel insecure, we check out what others have, what they wear, what they drive, where they go on vacation, and all other external measuring sticks. We have a pecking order in our minds, and we see where we are on that list. If we're far enough up the list, we feel okay, but if we're too far down, we crave the trappings that promise to make us look successful and beautiful. On the other hand, we may just be greedy and want more than what we have. Either way, craving things steals our hearts and ruins relationships.

The writer to the Hebrews tells us to recognize coveting, no matter what its cause, and get rid of it, replacing it with a deep sense of contentment. Where does the contentment come from? From acknowledging that everything we have and everything we are come from God. For our hearts to be filled with His grace and strength, we don't need anything else. The absence of things, however, is only part of the story of contentment. True contentment comes from a rich, real relationship with Christ. He promises to be as near as our breath, and He'll never leave us for a second.

A craving for things reveals an empty—or at least a partially empty—heart, one that can be filled and overflowing with the presence of our King, Savior, and Best Friend.

How much do you crave things? What do you hope they'll do for you?

In what way does Christ's presence give us true contentment?

"It is a dangerous thing to ask why someone else has been given more. It is humbling and indeed healthy to ask why you have been given so much." —CONDOLEEZZA RICE

PROSPERITY THEOLOGY—
REALLY!

Beloved, I pray that you may prosper in all things and be in health, just as your soul prospers. 3 JOHN 1:2

WE LIVE IN THE "AGE OF STUFF." Everywhere we look, we see the incredible wealth of our culture—and none of us want to be left out! In some Christian circles, leaders have adopted the desire for more possessions and pleasure, and they promise their followers that God wants them to have even more stuff.

Does God want us to prosper? Yes, but we need to be very careful not to put the cart before the horse. God's primary benchmark for prosperity is that we would be "rich toward God" (Luke 12:21), to love Him so much that all other desires pale in comparison. Jesus taught that true fulfillment comes from "losing our lives" in our affection and obedience to God, not by acquiring more possessions and enjoying more pleasures (see John 12:24-26).

Material possessions and health are desires—good, normal desires—but they aren't rights, and God doesn't promise them. Should we pray that God will give us prosperity in all things and in health? John did, and his devotion to Christ was unsurpassed. We can expect spiritual prosperity as we follow Christ, but we shouldn't demand that God give us the prosperity the world values. He's never promised that.

We should treat our desires very differently. We can have the utmost confidence that God uses every circumstance in our lives to deepen our love for Him and make our souls prosper, but we should hold our desires far more loosely. When they are fulfilled, we can thank God for His generosity. When they don't become a reality, we can refocus our hearts on true prosperity: the spiritual riches we enjoy.

What happens in our hearts when we demand worldly prosperity?

What are some adjustments you need to make to refocus your heart on true prosperity?

"As your positive confessions come forth, you will discover that the more blessings you thank God for, the more blessings you will have to thank God for."
—ZIG ZIGLAR

WHATEVER!

Finally, brethren, whatever things are true, whatever things are noble, whatever things are just, whatever things are pure, whatever things are lovely, whatever things are of good report, if there is any virtue and if there is anything praiseworthy—meditate on these things. PHILIPPIANS 4:8 { MEMORY VERSE

IF OUR BRAINS are the operating system, our thought patterns are the software our minds run on. To some degree, the software in all our minds is corrupted. We have trouble thinking correctly, so we get prideful in the good times and fearful in the bad. Paul reminds us that we have choices as to what we think about, and if necessary, we can do a clean install!

In his letter to the Philippians, Paul had given them encouragement and instructions. Now, at the end of the letter, he gives them his "final word," an instruction that will help them put all the pieces together. The key is to rivet our minds on truth, beauty, nobility, and honor—whatever is good and right and true.

Right thinking is a skill all of us can learn, even though our software will always have glitches in it until the day we see Jesus face-to-face. Focusing our minds on noble things and giving thanks can become habits as we practice them more and more, but negative, destructive, selfish thoughts creep in from time to time. When we find ourselves heading down the wrong thought trail, we don't need to beat ourselves up about it—we're only human—however, we can take definitive action to focus our minds again on whatever is true, noble, and praiseworthy. We may not be able to completely eliminate unhealthy thoughts, but we can act quickly to replace them. As Martin Luther said, "We can't keep birds from flying over our heads, but we can keep them from building nests in our hair!"

? } **How would you assess the effectiveness of your mental software?**

What are some practical things you can do to replace negative thoughts with positive ones?

" } *"Christian meditation is silent worship as you set the mind's attention and the heart's affection upon Godly aspirations."* —IKE REIGHARD

"We all need a daily check-up from the neck up to avoid stinking thinking, which ultimately leads to hardening of the attitudes." —ZIG ZIGLAR

ON SECOND THOUGHT

What things were gain to me, these I have counted loss for Christ. Yet indeed I also count all things loss for the excellence of the knowledge of Christ Jesus my Lord, for whom I have suffered the loss of all things, and count them as rubbish, that I may gain Christ. PHILIPPIANS 3:7-8

IN THIS LETTER, Paul had just recounted his impressive résumé (see Philippians 3:4-6). By birth, status, and accomplishments, he was at the top of the heap. When his name was mentioned in the region, everybody knew who he was. But then something happened: Paul met Jesus. Suddenly, Paul's world was turned upside down. Things that seemed so important before were now meaningless, and things that had seemed like annoyances became his priorities. Even more, the One who had been his enemy now was his friend and Savior. Meeting Jesus forced Paul to have second thoughts about everything in his life.

Our résumés, too, have elements of status, accomplishments, and other credits. We use them to gain acceptance, to earn respect, and to wield power. But Christ's claim on our lives changes everything. Those things may have been the most important truths about us in the past, and they may have shaped our goals and relationships, but now, they are "rubbish"—unimportant, secondary, forgettable.

Paul's explanation of the change in his perception tells us that his core sense of identity had radically altered. Why? Because knowing Christ and being known by Him zoomed to the top of Paul's Top Ten list of the most important facts about his life.

Jesus asked, "What does a man profit if he gains the whole world but forfeits his soul?" (see Matthew 16:26). The answer is, of course, nothing. All the wealth, prestige, awards, and pleasures of this life can't compare to the daily experience of God's amazing grace. There's no comparison.

Why do those things (wealth, status, pleasure, and so forth) seem so alluring to us?

What would it mean for you to value knowing Christ so much that all those things become secondary in your heart and in your priorities?

"God has a way of turning what you formerly treasured into trash, and what you once trashed becomes your most precious treasure." —IKE REIGHARD

NEITHER DEATH NOR LIFE

I am persuaded that neither death nor life, nor angels nor principalities nor powers, nor things present nor things to come, nor height nor depth, nor any other created thing, shall be able to separate us from the love of God which is in Christ Jesus our Lord. ROMANS 8:38-39 { MEMORY VERSE

NAGGING DOUBTS can rob us of peace—sometimes, they can rob us of our sanity. Some of us are sensitive and reflective, more susceptible to a questioning ember flaming into an inferno of doubt. *Did I do the right thing?* we wonder. *Did I do enough? Do the problems I'm facing show that God is angry with me? Has He turned His back on me? Will I ever feel confident again?*

Chapter 8 in Paul's letter to the Romans is one of the most encouraging selections of Scripture. It begins with the promise of "no condemnation" by God, and it ends with the promise of "no separation" from God. He holds us tightly in His hands, and He never lets go. To make the point, Paul gives us a list of physical, spiritual, and temporal boundaries that can't block God's transcendent love for us. No matter what we face, no matter where we go, no matter what powers are lined up against us, no created thing can come between us and the all-encompassing, never-ending love of God.

One of the most wonderful feelings in the world is a sense of profound relief when our doubts and fears evaporate in the warm glow of fresh confidence in God's greatness and grace. If we live long enough, even the most stouthearted among us will be tempted to doubt God. Paul's summary statement at the end of this faith-filled chapter is that when everything else around us crumbles, we can stand strong, knowing that the love of God never fails.

When were you (or are you) tempted to doubt God's love for you?

What does this promise mean to you?

"As far as I can see, that covers it all, and if we are not separated from the love of Jesus Christ, then He who has the power to save us not only will save us, but will keep us forever secure." —ZIG ZIGLAR

"I have come upon the happy discovery that this life hid with Christ in God is a continuous unfolding." —EUGENIA PRICE

THE MAN GOD CALLED A FOOL

God said to him, "You fool! This very night your life will be demanded from you. Then who will get what you have prepared for yourself?"

LUKE 12:20, NIV

IN THIS PASSAGE of Scripture, Jesus tells the parable of a rich man who had an exceedingly abundant harvest. The harvest was so fruitful that his barn was not large enough to store the crops, so he decided to build a larger storehouse to hold his wealth. Jesus explains that the rich man chose to "take life easy; eat, drink and be merry" (Luke 12:19, NIV).

The parable says that very night would be the end of the man's life. And while the man had made plans to build a new storehouse for his bountiful crop, he had failed to secure his salvation. God did not call this man a fool because he was wealthy or because he made plans to store his harvest; God called the man a fool because he found security in earthly prosperity instead of eternal security. The man's success had blinded him to the need for God in his life. You see, the man was thinking like the world thinks. He saw both his security and his worth in the things that he had accumulated.

The Bible tells us that we are not to store up treasure on earth but that we are to secure our treasure in heaven (see Matthew 6:19-20). So many times we can get caught up in what we think God forbids us to have, seeing God as some kind of cosmic killjoy who wants us to go without, when the reality is that He desires for us to prioritize our lives in such a way that we may have eternal significance.

Have you come to the point in your life where you experienced salvation?

Do you make decisions that are reflective of your awareness of eternal consequences?

"Salvation is from our side a choice; from the divine side it is a seizing upon, an apprehending, a conquest by the Most High God. Our accepting and willing are reactions rather than actions." —A. W. TOZER

HEARTSICK

Hope deferred makes the heart sick, but when the desire comes, it is a tree of life.

PROVERBS 13:12

WE'D LIKE TO THINK our faith is so strong that we're invulnerable to disappointments, but Solomon reminds us that we're still very human. Disappointment hurts, and in fact, it makes our hearts sick. The depth of our disappointment, of course, depends on the height of our hope. Small hopes, when thwarted, produce only minor setbacks, but shattered dreams devastate us. Our pain isn't a sign of immaturity; we're just responding normally.

If we think we should never be affected by unfulfilled hopes, we need to read the psalms. The writers often pour out their complaints about people who have let them down and situations that didn't go the way they had planned. These writers, though, didn't make the mistake of turning away from God. They pursued Him with gut-wrenching honesty, and sooner or later, God reminded them that He was still in control and that they could still trust Him.

When God answers our prayers and our hopes are fulfilled, we feel like jumping up and down, and we grow in our appreciation of God's goodness to us. We thank Him, we praise Him, and we rest in His goodness.

Either way, then, in disappointment or in fulfilled desires, our emotions are genuine and normal. The proper response in both cases is to turn to God, to pursue Him with all our hearts, and to dig deeper into His grace and wisdom to find comfort—or to praise Him for His grace and wisdom because He answered.

Describe a time when shattered hopes made your heart sick.

Do you feel permission to be truly honest with God about your disappointments? How would it help you to be honest with Him?

"Some men see things the way they are and ask 'Why?' I dream of the way things could be and ask, 'Why not?'" —GEORGE BERNARD SHAW

ALWAYS SUFFICIENT

[The Lord] said to me, "My grace is sufficient for you, for My strength is made perfect in weakness." Therefore most gladly I will rather boast in my infirmities, that the power of Christ may rest upon me. 2 CORINTHIANS 12:9

ONE OF THE HARDEST LESSONS for most of us to learn is that our points of weakness can become our greatest opportunities to experience God's strength. Too often, we deny we're weak and we miss wonderful steps of growth. God seldom demonstrates His amazing power, however, until and unless we admit we are powerless. And even then, He provides exactly what we need—not more and not less.

When Corrie ten Boom was a young woman growing up under Nazi domination, she told her father, "I'm not sure I can survive the strain."

Her father, a wise man, asked her, "Corrie, when you take the bus home each day, does the driver ask for a year's fare?"

"No, Father," she replied, not knowing where he was going with the question.

"Does he ask you for a week's fare?"

"No, Father, he doesn't. I only give him the fare for that ride."

Her father's eyes brightened, and he explained, "That's the way God's grace is for us. He always gives us what we need at the time we need it."

From time to time, all of us face situations when we feel submerged in confusion, pain, and difficulties. At those moments, we don't need grace and wisdom for the whole solution. We just need them for the next step. God will give us exactly what we need at the time we need it—probably not more and certainly not less.

How have you seen God's strength demonstrated when someone admitted his or her weakness?

Is there a situation in your life right now in which you need God's strength? In what way are you weak?

"The Lord gets His best soldiers out of the highlands of affliction."
—CHARLES HADDON SPURGEON

TWICE BLESSED

The LORD restored Job's losses when he prayed for his friends. Indeed the LORD gave Job twice as much as he had before. JOB 42:10

JOB NEVER SAW his troubles coming. In the introduction to his story, we find out the reasons behind Job's suffering (see Job 1:6–2:7), but Job never had a clue when he endured each trial. As we read the account, we see that Job wondered why God allowed all these terrible things to happen to him. Some friends came by, but instead of giving Job comfort and wisdom, they insisted that he must have done something really bad for all this to have happened. (Thanks a lot, guys!)

Job kept asking God why, and God finally showed up, but not with the answer to his question (see Job 38–41). Instead, God reminded Job that He was God and Job was not. There was no need to ask that question any longer, God told him. "Just know that I'm God, and you can trust Me," He said. (But at least God said to Job's friends, "You're no help!")

Job could have been really angry with his friends for giving him bad advice and assuming his problems were entirely his fault, but he chose a different course: He prayed for them. When he prayed, God opened heaven's doors and gave Job twice as much wealth as he had before. He was twice blessed. He still didn't understand all that had happened, but he trusted God anyway. And God really likes it when we trust Him.

What do we need to trust about the character of God when we don't understand what's going on in our lives?

What was the correlation between Job's prayer for his friends and God's blessing?

"Adversity is the diamond dust heaven polishes its jewels with." —ROBERT LEIGHTON

WRESTLING WITH GOD

Jacob was left alone; and a Man wrestled with him until the breaking of day.

GENESIS 32:24

SOME OF US FEEL GUILTY for questioning God, but human faith has a long tradition of wrestling with Him. Jacob's life had been characterized by lies and deceit. Over and over again, he resorted to deception to get what he wanted, but finally, his sins caught up with him. It was nighttime, and the next day he would face the brother he had defrauded. Jacob feared for his life, and he was desperate for God's help.

In a wonderful act of grace, God stepped into the ring on that dark night to wrestle with Jacob. The two went after each other. Jacob begged God to bless him and protect him, and surprisingly, God seemed to let Jacob win the fight. At the end, though, God touched Jacob's side and dislocated his hip. Walking with a cane would be a permanent reminder for Jacob to lean on God instead of on his own cunning.

God never criticizes us for asking questions, or even for being angry with Him when we ask questions. He can take it, and He is thrilled that we will pursue Him even—and especially—when we feel so hurt and angry. Our wrestling match may end with a flash of insight that gives us the answer to our problem, but more often, God reminds us that He is God and that He rules in the affairs of men and nations. We, like Jacob, have to keep leaning on Him as we limp along in life.

Our struggle with God, though, deepens and enriches our lives. We'll never forget that He didn't blast us into oblivion and that He didn't run away. He wants a relationship with us even when we want to wrestle.

Describe a time when you wrestled with God. What was it about?

How does wrestling with Him change us and deepen our faith?

"Trouble handled rightly honors God and strengthens us." —**IKE REIGHARD**

SOME MORE THAN OTHERS

The very hairs of your head are all numbered. MATTHEW 10:30

YES, THE TITLE of today's devotional, paired with the verse, is supposed to provoke a smile. For some of us, God's job of counting the hairs on our heads is getting easier—in fact, too easy! But there's an important lesson in our humor. God is aware of the changes we experience, and the impact of those changes, in every area of our lives. He knows, He cares, and He's present to give us support and guidance every step of the way.

Change is difficult. Studies show that people fear change almost as much as speaking in public. In fact, the fear of change is the most common fear we experience. When our world is shaken, we lose our bearings, we feel insecure, and we grasp for anything that can bring us certainty. Though *our* world may be shaken, *God's* world remains steady and solid. Change never threatens God because He knows what is going to happen before it happens, and He sees the end with crystal clarity when we see our future through a mist.

A common reaction to change is worry. We believe that if we think about our problem enough, we can figure it out. Sometimes that's true, but often, our copious reflections lead only to more worry, more confusion, and genuine despair. When we start to worry, we can remember that God knows everything about every aspect of the change we're experiencing. His infinite knowledge and His genuine compassion can relieve our worries and give us confidence in His future for us, no matter how many hairs we're losing.

Oops. There goes another one.

How do you normally respond to change?

When we experience change, how is it helpful to remember that God is omniscient?

"The Lord who has everything we need also knows our needs before we even think about them. And He is anxious to give them to us who are His." —ZIG ZIGLAR

WORDS YOU CAN BUILD ON

Let no corrupt word proceed out of your mouth, but what is good for necessary edification, that it may impart grace to the hearers. And do not grieve the Holy Spirit of God, by whom you were sealed for the day of redemption.

EPHESIANS 4:29-30 { MEMORY VERSE

WORDS HAVE THE POWER to heal or destroy, to build up or tear down. Corrupt words of condemnation or name-calling have the force of a sledge-hammer to crush people. Gossip and sarcasm are just as destructive, but they are corrosive, taking longer to wear away a person's confidence and ruin a relationship.

Paul doesn't advise us to cut back on the harmful words that we say to one another. He doesn't suggest that we stop saying the obviously damaging words but continue the secret ones. He commands that we cut them all out now and replace them with words that build people up.

Yeah, but what if someone bored us, ignored us, told a friend about something stupid we did, or lied about us? Maybe that's true, but that's still no excuse. Every word we utter must meet the standard of God's holiness and love for that person. We should look for good in others and affirm it, and we must notice their successes and celebrate with them. If they have hurt us, we should speak the truth for the purpose of restoration, not condemnation. Our motive changes our language and our demeanor, and perhaps other people's responses.

Our words, though, don't have only a horizontal impact; they also affect the Holy Spirit. Paul tells us that the way we speak to one another can grieve (or, we can assume, please) the Spirit. Don't miss this. God's emotions are affected by the way we treat one another.

Have you made Him smile today?

What negative, harmful language do you need to stop using?

Think of three or four common conversations in which you often use crushing or corrosive language, and plan positive statements for each one.

"If it is painful for you to criticize your friends, you are safe in doing it. But if you take the slightest pleasure in it, that's the time to hold your tongue."
—ALICE DUER MILLER

"When you experience your freedom to express yourself at the lowest level, you ultimately condemn yourself to live at that level." —ZIG ZIGLAR

NO PAIN, NO GAIN

Our light affliction, which is but for a moment, is working for us a far more exceeding and eternal weight of glory, while we do not look at the things which are seen, but at the things which are not seen. For the things which are seen are temporary, but the things which are not seen are eternal.

2 CORINTHIANS 4:17-18

AS WE GROW IN OUR FAITH, we develop the capacity to see things differently than before. In the beginning, we are able to see only the people, places, and circumstances that are visible, and our choices are geared to make our lives today as successful and comfortable as possible. Gradually, though, by reading the Scriptures, interacting with mature believers, and praying, we learn to perceive an invisible, spiritual world. As strange as it may seem, we begin to live for things we can't see with our physical eyes.

In the beginning, problems are a threat to our security and success, so we avoid them as much as possible, and we fear them when we can't avoid them. For some of us, even the smallest difficulties seem to be enormous calamities because they threaten us to the core. Living for Christ, though, changes everything. Every problem is a stepping-stone of growth, and every difficulty is an opportunity to trust God more deeply, to follow Christ's example of selfless service, and to experience God's presence. We realize that every problem we face, as overwhelming as it may look to us, is just a dot on the infinite line of eternity. But we don't live for the dot; we live for the line.

When we perceive our problems through the lens of the Spirit, we respond with courage and with the confidence that God will reward us when we see Him face-to-face. Our faith-filled response to pain results in great gain.

What does it mean to see things with spiritual eyes? How much are you seeing life this way?

Think about the problems you face today. What difference will it make to look beyond the visible to the invisible realities of a situation?

"Even in tragedy, God through His Word offers hope for those who seek and believe. It starts with the promise of a better tomorrow, of life everlasting, of eternal peace. It's called faith, and it offers hope where none existed." —ZIG ZIGLAR

GETTING STRAIGHT

There was a woman who had a spirit of infirmity eighteen years, and was bent over and could in no way raise herself up. But when Jesus saw her, He called her to Him and said to her, "Woman, you are loosed from your infirmity." And He laid His hands on her, and immediately she was made straight, and glorified God. LUKE 13:11-13

THE CULTURE OF JESUS' DAY was a man's world. Women, and especially sick women, were overlooked, if not ridiculed. In a synagogue on a Sabbath day, Jesus noticed a woman in need, and in a culturally incorrect move, He asked her to come to Him and then healed her.

The woman had been crippled for eighteen years. Had she prayed for deliverance? Certainly, but no answer came. Did she know the cause of the problem? Maybe—maybe not. Did she remain faithful to God during those many years of disappointment? Yes, she was still worshiping God that Sabbath. For all those years, her spine had been fused together. Her condition was probably painful, and certainly embarrassing, but she continued to pursue God.

Sometimes, God chooses a particular moment to step into our pain and change everything. He doesn't do it often, but when He does, it's amazing! On that particular day, Jesus summoned the woman. She had tried to be as invisible as possible for all these years, but now the visiting rabbi had singled her out. She obeyed and moved toward Him. He reached out His hand and touched her back. Immediately, the bones loosened and she straightened up. She praised God!

Why does God choose to miraculously heal one person and not another? Why does He delay for decades in some cases but heal quickly in others? These are valid questions, but not ones we'll get answers to in this life. All we need to know is that if we remain faithful, sooner or later, in this life or the next, a miracle will happen.

How do you think the woman felt the day before this event, at the moment Jesus called her to come forward, and when He healed her?

Does this give you confidence that Jesus will one day perform a miracle in your life? Why or why not?

"If you truly want to measure the success of a man, you do not measure it by a position he has achieved, but by the obstacles he has overcome."
—BOOKER T. WASHINGTON

GOD'S 9-1-1

He who dwells in the secret place of the Most High shall abide under the shadow of the Almighty. PSALM 91:1

THROUGHOUT THE COUNTRY, every child, teenager, and adult is drilled to call 9-1-1 in times of trouble. Whether or not the problem is grave, or we don't know the person who is in trouble, we dial that number. In an emergency of any kind, day or night, 9-1-1 is the number we call because it's our connection to every emergency service in the city. In the same way, God has given us a 9-1-1 number to call no matter what our needs may be: We simply call on Him anytime, anywhere, for anything. He's available to help.

We have confidence in our community's fire department, police, and emergency personnel because we know they've been screened and trained, and we've heard about their exemplary service to other people. Similarly, we have confidence in God because He is God Most High, the Almighty King. "Most High" is the name for God that signifies His role as the sovereign ruler of the universe. Nothing escapes His notice, and nothing is beyond His wisdom to grasp. "Almighty" is the translation of the name *El Shaddai*, which means "all sufficient." God's power is beyond all other force in the universe. He reigns supreme.

God is awesome in His power, but He is tender in His love. He invites us into the "secret place" where we spend time with Him, and we live "under the shadow" of His gracious protection.

How quickly or slowly do you turn to God when you need help?

How do His names encourage you to turn to Him more quickly?

"Be assured, if you walk with Him and look to Him and expect help from Him, He will never fail you." —GEORGE MÜLLER

PRAYING FOR LEADERS

I exhort first of all that supplications, prayers, intercessions, and giving of thanks be made for all men, for kings and all who are in authority, that we may lead a quiet and peaceable life in all godliness and reverence. For this is good and acceptable in the sight of God our Savior, who desires all men to be saved and to come to the knowledge of the truth. 1 TIMOTHY 2:1-4

IT'S EASY TO COMPLAIN about national politicians, corporate managers, bureaucrats at every level of government, and church leaders, but instead, Paul tells us to pray for them—and even to thank God for them! Certainly, God wants to work in these leaders' lives so they come to know and follow Him, but Paul has an even broader view in mind. Good governance provides peace and stability so that the gospel can be spread unhindered to people next door as well as to the remotest parts of the earth. When our attention and resources aren't absorbed by wars, bickering, and conflicts of all kinds, we can invest our energies in the things that really matter: Christ and His Kingdom.

Paul didn't suggest that we agree with all politicians. After all, the top leader in his world was a Roman emperor who had no sympathies for Christians. But that didn't matter to Paul. His eyes were fixed on an invisible Kingdom where God reigns and where grace and forgiveness are the highest virtues. The reality of life in this world is that we can get caught up completely in the things that are seen but neglect the things that are unseen. Political power (and any other kind of authority) can serve the Kingdom by providing peace and stability. Then we can focus on what matters most.

When you think of our political, corporate, and religious leaders, pray for them, for the peace they can provide, and for the gospel to spread under the umbrella of their authority.

How do you usually think and talk about your political, corporate, and religious leaders?

Take some time now to pray for them and for the cause of Christ to spread.

"It is impossible to rightly govern the world without God and the Bible."
—GEORGE WASHINGTON

MINISTRY THAT LASTS

If anyone builds on this foundation with gold, silver, precious stones, wood, hay, straw, each one's work will become clear; for the Day will declare it, because it will be revealed by fire; and the fire will test each one's work, of what sort it is. If anyone's work which he has built on it endures, he will receive a reward. 1 CORINTHIANS 3:12-14

A DAY IS COMING, Paul tells us, when each believer will stand before Christ to get a report card of our actions on earth. This isn't the judgment of unbelievers at the great white throne. Instead, this one is designed to reward believers for every action we take to honor God. Christ is our firm foundation. The question is, What are we building on it?

All our attitudes and actions, since the day each of us trusted in Christ, will pass through a fire to be tested. Some of our deeds are like gold, silver, and precious stones, which will pass through the fire unscathed. But some are like wood, hay, and straw, which are incinerated by the fire.

The startling insight is that what you and I do today will pass through Christ's fire on that day. We have the opportunity to make that a really good day or a really bad one. The choices we make now will make a difference then.

The promise of rewards (and threat of ashes in our hands) motivates us to take a long, hard look through the eyes of Christ at the choices we made yesterday. Did we take an extra minute to listen to someone? Did we speak an affirming word? Did we put the accurate number on the expense report? Did we avoid exaggerating when we gave the report? And did we do the right thing because we're convinced that God's "Well done!" is more important than any accolades and possessions we can ever achieve?

What choices will we make today?

If Christ gave you a report card today, how would He grade you up to this point in your journey of faith?

What are two or three things you need to change to get a better report card?

"Trying to do the Lord's work in your own strength is the most confusing, exhausting and tedious of all work. But when you are filled with the Holy Spirit, then the ministry of Jesus just flows out of you." —CORRIE TEN BOOM

BURNING BRIGHT WITHOUT BURNING OUT

When [the disciples] found [Jesus], they said to Him, "Everyone is looking for You." But He said to them, "Let us go into the next towns, that I may preach there also, because for this purpose I have come forth." MARK 1:37-38

JESUS NEVER LET POPULARITY go to His head, and He didn't let opposition get Him off track. Throughout His ministry, He kept His eyes fixed on the purpose the Father had given Him. Early in His ministry, He was immensely popular (see Mark 1:32-33). Crowds flocked to Him to listen and be healed of sicknesses. We can imagine the disciples' enthusiasm. "Man, they love this guy!" "He's got them right where He wants them!" "This is going better than we ever dreamed!"

In a stunning decision, Jesus told them, "Pack your bags, guys. We're outta here." Nothing, not even the greatest successes and popularity, could keep Jesus from doing what He came to do: tell everyone everywhere the Good News.

Both failure and success can drive us to exhaustion. Failure fills us with fear and shame, and we dedicate ourselves to avoid failure at all costs. But success can be intoxicating. The adrenaline rush propels us to do more, be more, and please people more, but before long, our emotional tank runs dry. The only way we can burn bright without burning out is to rivet our hearts on God's purpose and stay true to it through the ups of success and popularity and the downs of failure and despair. That's a decision we should make before these ups and downs occur, but more realistically, it's a course correction we make when we've gotten off course a time or two.

Either way, focus on God's purpose, and say no to anything that gets in the way.

How can fear of failure or the intoxication of success take our eyes off God's purpose for our lives?

Do you need to make a midcourse correction at this point? Explain your answer.

*"In my mind there is no doubt that those who use their talents to serve the Lord will truly enter into the joy of the Lord now." —*ZIG ZIGLAR

LOVE IS ALL THAT LASTS IN HEAVEN

And now abide faith, hope, love, these three; but the greatest of these is love.

1 CORINTHIANS 13:13 { MEMORY VERSE

WHY DID PAUL SAY that the greatest of these three traits is love? Perhaps it's because in heaven, we won't need faith and hope. We'll live in the presence of God, and all our faith and hopes will be realized. Love, though, will remain in all its glory.

"Real love ain't syrupy," the gruff old believer related. "It's tough as nails." He's right. Many people have a romantic view of love. We sing silly love songs and daydream about the perfect evening with our spouse or a date. Genuine love is, in fact, incredibly idealistic, but not distant. It summons the very best motives and noblest actions from the depths of our hearts, and it sometimes calls for the most heart-wrenching sacrifices we can imagine.

Love is *the active pursuit of the best for another person*. It involves our emotions, wills, and energy. It notices needs with clear-eyed perception and refuses to walk away. Paul's multifaceted description of love is often read at weddings, and appropriately so, because the stresses and conflicts inherent in two individuals' becoming one require objectivity, honesty, forgiveness, patience, and kindness—in other words, authentic love.

This kind of love, though, is also a necessity when a toddler asks the 396th question of the day, when a teenager turns her back on all she believed in, and when a friend disappoints us.

Genuine love can be praised in a beautiful song, but it comes to life in the cauldron of painful experiences. There, we find out what we're made of. There, we discover how selfish we really are, and we choose to trust God to transform us. And there, as we make even feeble attempts to love others, we experience God's love more deeply than ever before.

Whom do you know who exemplifies genuine love?

What is one thing you can do today to follow that person's example?

"I think that love is the only spiritual power that can overcome the self-centeredness that is inherent in being alive. Love is the thing that makes life possible or, indeed, tolerable." —ARNOLD TOYNBEE

"One reason I love the Lord so much is explained in Luke 7:47: 'To whom little is forgiven, the same loves little.' In my case, much was forgiven, so I love much." —ZIG ZIGLAR

THE GOOD LIFE

*Who is wise and understanding among you? Let him show by good conduct
that his works are done in the meekness of wisdom.* JAMES 3:13

GROUNDED. UNFLAPPABLE. Got it together. A few people among us seem
to have learned the secret of life. When others around them are losing their
cool, these people remain calm, think clearly, and make good choices. No,
they aren't supermen and superwomen, and no, they aren't on drugs. They've
learned to tap into God's wisdom.

The Scriptures give us a thousand snapshots of wisdom, and the Proverbs
paint many pictures of wise living. People who are wise have a deep reverence
for God, first of all. They are in awe of His power and love, and their trust in
Him permeates their response to every situation, every interaction, and every
decision. A shift has taken place in their hearts: They have learned to care
more about God's purposes than their own selfish desires. They've found out
that pursuing God's design with an open mind and a full heart leads to the
richest life possible.

At work, they function with integrity, and they make everyone around
them more successful. At home, their spouse and children know they are loved
and safe and they enjoy being with one another. They have learned to handle
money wisely, and they receive God's many gifts with a heart of thankfulness.
They never brag, because they don't have to prove themselves, and they resolve
conflicts so that each person comes out with his or her reputation intact.

Is this kind of life possible? Yes, and it begins with an honest assessment
of our current condition.

Give yourself an honest assessment of your life at this point.

In what areas do you need to grow in God's wisdom?

*"That best portion of a good man's life: His little, nameless, unremembered acts
of kindness and of love."* —WILLIAM WORDSWORTH

DRAW NEAR TO GOD

Draw near to God and He will draw near to you. Cleanse your hands, you sinners; and purify your hearts, you double-minded. JAMES 4:8

A PERSONAL RELATIONSHIP with God has always been an amazing thing to contemplate. The Scriptures tell us that God's love is as comforting as a mother's tender care, but they also remind us that He is a consuming fire! How do we relate to a God like this? James gives us some suggestions.

Our relationship with God begins with His invitation. Isn't it amazing that Almighty God stoops low to communicate with *us*? We offer Him nothing, yet He gives us Himself. James tells us that our efforts to pursue God will certainly be rewarded, but we shouldn't come to Him with a cavalier attitude. Like the priests who cleansed themselves before entering the Temple, we, too, need to cleanse ourselves if we are to experience God's presence.

James also addresses our actions and our attitudes. Our "hands" represent our choices, either to obey God or act selfishly. Our "hearts" reflect our attitudes and perspectives. James reminds us that we are too often "double-minded," pulled between God and money, spiritual riches and earthly treasure, our position in Christ and our position at work or church.

It's easy for us to drift along each day without a thought of how dirty our hands and hearts may be—until we think about entering God's presence. When we bow before the Holy One, He shines His light on the dark recesses of our lives and points out any dirt He finds there. At that moment, we can turn and walk away or we can say, "Yes, Lord. I see it too. Thank You for forgiving me." And we draw near to Him.

Why is cleansing important for us as we draw near to God?

Do you long to draw near to God? Explain your answer.

"The first duty of the gospel preacher is to declare God's law and to show the nature of sin." —MARTIN LUTHER

EXCESS BAGGAGE

Since we are surrounded by so great a cloud of witnesses, let us lay aside every weight, and the sin which so easily ensnares us, and let us run with endurance the race that is set before us, looking unto Jesus, the author and finisher of our faith, who for the joy that was set before Him endured the cross, despising the shame, and has sat down at the right hand of the throne of God.

HEBREWS 12:1-2

WHEN OLYMPIC MARATHON RUNNERS get ready for a race, they give plenty of attention to their gear. The race may be long, but often only a few seconds separate runners at the finish line. Because every ounce—and every portion of an ounce—counts, the runners find every possible way to eliminate excess weight. In fact, it's an obsession for them. Shorts and shirts are made of the thinnest, lightest material. Most of them don't wear socks, and if they do, the socks are very lightweight. Their shoes, the heaviest item in their wardrobe, have gone through technological transformations so they are as light as can be. Nothing is going to slow down these runners.

The writer of Hebrews compared the Christian life to a long-distance race, and he told us to get rid of excess baggage and sin in our lives. Many of us carry around *baggage* of neglected areas that have become bloated or weak, such as how much money we spend, a lack of exercise, too little time with our families, or watching too much television. Our *sins* are areas of disobedience that weigh us down with guilt and fog our vision of God's purpose in our lives.

What do we do about these things? First, we need to recognize the negative impact they have on us. Yes, we're still running, but not as far or as fast as we could run without them. When we look to Jesus and are free from the weight of baggage and sin, we can run toward Him and His purpose for our lives even faster.

What are some things that are slowing you down in your race of faith?

What are you going to do today about those things?

"It is cynicism and fear that freezes life; it is faith that thaws it out, releases it, and sets it free." —HARRY EMERSON FOSDICK

GIVE YOURSELF AWAY

Be imitators of God as dear children. And walk in love, as Christ also has loved us and given Himself for us, an offering and a sacrifice to God for a sweet-smelling aroma. EPHESIANS 5:1-2

IN A SENSE, all of us give ourselves away and smell like something to the people around us every day, but what do we give, and what do we smell like? In his letter to the Ephesians, Paul sets the standard very high. God wants us to give ourselves to others in the same way Jesus gave Himself to us: unreservedly—with kindness, boldness, and amazing love—taking great risks of being misunderstood and rejected.

When we think about those traits and the impact they have on others, it's easy to envision a huge, fragrant, beautiful bouquet of flowers filling the room with their wonderful scent. All our senses are drawn to the bouquet, and we delight in it, not rushing along to check off the next thing on our to-do lists. God wants each of us to have that kind of impact on people around us because of the sweetness and love we show them.

Is it possible to be that loving? Only if we imitate God the way a dearly loved child imitates his or her parent. The source of our love for others is our experience of the deep, rich, transforming love of God. We can look at it from another angle too: If we don't demonstrate much love for people around us, perhaps we need to experience more of God's love to fill our tanks so they overflow in love for those around us.

What, do you think, do you smell like to others?

What do you need to do to fill your tank with God's love for you?

"The secret to a life of fulfillment is learning to give yourself away."
—JEAN HENDRICKS

GOD'S VESSEL

In a great house there are not only vessels of gold and silver, but also of wood and clay, some for honor and some for dishonor. Therefore if anyone cleanses himself from the latter, he will be a vessel for honor, sanctified and useful for the Master, prepared for every good work. 2 TIMOTHY 2:20-21

GOD HAS GIVEN US an incredible opportunity to choose the value of our lives. When we go to the department store, we find finished goods for sale. Someone has made the choice to make a bowl out of pottery or of silver, to make a platter out of wood or of bone china. The items themselves cannot choose to be used for honorable or dishonorable purposes; we the buyers are responsible for that. In the spiritual world, though, we are able to choose to be valuable or worthless, full of honor and useful to God or dirty and broken, not serving any purpose.

Paul wrote in 2 Timothy that you and I can cleanse ourselves and become useful to God. To be cleansed, though, we first need to see the dirt. Far too often, we rationalize, minimize, or excuse our sins. We say, "It doesn't really hurt anybody," "It wasn't that bad," or "I couldn't help it." But those responses leave us dirty and unusable. Early in our Christian experience, the Spirit shines His light on public, obvious sins, and as we grow, His light reveals more subtle and hidden sins such as pride, jealousy, and resentment.

At any point that the Spirit reveals sin in our lives, we have the opportunity to choose our response: We may choose to say yes and repent, to say no and continue in sin, or to act as if we didn't get the message and stay stuck in our sinfulness. When we have the courage to say yes to God, He moves in our hearts to cleanse us, heal us, motivate us, and give us opportunities to serve Him. When we say yes, He prepares us "for every good work." It's a pretty good deal.

What does it mean to be usable to God? What are some ways He uses you?

Is the Spirit pointing out any sin in your life that you need to repent of? If so, how will you respond?

"Do not have your concert first, and then tune your instrument afterwards. Begin the day with the Word of God and prayer, and get first of all into harmony with Him." —HUDSON TAYLOR

A GREAT EXCHANGE

Let all bitterness, wrath, anger, clamor, and evil speaking be put away from you, with all malice. And be kind to one another, tenderhearted, forgiving one another, even as God in Christ forgave you. EPHESIANS 4:31-32

ALL OF US LIVE on an emotional watershed. On one side, if anger builds and festers, it turns to resentment and bitterness, souring every relationship. On the other side, if forgiveness becomes a way of life, we grow in love, compassion, and a deeper appreciation for God's forgiveness of our own sins.

No matter how much we've been hurt, and no matter how much we've used our resentment to give us a sense of identity as the one who was wronged, we can experience a great exchange—one that will revolutionize our lives. The key, Paul explains, is to focus first on the forgiveness we've experienced in Christ. The more deeply we grasp our sinfulness and God's grace, the more we'll be able and willing to forgive those who hurt us.

The warmth of God's grace melts our resentment, cools our tongues, and replaces our anger with love. It doesn't mean the wound didn't happen or that it doesn't hurt, but it means we choose to focus on God's grace instead of our wounds and live in thankfulness instead of demanding justice.

Living on the side of forgiveness, love, and kindness is a decision and a process. We recognize the damage resentment causes and we choose to forgive, but if the wound is deep, God often takes us through layers of pain, grief, and forgiveness until the vat of bitterness is drained dry.

Whom do you know who has exchanged resentment for forgiveness and love?

Are there some people in your life for whom you've harbored some resentment? If so, begin the exchange.

"Things you say in a matter of seconds are never forgotten in a lifetime."
—IKE REIGHARD

GOOD NEWS

[Jesus] said to [the disciples], "Go into all the world and preach the gospel to every creature." MARK 16:15 { MEMORY VERSE

JESUS LEFT US with the great commandment to love God with all our hearts (see Mark 12:30) and the great commission to take the message to everyone on the planet. Both of these apply to every believer, not just those to whom He appeared that day or to pastors in churches today. If you're a believer, these statements are written on your job description. How's it going so far?

Too often, we treat the good news of Christ as if it's the news that our favorite team won the big game. We're excited, but it doesn't change how we live each day. The great commission, though, is about life and death, heaven and hell. It's about sharing the best news ever announced, and those entrusted with it have the unspeakable privilege and heavy responsibility to get the news out to every person.

Jesus was very clear: Those who believe will be rescued from sin and death, but those who don't will experience God's righteous judgment. He could have chosen a different way to get the message out, but He chose you and me. We can see it as a burden, or we can see it as the greatest privilege anyone has ever received. God calls us His ambassadors to a lost world (see 2 Corinthians 5:19-20). We represent the King of kings, and we can be both proud of our role and humble that He would entrust His venture to people like us. Our primary motivation comes, though, from remembering that we, too, were lost, but now we're found.

How does it feel to know that the greatest commandment and the great commission are on your job description?

What changes do you need to make to represent Christ more effectively?

"The Gospel is only good news if it gets there in time." —CARL F. H. HENRY

"Each of us must start from where we are with what we have and go from there. Then God will take the knowledge we have, expand it, and use our witness to claim others for Himself." —ZIG ZIGLAR

PASS IT ON

The things that you have heard from me among many witnesses, commit these to faithful men who will be able to teach others also. 2 TIMOTHY 2:2

WE MAY THINK we invented viral marketing, but Paul used it almost two millennia ago. Viral marketing occurs when a product or service generates enough enthusiasm to cause people to tell their friends and business associates about the product or service. The life-changing truth about Christ works the same way.

Paul invested tremendous resources in Timothy. He spent lots of time with him, prayed with him and for him, and showed him how to lead people. Day and night, in every kind of circumstance, Paul taught and modeled the truth for Timothy. Paul didn't expect the chain to stop there. He told Timothy to pass along everything he had learned, but not just to anybody. He carefully instructed Timothy to set the standard very high: Select "faithful men" who have the heart and the skills to teach others. These men would then do the same thing, selecting great leaders and imparting God's truth to them, and they'd do the same with people they selected.

The Christian faith isn't like a box of cereal on the shelf that people can buy on a whim. Throughout the world, people who become believers are won because men and women have caught the "virus" from faithful, skilled, passionate men and women who were "infected" by others.

Today, most of us can look back at a generation or two of faithful people who, like Paul and Timothy, were part of the viral marketing of the Christian faith. How are we doing at moving it forward?

Why is it important to select faithful people to invest our time in?

How are you doing in imparting the faith to faithful people? Explain your answer.

"When love and skill work together, expect a masterpiece." —JOHN RUSKIN

WORTH FIGHTING FOR

I am already being poured out as a drink offering, and the time of my departure is at hand. I have fought the good fight, I have finished the race, I have kept the faith. 2 TIMOTHY 4:6-7

PROFESSOR HOWARD HENDRICKS quoted a businessman who lamented, "I've spent my life climbing the ladder of success, only to find that it's leaning against the wrong wall." Effort isn't enough. Even adding a healthy measure of passion isn't enough. Our energy and emotion have to be spent on something worth fighting and dying for. It's the ultimate object of our life that gives it meaning.

Paul had fought like a madman! Years earlier, an encounter with Jesus made him realize that his ladder was leaning against the wrong wall. Suddenly, he found a cause that was worthy of every ounce of his being—and he gave it his all. He devoted his considerable intelligence, his heart, his leadership gifts, his time, and all the rest of his resources to that single, consuming cause: Jesus Christ.

He enjoyed incredible successes, and he experienced tremendous difficulties. He was beaten, stoned, whipped, and imprisoned. He was betrayed and misunderstood. But a clear eye on his cause gave him purpose, energy, and the will to keep fighting for Christ no matter what obstacles he encountered.

Now, at the end of his life, he looked back with, we can imagine, a sigh and a smile. He had fought hard. He had fought for a cause that was worthy of his efforts. And he wasn't sorry one bit.

How would you define and describe the wall your ladder is leaning against?

Is Christ a cause worth fighting for? Why or why not?

"What our deepest self craves is not mere enjoyment, but some supreme purpose that will enlist all our powers and will give unity and direction to our life. We can never know the profoundest joy without conviction that our life is significant—not a meaningless episode. The loftiest aim of human life is the ethical perfecting of mankind—the transfiguration of humanity."—HENRY J. GOLDING

UNCHANGING

Jesus Christ is the same yesterday, today, and forever. HEBREWS 13:8

LIFE CAN BE SO CONFUSING, and the Christian life can be even more mind boggling! Just when we think we have it figured out, God throws us a curve, and we wonder if we've understood anything at all. What happened? Did we miss what God was telling us to do? Was He too busy to pay attention? Did He change His mind?

God's will and ways have always included a fair share of mystery. (Beware of those who claim to know God's perfect will for every detail of life—especially for *your* life!) In the list of heroes of the faith, which we find in Hebrews 11, we see that many of them endured setbacks and confusion as they pursued God with their whole hearts.

In this life, we can see only the back side of the tapestry, and quite often we can't figure out the image God is producing on the front side. In those times—and every person who genuinely wants to follow God experiences them from time to time—we have to go back to what we know is true about God. The writer of today's verse reminds us that Jesus Christ never changes. His love, power, and authority existed in eternity past, and they will exist eons and eons into the future. They are real today, even if we don't see them, feel them, or believe them.

Even when everything around us seems to be changing, we can trust that Christ's heart, His purposes, and His love for us are still as strong as ever.

When times are tough, what kinds of questions do you ask?

How does it help to remember that Christ never changes?

"Great truths that are stumbling blocks to the natural man are nevertheless the very foundations upon which the confidence of the spiritual man is built."
—H. A. IRONSIDE

START EACH DAY RIGHT

This is the day the LORD has made; we will rejoice and be glad in it.

PSALM 118:24

DEAD-END JOBS. Strained relationships. Feelings of emptiness. Too often, we dread getting up in the morning to face another day of struggles and disappointments. But it doesn't have to be this way. Perspective makes all the difference, and if we have a strong sense of hope in a God of infinite possibilities, the whole world opens up to us.

Imagine Jesus' disciples getting up each morning. Do you think they dreaded the day? Not a chance! As they sat by the fire while munching on their fish breakfast, they probably looked at one another as if to say, "I wonder what He's going to do today!" Whatever it was, it would be fantastic!

Every day was amazing. They watched Jesus heal the sick, raise the dead, cure lepers, argue with the rigid religious leaders, laugh, cry, teach thousands, calm storms, cast out demons, pray all night, and get away to relax. As they packed up their meager belongings to hit the road, we can almost hear them say, "I can't wait to see what's going to happen today."

He's with us, too. We don't walk on dusty roads in Palestine, but Christ is with us in the boardroom, the bathroom, and the bedroom. He has made each day—including this day—for each of us to experience His presence and His power. The disciples often didn't understand what He was doing, and there will be times we don't get it, either. But each day is a gift from God for us to watch Him work in us, around us, and through us.

What would it have been like to be one of the disciples and watch Jesus every day?

How does it affect your attitude about today to realize that you walk with the risen Christ and that today is His gift to you?

*"I'm convinced that millions of people today don't know the Lord because of the long-faced, poor, suffering-little-me, self-sacrificing, tell-everybody-all-their-troubles Christians who act like their second birth was just as painful to them as their first one was to their mothers." —*ZIG ZIGLAR

SEEING THE INVISIBLE

Faith is the substance of things hoped for, the evidence of things not seen.

HEBREWS 11:1

IN EVERY ASPECT of our lives, we exercise faith. We sit in a chair, having faith that it won't collapse under our weight. When we come to a green light, we trust that cars coming the other way will stop because those drivers are facing a red light. When it comes to the spiritual realm, however, some of us think that we have nothing substantial on which to base our trust. But that's not the case.

Though the spiritual realm is invisible, God has given us plenty of clues about His power, love, and faithfulness. Nature reveals the creativity and power of God, and the life of Christ is the supreme demonstration of God's character and His purpose for us. Still, faith, by its nature, remains a mystery. We trust in God today, looking back at the substance of Creation, the life of Christ, and the stories of countless believers who found God to be faithful in their lives. The choice to trust Him today, however, is our challenge. We don't see Him, and we don't audibly hear Him, but God has given each of us a sense that He is there and that we can trust Him.

The preamble to the "Hall of Faith" in Hebrews 11 blends the two concepts: first, the utter reliability of God in the past and as seen in nature and, second, our trust in God's invisible hand today. Faith stands on the past and confidently reaches out for the future, trusting that what God did in the past He will do one more time—for us.

In what ways is our faith based on the visible and tangible? on the invisible and intangible?

What does God want you to trust Him to do today?

"Faith is a passionate intuition." —WILLIAM WORDSWORTH

DREAMS CAN COME TRUE

Every valley shall be exalted and every mountain and hill brought low; the crooked places shall be made straight and the rough places smooth; the glory of the LORD shall be revealed, and all flesh shall see it together; for the mouth of the LORD has spoken. ISAIAH 40:4-5

PEOPLE SAY that the night is darkest just before the dawn. Certainly, the children of Israel in the time Isaiah was written felt their situation was as black as it could be. The cruel Babylonian empire had overrun them. God had warned them over and over again that He would punish them for their repeated sins, but they had rebelled against Him. Now, they were suffering the drastic consequences of their behavior.

In a remarkable sign of grace, God spoke to them through Isaiah to reassure them of His good intentions for them. In their despair, they felt like giving up, but God reminded them that He could make their wildest dreams—of freedom, peace, and joy—come true.

God's promise of blessing and change found in the passage above carries two separate meanings. First, it assures the people of Israel that God would rescue them from Babylon. The second application will occur when Jesus returns to earth. On that day, He will appear in the clouds with angels blaring trumpets (see Matthew 24:30-31) as the world watches (on every network and cable news station!). On both occasions—the return to Israel from Babylon and Christ's return to earth—people experience miraculous transformation, injustice is replaced by God's justice, and righteousness rules.

All of us long for wrongs to be made right. We may not be in as difficult a spot as the children of Israel in captivity, but all of us experience forms of injustice in our lives. Someday, though, God will make everything right. It's His promise.

What injustices would you like to see God make right?

What will it look like when God does it?

"I have a dream that one day every valley shall be exalted, and every hill and mountain shall be made low, the rough places will be made plain and the crooked places will be made straight and the glory of the Lord shall be revealed and all flesh shall see it together."—**MARTIN LUTHER KING JR.**

GOD'S DELIGHT

Thus says the LORD: "Let not the wise man glory in his wisdom, let not the mighty man glory in his might, nor let the rich man glory in his riches; but let him who glories glory in this, that he understands and knows Me, that I am the LORD, exercising lovingkindness, judgment, and righteousness in the earth. For in these I delight," says the LORD. JEREMIAH 9:23-24

A CASUAL WALK past the magazine rack at a bookstore shows us what people value: beauty, wealth, lavish spending, physical strength, pleasure of every description, and political and corporate power. Millions of people read about these things, daydream about them, and work hard to have more of them. But God says, "If you pursue these, you miss the whole point of life."

We glory in the people, places, and things that give us the most pleasure. We think about them, we praise them, and we can't wait to tell our friends about them. The truly wise person, God says, doesn't glory in what's tangible in this world, but in the intangible thing of inestimable value: having a rich, rewarding relationship with God.

We become like what fills our minds. If we focus on beauty and riches, we'll compare ourselves and everything else to those traits. But if the character of God fills our minds, we'll become more like Him. What does that look like? God overflows with loyal love, accurate judgment and wisdom, and righteous choices that help people. When we rivet our thoughts increasingly on God, He works these traits into us, too.

Becoming more like God, though, isn't just hard work and self-discipline. Walking hand in hand with God—leaving the things that promise life but deliver death and making choices that honor God—brings delight to us and to God.

It's our choice: the visible and worthless, or the intangible and valuable.

Why do tangible things such as beauty and wealth look so attractive to us? What do they promise us? What do they deliver?

How would your life be different if you truly delighted in loving-kindness, wisdom, and righteousness?

"The chief cause of failure and unhappiness is trading what you want most for what you want now." —ZIG ZIGLAR

LEAD BY EXAMPLE

Let no one despise your youth, but be an example to the believers in word, in conduct, in love, in spirit, in faith, in purity. 1 TIMOTHY 4:12

GOD HAS GIVEN all of us skills and talents, but He is more interested in the character of the man or woman who uses these abilities. Certainly, we can be good examples to others who watch us model the skills we use in our work. They can learn a lot from us. But they can learn even more by watching how we treat our spouses and children and our fellow employees, how we respond to annoying people and difficult situations, and how we talk about corporate executives when they make poor decisions.

In the business world, we may expect people to look out for themselves, to do whatever it takes to climb the corporate ladder, and to use people every step of the way. When a Christian goes out of his or her way to care for someone who is hurting, overlooks petty offenses and takes steps to resolve big ones, finds something else to do when the rest of the team goes to a strip club, and exudes a positive attitude while being ruthlessly honest about difficulties—people notice!

All of us have a hundred choices to make each day. We may not recognize many of them because we're so steeped in habitual attitudes and behaviors, but we have constant opportunities to demonstrate love or selfishness, faith or doubt, hope or complaints, purity or sinful passion. Habits can be broken, but not without heartfelt prayer and tenacity to make different choices. If we choose to be Christ's examples to those around us, we're in for a great ride of seeing Him touch people through us. Don't miss it!

Who is the best "leader by example" you know? Describe that person's impact on others.

What new choices do you need to make, and what new habits do you need to develop?

"Charisma may place you at the front of the line. Only character will keep you there." —IKE REIGHARD

THE GREAT THING ABOUT GREAT THINGS

Call to Me, and I will answer you, and show you great and mighty things, which you do not know. JEREMIAH 33:3 { **MEMORY VERSE**

GOD'S PROMISE to answer the prayers of His people was given at a time of desperate need. The children of Israel were in deep trouble—in slavery under the brutal, vicious Babylonian regime. Survival was uppermost on their minds, but God had bigger, more wonderful plans for them than merely surviving. In fact, God's plans for them were beyond their comprehension.

The promise was clear and strong, but the path to deliverance wouldn't be easy. If the children of Israel responded, they would experience the cleansing of suffering before God would free them and restore them to their land. Later, when they made the trip from Babylon back to Israel, they laughed and cried because they were so happy (see Psalm 126).

For us, too, saying yes to God doesn't guarantee a smooth ride. God's great promises often involve great challenges to test our faith in and our loyalty to Him. As we respond to His promise, we need to have our eyes and ears open. God's path of freedom may first take us where we suffer in order to purge our hearts of impure desires, and God's path to blessing may wind through loss.

Through it all, we will cling to God's promise. More than that, we will cling to God Himself. We will reflect on His goodness and greatness and remember how He worked in the lives of men and women who trusted Him with their lives, their hopes, and their futures. And we will trust Him too.

Can we, then, trust God's promise to give us freedom and blessings? Explain your answer.

What does your yes to God mean today?

"The thing is to understand myself, to see what God wishes me to do ... to find the idea for which I can live and die." —**SØREN KIERKEGAARD**

"I would rather have plans changed with God's blessings than fulfilled plans without His blessing." —**ZIG ZIGLAR**

MEASURING UP TO JESUS

He Himself gave some to be apostles, some prophets, some evangelists, and some pastors and teachers, for the equipping of the saints for the work of ministry, for the edifying of the body of Christ, till we all come to the unity of the faith and of the knowledge of the Son of God, to a perfect man, to the measure of the stature of the fullness of Christ. EPHESIANS 4:11-13

A CHRISTIAN LEADER once commented, "Christ's followers today have done what His enemies could never do—we've made Him boring." What a travesty! If we focus our attention on bad news and gossip about Christians, we will miss God's incredible, visionary, optimistic purpose for every believer: to grow so much in our faith that we shine like beacons to everyone around us!

Yes, the road is long and tough, and yes, God is working with clay that has a lot of lumps in it, but God is able to work miracles if we'll trust Him. One of those miracles, one that our neighbors are looking for, is love among Christians. Our friends and neighbors have heard about church members arguing about the flowers planted out front or the extra things done for the wedding of someone's daughter. They know about the vicious arguments and church splits, and they're sick of hearing about them! So are we.

God's vision for each church is that we would grow so much in our love for God that we'd love people the way He loves them: unconditionally and passionately. He wants us to be filled up with Christ's grace, truth, and purpose so that everything we do will reflect Him to those around us.

Can that vision really happen? Not if we're content with having lukewarm affection for God, tolerating people instead of loving them, and just getting by in our efforts to touch others' lives.

Describe what God's vision for your church might look like.

What are you doing to contribute to this vision being fulfilled?

"If a hypocrite is standing between you and God, it just means the hypocrite is closer to God than you are." —ZIG ZIGLAR

ALL THINGS NEW

God will wipe away every tear from their eyes; there shall be no more death,
nor sorrow, nor crying. There shall be no more pain, for the former things have
passed away. Then He who sat on the throne said, "Behold, I make all things
new." And He said to me, "Write, for these words are true and faithful."

REVELATION 21:4-5

ALMOST THREE MILLENNIA AGO, Solomon observed that God had placed a desire for eternity in our hearts (see Ecclesiastes 3:11). We long for heaven. Intuitively, people know there's something beyond this life. Men and women of every culture and every age have tried to identify what it might look like, and we're given a glimpse in John's Revelation.

A day is coming when all wrongs will be made right, every pain will be comforted, and every tear dried. All of the confusion, doubt, and heartache will pass away. Bitterness, resentment, and strains of every kind in every relationship will vanish. In their place, God will make "all things new."

To tantalize us, God doesn't give us more than a shadowy look into that glorious time. We can, though, make some assumptions. Those things that give us joy now will be magnified incredibly. Love, affirmation, understanding, and encouragement will thrill us because they will be untainted by any hint of selfishness. We'll laugh more heartily than ever before, and we'll be challenged to worship God more effectively and wholeheartedly. And those things that cause pain now will vanish in the light of God's amazing love.

For centuries, those who thought, talked, and sang about heaven were those who experienced oppression in this life. Slaves, the chronically poor and destitute, sick and disabled people, and prisoners have always longed for heaven's door. The rest of us, though, will marvel when we get there because heaven will be so much more wonderful than our lives now.

Think about it. It'll do you good.

How do you think heaven will be different from your life now?

What do you look forward to most?

"When the darkness of dismay comes, endure until it is over, because out of it will come that following of Jesus which is an unspeakable joy." —**OSWALD CHAMBERS**

STARTING OVER

I went down to the potter's house, and there he was, making something at the wheel. And the vessel that he made of clay was marred in the hand of the potter; so he made it again into another vessel, as it seemed good to the potter to make. JEREMIAH 18:3-4

THE BIBLE AND THE HISTORY of people of faith give us a rich record of God's not giving up on us when we fail. Abraham was a coward who twice lied about his wife's identity to protect himself, but God transformed him into the father of our faith. Jacob was a deceiver who lied over and over again, but God touched him and made him the father of the twelve tribes. Peter denied Jesus, but a few days after the Resurrection, Jesus met him to reaffirm his acceptance, and Peter became the leader of the early church. The list of men and women who started over is almost endless.

Jeremiah gives us an image of God as the potter and us as the clay. God works diligently to form us and transform us into useful, beautiful vessels, but sometimes things don't work out. It's not the potter's fault; a flaw in the clay causes the problem. But God doesn't wad us up into a clay ball and fling us away. He lovingly starts over, eliminating the flaw and adding the elements of the Spirit, the accountability of friends, and the guidance of the Word to start shaping us again.

The process of producing a beautiful pot isn't fast. The potter takes time, carefully crafting the clay into shape for its intended use. In the same way, when God starts over with us, we may not become instantly useful. It takes time and the skill of the Potter to shape us. Sooner or later, though, we'll be useful again.

What kind of flaws can make us unusable to the Potter?

What's your role and what's God's role in shaping you?

"The God who made you can make you over." —ZIG ZIGLAR

JESUS LOVES THEM

Jesus said, "Let the little children come to Me, and do not forbid them; for of such is the kingdom of heaven." MATTHEW 19:14

IN ANCIENT PALESTINE, men ruled over society. Women were second-class citizens, and children followed in a distant third place, just above the despised Samaritans. As we read the accounts of Jesus' life, we find that He turned things upside down. Instead of fearing the powerful religious leaders, He argued with them, and He broke the molds of accepted religious behavior they had so carefully constructed. Instead of ignoring women, He reached out to them again and again, including them in His circle as equals. And the snotty-nosed, loud, out-of-control children? Jesus honored them by welcoming them into His inner circle, into His life, and into His heart.

In our society, children occupy a prominent place. Many couples construct their schedules around their children's sports and hobbies, and the needs of the children are a high priority in any decisions in family life. But far too often, we neglect the emotional and spiritual needs of our children. We're so tired from working so hard that we don't have much energy to devote to them.

We need to take our cues from Jesus. We don't have more responsibilities than He had! We need to see our children the way He sees them and treat them with respect, patience, and love. If He could carve out time to value children, we can too.

To what extent are children in your life a joy, an annoyance, or a burden?

What are some things that need to change so that you can devote more emotional energy and time to them?

"Start your child's day with love and encouragement and end the day the same way." —ZIG ZIGLAR

COMPLETE INSPIRATION

All Scripture is given by inspiration of God, and is profitable for doctrine, for reproof, for correction, for instruction in righteousness, that the man of God may be complete, thoroughly equipped for every good work.

2 TIMOTHY 3:16-17

EVERY WORD OF SCRIPTURE is inspired, which means "God-breathed." God worked through the writers' personalities and backgrounds to communicate His message to us. We may not understand exactly how this happened, but we can be certain that the message they wrote was, and is, God's divine Word.

God's truth transforms lives, but not by magic. As we listen and study it ourselves, it becomes "profitable" to us by changing our lives. The Bible teaches us truth about the greatness and grace of God and about the human need for forgiveness. It instructs us in relationships of every kind. When our lives are in alignment with God's will, the Scriptures affirm our direction; when we're off base, it shines its light on our selfishness and disobedience. The Bible gives us new tracks to run on, directing us to live in ways that honor God and bring fulfillment to us. And ultimately, our humble and willing response to God's truth shapes us so that God can use us to accomplish His purposes in others' lives.

Today, we can read scores of translations, and we can download hundreds of files of the Bible. In addition, we can listen to messages by many of the finest teachers of our day. If the benefits of studying God's Word are so great, and it is so readily available, why don't we read and study it more deeply and more often?

Describe a time when Bible study really excited you.

What are some resources you can use and ways you can make Bible study a higher priority?

"There are some promises in the Bible which I have never yet used; but I am well assured that there will come times of trial and trouble when I shall find that that poor despised promise, which I thought was never meant for me, will be the only one on which I can float. I know that the time is coming when every believer shall know the worth of every promise in the covenant." —CHARLES HADDON SPURGEON

THERE'S NOTHING LIKE A BIG BROTHER

The LORD is my light and my salvation; whom shall I fear? The LORD is the strength of my life; of whom shall I be afraid? PSALM 27:1

IN THE CLOSING PAGES of Harper Lee's Pulitzer Prize–winning novel, *To Kill a Mockingbird*, young Jem Finch escorts his sister, Scout, home from the school Halloween party. As they walk through the woods in the darkness, a deranged man attacks the little girl. Jem throws himself at the attacker. In the melee, Jem is thrown to the ground and breaks his arm.

This classic story of a noble, single-parent attorney and his rambunctious kids captured hearts of generations of readers and movie fans, in part because it depicts the warmth and loyal love of an older brother for his sister. We all long for an older brother like Jem to give us wisdom, protect us, and get us out of trouble (or most of it, anyway), and we have one. David's confident assertion is that God is our light and our strength. With Him by our side, we won't wilt in fear when we are threatened.

David, we should remember, had plenty to fear. Family and friends betrayed him, King Saul attacked him and chased him over the desert, and David found himself close to death on many occasions. But through it all, the Lord led him, provided for him, and protected him.

What threatens you and me today? When we feel hurried and harried and we believe that no one else understands or cares, we can remember how Jem took care of Scout, and even more, how God took care of David.

What would it mean for you to see the Lord as a loving, strong big brother?

What are some situations in your life right now in which you could use a big brother like that?

"Worry is stewing without doing. It's interest paid on trouble which never comes due." —ZIG ZIGLAR

CAN YOU LOVE THE UNLOVELY?

[Jesus said,] "Love your enemies, bless those who curse you, do good to those who hate you, and pray for those who spitefully use you and persecute you."

MATTHEW 5:44 { MEMORY VERSE

IT MAKES PERFECT SENSE to love people who love us and hate those who hate us. That's just the way the world works!

But it's not the way the Kingdom works. Jesus acknowledged the law of human nature, but He calls us to be different, radical, and countercultural. He wants us to go completely against our basic human natures and love the people who annoy or antagonize us, do kind things for the people who actively try to hurt us, and ask God's blessing for those who curse us and do everything in their power to cause us pain.

It doesn't make sense—until we realize that's exactly the way God has treated us. We had nothing to offer Him except our arrogance, rebellion, and apathy. For years, many of us looked at the Cross and said, "Who cares?" God gave the most He could give when Christ stepped out of eternity into time to die a horrible death for us, but for a long time, we looked the other way. We were so preoccupied with our own selfish desires that we didn't think much about other people or God. But through it all, God kept loving us, doing good for us, and giving us a wealth of gifts when we deserved only punishment.

In any relationship, and especially any strained relationship, we have a choice: to be like God or to be like all other selfish people on the planet. If we choose selfishness, we're on our own, but if we make the hard decision to pursue God and make our lives a display case of His grace, He has promised to lead us, fill us, and use us to change lives.

In what ways is "loving the unlovely" like God?

What steps can you take today to be a display case of God's grace?

"Loving the lovely is an easy test to pass. Loving the unlovely requires much patience and wisdom." —IKE REIGHARD

"The best way for our faith to grow and expand is by expressing that faith to others." —ZIG ZIGLAR

EMBRACE THE DARKNESS

Moses said to the people, "Do not fear; for God has come to test you, and that His fear may be before you, so that you may not sin." So the people stood afar off, but Moses drew near the thick darkness where God was.

EXODUS 20:20-21

TIMES OF DARKNESS come to all of us. We may experience tragic, inexplicable loss; confusion; failure; rejection; or for some of us, spiritual emptiness. Our response in these moments often is the product of our previous encounters with God. If we have developed trust in God in the light, we'll embrace Him in the darkness, and in fact, we'll even embrace the darkness as His path for us.

Moses had just come down from the mountain and delivered the Ten Commandments to the people. The message didn't come by e-mail. Lightning struck, thunder boomed, trumpets blared, and thick smoke surrounded the mountain and blotted out the sun. The people cowered at the magnificent and terrifying display of the majesty of God! They insisted that Moses talk to them—they didn't want to hear God's voice because they thought they would die!

Moses, though, wasn't terrified. His experiences with God at the burning bush, in his confrontations with Pharaoh, at the Red Sea, in providing water from the rock as well as manna and quail from the sky, and on the mountain that very day all convinced him that God was trustworthy no matter what circumstances he faced.

His faith in God was so strong that when the people backed away from the darkness, Moses moved toward it. He was convinced God was there, and he wanted to connect with Him as much as possible.

When we experience darkness, we'll back away if our faith is weak, but we'll move into it if our faith has been strengthened by years of experience in seeing God's faithfulness, grace, and power.

How do you usually respond in times of confusion and darkness?

What do you need to do to strengthen your faith so that you move toward God in times of darkness?

"Anxiety is not only a pain which we must ask God to assuage, but also a weakness we must ask Him to pardon." —C. S. LEWIS

MORE THAN CONQUERORS

Who shall separate us from the love of Christ? Shall tribulation, or distress, or persecution, or famine, or nakedness, or peril, or sword? . . . Yet in all these things we are more than conquerors through Him who loved us.

ROMANS 8:35, 37

OUR INTERPRETATION of difficulties determines our response to them. If we believe we deserve that God give us a smooth, relatively pain-free life, always on the upward path of greater success, we'll be devastated (and shocked) when we experience trouble. *Hey*, we'll wonder, *what's this about?* Unrealistic expectations inevitably lead to resentment, and soon, our hearts grow cold toward God.

In this oddly triumphant passage, Paul doesn't shrink from the fact that following Christ in a fallen world sometimes includes genuine suffering. In fact, his list of troubles covers the spectrum from general distress to the point of a sword. Don't be surprised, Paul reminds us, when you encounter problems, and don't forget God's presence and love, either.

Nothing, absolutely nothing, can separate a believer from the personal attention and deep love of Christ. When we're being beaten up, Christ's compassion only intensifies. When we are wise enough to realize that difficulties don't mean God doesn't care, we'll trust Him in the middle of our darkest nights and most threatening days.

When we trust God in the midst of difficulties, we don't just grit our teeth and hang on until the pain stops. More than ever before, we trust in His wisdom to guide us, His presence to comfort us, and His strength to support us. Instead of barely making it, we become "more than conquerors." Our interpretation of the problem, though, is the key that unlocks our response.

When you experience difficulties, how do you normally interpret the situation? How realistic are your expectations?

What would it look like for you to be more than a conqueror in difficult times in your life?

"There are two things to do about the gospel—believe it and behave it."
—SUSANNA WESLEY

STRENGTH IN WEAKNESS

I take pleasure in infirmities, in reproaches, in needs, in persecutions, in distresses, for Christ's sake. For when I am weak, then I am strong.

2 CORINTHIANS 12:10

MANY YEARS AGO, a man was arrested in the Soviet Union. After a sham trial, he was sentenced to twenty years of hard labor in the Siberian gulag. Seven days a week and fourteen hours a day, he worked in fierce cold in winter and swarms of ravenous insects in summer. Some men died from exhaustion, and most of the survivors became bitter and hardened. This man, though, found Christ, and his days of labor took on new meaning. He learned to thank God for the meager food ration the prisoners were given, and he learned to experience joy in that desolate place. A few Christian friends there were the light of his life, and he was able to find peace. On the day he was released, the man walked out the gates, turned, and to the astonishment of the guards, kissed the walls of the prison camp. "Here," he explained, "I found God, and He found me, and I am so thankful."

Suffering is a given for us. We naturally try to construct our lives to avoid it if at all possible, but sooner or later, suffering weasels its way into our experience. At that moment, we either embrace it as a tutor to teach us the deepest, richest lessons of life, or we despise suffering and our hearts grow hard and cold.

Weakness isn't fun and isn't pretty, but admitting our weaknesses to God is the first step in trusting Him and experiencing His great strength. Paul was so convinced that suffering produces good that he took pleasure in it! But suffering itself didn't produce perception, wisdom, and strength in Paul's life—suffering *for Christ's sake*, trusting Him to turn it into something good, produced the fruit.

How do you normally respond to suffering?

How would it help to believe God can turn suffering into something good in your life?

"God is not looking for brilliant men, is not depending upon eloquent men, is not shut up to the use of talented men in sending His Gospel out in the world. God is looking for broken men, for men who have judged themselves in the light of the Cross of Christ. When He wants anything done, He takes up men who have come to an end of themselves, and whose trust and confidence is not in themselves but in God." —**H. A. IRONSIDE**

BRINGING COMFORT

Blessed be the God and Father of our Lord Jesus Christ, the Father of mercies and God of all comfort, who comforts us in all our tribulation, that we may be able to comfort those who are in any trouble, with the comfort with which we ourselves are comforted by God. 2 CORINTHIANS 1:3-4

NOBODY LIKES PAIN. We naturally wonder, *Where is God when it hurts?* and *Why is this happening?* The Scriptures tell us that suffering may occur from a variety of causes, including natural disasters, the consequences of our own sins, and the effects of others' sins against us. Whatever the cause, and whether we ever figure it out, our response can include two things: turning to God for comfort and then comforting others who are in pain.

God never promised a pain-free life. Some preachers claim God will give people unlimited prosperity and health, but those promises prove to be cruel hoaxes to those who believe them. Instead, God promises that our pain will never be in vain. No matter what we experience and whether we ever learn the reason or not, God is willing to enter into our pain with us, to give us a sense of His presence, and to provide genuine comfort for us. The process may be short or long, but if we cling to God, we'll experience His mercy and comfort. Then, and only then, will we be able to comfort others who feel just as much despair, emptiness, and heartache as we felt in the midst of our pain.

When we've experienced true comfort, we realize that pat answers do more harm than good and that simple solutions seldom help at all. A friend "just being there" is often the greatest comfort we can experience, and when people around us are suffering, we use few words as we stay near them.

First, though, we experience God's kindness, tenderness, patience, and love in our darkest moments. This experience is our greatest resource in comforting others.

Describe a time when you were hurting. What questions did you ask? What brought real comfort?

Who are some people around you today who need to be comforted? What will you do?

"There is nothing you will ever face that you and God can't handle. The Lord promises us He will give us the grace to bear whatever burden comes our way."
—ZIG ZIGLAR

PATIENCE

Take the prophets, who spoke in the name of the Lord, as an example of suffering and patience. Indeed we count them blessed who endure. You have heard of the perseverance of Job and seen the end intended by the Lord— that the Lord is very compassionate and merciful. JAMES 5:10-11

WE WANT THE CHARACTER quality of patience, but we don't want to go through the curriculum to learn it! We'd love to have the life of Christ effortlessly poured into us like a transfusion, but spiritual life doesn't work that way. More often, faith is built in the crucible of doubts, hope develops when we face despair, and genuine love blooms in relationships with the most difficult people. In the same way, patience becomes a reality in us because we cling to God during times when we long for quick, complete solutions to our problems.

Look at the prophets, James tells us, as examples of people in whom God gradually built the character quality of patience. All the prophets endured tremendous hardships, but none like Job did. He experienced calamity after calamity, followed by misunderstanding and accusations of friends—including his wife's "encouragement" to curse God and die! (See Job 2:9.) But through long, excruciating times of intense suffering, confusion, and spiritual darkness, Job continued to cling to God. In the end, God showed up. Even then, God didn't explain the whys to him. He simply convinced Job that He was, after all, the God of the universe, and he could trust Him (see Job 38–41).

Could it be that God has been trying to form the quality of patience in us by putting difficulties, obstacles, and obstinate people in our lives? God's curriculum for all of us includes several courses on Patience 101, 201, and 301. Will we try to skip school, or will we be good students and learn our lessons?

What are some times in your life when God tried to teach you patience? What kind of student were you?

What do you need to know about God in order to respond better in His classroom?

"How far you go in life depends on you being tender with the young, compassionate with the aged, sympathetic with the striving and tolerant of the weak and the strong. Because someday in life you will have been all of these."
—GEORGE WASHINGTON CARVER

BROKEN TO BLESS

Make me hear joy and gladness, that the bones You have broken may rejoice. . . . Restore to me the joy of Your salvation, and uphold me by Your generous Spirit. Then I will teach transgressors Your ways, and sinners shall be converted to You. PSALM 51:8, 12-13

AUTHOR HENRI NOUWEN said that only those who are "wounded healers" have the credibility and compassion to enter into another person's pain and provide genuine comfort. King David would have agreed. He had blown it big time! He'd committed adultery with Bathsheba and conspired to murder her husband, Uriah. In this beautiful and poignant psalm of repentance, David pours out his heart to the Lord, trusting Him to forgive.

The "bones" represent David's entire life. When his friend Nathan confronted him about his sin, David was shattered (see 2 Samuel 12:1-13). He immediately confessed what he had done, and he began the process of restoration. First, though, he had to come to grips with the horrible nature of his actions. Once, he had danced before God because he delighted in Him, but now he felt only sadness and guilt. Once, he had stood strong and bold to kill a giant, but now he felt terribly weak and small. Restoration couldn't come from self-effort. God had to accomplish it by convincing David of His great mercy and grace.

Those who have been restored from wounds or sins have much to offer others who suffer. Broken and mended, stronger than ever, these people have a perspective on pain that goes beyond books. They have looked into the darkness, and God has met them there. Their experience of restoration has earned them the credibility to speak truth with authenticity to others who have been broken by sin or loss. Wounded healers have the joy and responsibility to impart what they've learned to others, and they keep paying it forward.

How would you define a "wounded healer"?

In what way does a restored sinner or someone who was wounded but now healed have credibility to help others?

"Brokenness is not a revival. It is a vital and indispensable step toward it."
—ARTHUR WALLIS

GOD NEVER SLEEPS

Behold, He who keeps Israel shall neither slumber nor sleep.

PSALM 121:4 { MEMORY VERSE

MANY PEOPLE OUTSIDE the church look at us and criticize us for being "plastic" or "phony." They say we give glib answers to difficult questions, or worse, we don't even ask the questions in the first place! The writers of the Bible, though, were never criticized for this problem because they were so painfully honest. In fact, people who study ancient literature say the Bible is unique because, unlike other ancient texts, its heroes all have clay feet. Time after time in the Bible, we find people who wonder if God really cares. They express anger, despair, fear, and confusion, and God is delighted for them to approach Him with raw emotions and exposed hearts. Time after time, God rewards honesty with fresh insights and renewed confidence in Him.

In this psalm, the writer, who is on his way to Jerusalem, is afraid because he's going through hills full of thieves. "Who's going to help me?" he cries (see Psalm 121:1). "I wonder," he seems to ask, "if God is aware of the danger I'm in. Is He paying attention, or is He asleep?"

Once again, God rewards honesty with hope. The process of wrestling with his doubts strengthens the psalmist's faith. Whether it took a long time or it happened quickly, we don't know, but God let him know that He is fully aware and fully present, even in the most threatening situations.

Each of us goes through times when it seems that God has taken a nap and forgotten about us. In those moments, our honesty is a door to closer communication with God, and eventually, more hope, understanding, and confidence in Him.

When have you felt that God was taking a nap and you were on your own?

Does being honest with God about your doubts and fears seem right to you? Why or why not?

"The future is as bright as the promises of God." —WILLIAM CAREY

"It's nice to know that you don't have to sit up at night and worry, because God is going to be up all night, anyhow." —ZIG ZIGLAR

NO DOUBT ALLOWED

Let him ask in faith, with no doubting, for he who doubts is like a wave of the sea driven and tossed by the wind. JAMES 1:6

JAMES HAD DESCRIBED the challenge and the benefits of trusting God during difficult times. Problems test our faith, he explained, and in the crucible of struggle, we develop the quality of endurance (see James 1:2-3). As we continue to trust God in hard times, we grow up spiritually, and our faith matures into a deep, strong trust in God through thick and thin.

To get where God wants us to go, we desperately need His wisdom so we understand His purpose and processes along the way. He has promised to give us His wisdom generously, but there's a catch: We have to ask in faith and not doubt.

In times of trouble, we naturally doubt just about everything, including our abilities, our understanding, other people's motives, the path forward, and God's goodness. We can get so wrapped up in trying to figure things out on our own that we almost go crazy! James calls this confusion being "like a wave of the sea driven and tossed by the wind." The winds we experience during hard times are all the conflicting thoughts, differing advice from friends, and emotions that can swing between blind hope and deep despair.

When we "ask in faith," we humbly acknowledge that we don't have the answers and we're turning to God for His help. We need to consider our ways, but we don't want to become obsessed with every possible contingency so that we lose sleep. We also trust that God will, in His way and in His timing, give us the direction we need. We don't demand an instant answer. We ask, and we wait confidently. During the wait, God often leads us to truth in His Word and to wise believers who give us valuable insights. Then, when we sense that God has, in fact, given us His wisdom, we act.

Describe situations when you felt confused and needed God's wisdom. Did you ask "in faith"?

How would you explain what it means to ask for God's wisdom without doubting?

"God's laws work all of the time, not just some of the time, and they work whether you believe in them or not." —ZIG ZIGLAR

THE KEY TO PLEASING GOD

Without faith it is impossible to please Him, for he who comes to God must believe that He is, and that He is a rewarder of those who diligently seek Him.

HEBREWS 11:6

IN THE BOOK OF GENESIS, we read about the life of Enoch, a man who walked with God so closely that God plucked him out of this life and into heaven instead of bothering with the normal transition of death (see Genesis 5:23-24, NLT). The writer to the Hebrews explains that God did this because He was pleased with Enoch (see Hebrews 11:5). The author, though, wants to make it clear what gave pleasure to God: Enoch's faith. You and I, too, can make God smile by trusting Him.

Unlike some of the world's religions, Christianity isn't primarily adherence to a set of principles, concepts, or laws. It is a relationship with Almighty God, who responds emotionally to our attitudes and behavior. Our faith pleases Him, and our lack of faith grieves Him.

The writer expands on the concept of a personal relationship with God by reminding us that God rewards those who pursue Him. God isn't a vending machine that dispenses blessings or curses depending on the currency of behavior we put in the slot. He knows us as a friend knows a friend or, even better, as a parent understands his or her child. He delights in giving us good gifts, and we make Him sad when we don't appreciate what He does for us.

The key to pleasing God is having faith that He exists, that He is personal, and that He delights in rewarding even our feeble efforts to know Him better.

Is He personal to you? Do you give Him reasons to smile?

How differently do we respond when we believe God is personal instead of like a vending machine?

Is your faith making God smile? Why or why not? What can you do to strengthen your faith?

"If we have Christ with us, we can do all things. Let us not be thinking how weak we are. Let us lift up our eyes to Him and think of Him as our Elder Brother who has all power given to Him in Heaven and on earth. He says, 'Lo, I am with you alway, even unto the end of the world.'" —D. L. MOODY

QUÉ SERÁ, SERÁ

That which has been is what will be, that which is done is what will be done, and there is nothing new under the sun. ECCLESIASTES 1:9

SOLOMON SHREWDLY OBSERVED the way life works, and he never sugarcoated reality. In this verse, Solomon seems to be saying that we have to accept things the way they are because few things ever change, but he's also acknowledging the value of constancy in our universe and in our daily lives.

We take many things for granted because they've been consistent for so long. The rhythm of days, weeks, seasons, and years never changes. Up is always up, and down is always down. Consistency can be really boring if we're talking about our daily routines, but constancy in the physical world is a wonderful (if often overlooked) gift from God! And in our advanced culture today, we enjoy even more constancy because most of us don't have to worry about the weather to see if our crops will grow so we can eat. Certainly, we experience variations in things like our choice of foods and risks like new relationships and business decisions, but in many respects, we live in a remarkably stable environment.

God gives us our surprisingly constant world so that we don't have to spend our energies on survival. We can devote our creativity to things that will make a difference: caring for people and taking risks to accomplish great things for God.

What are some things you appreciate about God's gift of constancy?

How can you use the security of constancy to focus your energies on things that matter?

"One cure for boredom is to forget yourself through activities which bring you in touch with people and ideas outside yourself." —BLANCHE MCKEOWN

ETERNITY IN THEIR HEARTS

He has made everything beautiful in its time. Also He has put eternity in their hearts, except that no one can find out the work that God does from beginning to end. ECCLESIASTES 3:11

IN EVERY AGE, culture, religion, and nation, people have an innate awareness that life transcends what they can see, taste, feel, and smell. All of them know a supernatural world exists, though they may pursue it in different ways. People may try to define the supernatural world or categorize it into "steps" or "paths" or "gods" or "laws" but people's meager attempts to put labels on God fall far short. Even we Christians, who have the truth of the Scriptures to tell us about God, recognize that He is far greater than we can conceive.

Certainty and mystery—these two opposing facts of life give us a firm foundation but keep us amazed at the greatness and goodness of God. Creation shouts that God exists, and history declares that He became a man and died for our sins two millennia ago. About these things, we can be certain. But in this life, we often can't see the hand of God working in individual lives—especially our own! His ways are mysterious and sometimes bewildering.

Great art often combines certainty and mystery to intrigue us. That's part of what makes it beautiful. In the same way, God blends those traits in our lives and in our world to make "everything beautiful in its time."

Do you feel more comfortable with certainty or with mystery?

What are some reasons you need the other trait in your life and in your walk with God?

"Live near to God and all things will appear little to you in comparison with eternal realities." —**ROBERT MURRAY M'CHEYNE**

AN IMMORTAL LEGACY

I know that whatever God does, it shall be forever. Nothing can be added to it, and nothing taken from it. God does it, that men should fear before Him.

ECCLESIASTES 3:14

DOES WHAT WE DO for God really matter? Sometimes we wonder. We look around at others who don't care about God but seem to be getting ahead far faster than we are, and we get discouraged. We need to remember that for all of eternity, God will honor every moment we trust Him, every word we say to communicate His truth, and every move we make to follow His leading. All these things are not only done *for* Him but done *by* Him as He works in our hearts. Nothing is wasted. Nothing is forgotten.

If we live for the applause of people, we often will be disappointed. But if we live with a deep reverence for the One who is both King and Savior, we realize that He is the One who ultimately holds the measuring stick and determines which kind of life has real value.

We all leave a legacy, but God determines the eternal value of our lives. We can live each day with the confidence that God will one day measure our lives and give them a grade. On that day, some who appeared to be really successful might find they weren't so hot after all, and God will smile at some who were faithful and loving but overlooked.

What are you doing these days that has eternal value?

What adjustments do you need to make so that your legacy is more pleasing to God?

"The greatest investment you can make in this world is in God's Word and God's people. They are two things that last forever and pay eternal dividends."
—RICK WARREN

WHEN LESS IS MORE

Better a handful with quietness than both hands full, together with toil and grasping for the wind. ECCLESIASTES 4:6

MANY OF US ARE AFFLICTED with the "go, go, go disease." Somehow, we've developed the core belief that we can't be happy unless we have our lives full of activities. But the disease leaves us feeling exhausted. Our most cherished relationships become shallow and tense, and we become confused because we're trying so hard but feel so empty. We're "grasping for the wind."

In our light-speed culture, one of the marks of true wisdom is the determination to carve out time and space to reflect, rest, and recharge our emotional batteries. Creating "margin" in our lives doesn't just happen. We have to schedule it, value it, and then protect it from the onslaught of voices that scream, "You've got to do this, too!"

The price we pay for creating these regular times is that we have to say no to some activities, but we need to be honest about the price we've paid for saying yes to too many things. Making margin a priority reduces stress, increases fulfillment, and leads to richer relationships with God and every person in our lives. Is it worth the effort?

What are some of the effects of "go, go, go disease" in your life and in the lives of those you love?

What do you need to do to carve out time and space for yourself?

"My God, give me neither poverty or riches, but whatsoever it may be. Thy will to give, give me with it a heart that knows humbly to acquiesce in what is Thy will." —GOTTHOLD EPHRAIM LESSING

NEVER ENOUGH

He who loves silver will not be satisfied with silver; nor he who loves abundance, with increase. This also is vanity. ECCLESIASTES 5:10 { MEMORY VERSE

IN ADDICTIONS LIKE ALCOHOLISM, people experience a phenomenon called tolerance. A person's body gets used to the level of alcohol being consumed, so he or she has to drink more to get the same effect. And the process continues as the body adjusts to taking in more and more.

The same phenomenon occurs in the world of money and possessions, but in this case, tolerance is a psychological effect. People believe that the next rung up the ladder will give them the happiness they long for, so they work hard to get there. When they achieve it, they feel great—even euphoric—for a little while. But soon, the feeling wears off, and the next rung comes into view. The pursuit of more always promises ultimate fulfillment, but it always leads to deep disappointment. It is, as Solomon observed, vanity—empty and futile.

The solution to the problem of tolerance in money and possessions isn't to get more and more. It's to kick the habit! We need to step back, take a hard look at the compulsion to acquire, and confess our sin to God. He will forgive us, give us wisdom, and put us on a path of filling our lives with things that really satisfy.

Do you agree or disagree that for many people, the lure to acquire is like an addiction? Explain your answer.

What changes do you need to make in your perception of what will really satisfy you?

"Money never made a man happy yet, nor will it. There is nothing in its nature to produce happiness. The more a man has, the more he wants. Instead of filling a vacuum, it makes one. If it satisfies one want, it doubles and triples that want another way. That was a true proverb of the wise man; rely on it: 'Better is little with the fear of the Lord than great treasure and trouble therewith.'"
—BENJAMIN FRANKLIN

"Money will buy you a bed, but not a good night's sleep; a house, but not a home; a companion, but not a friend." —ZIG ZIGLAR

FOOLISH SONGS

It is better to hear the rebuke of the wise than for a man to hear the song of fools. ECCLESIASTES 7:5

"I DIDN'T ENJOY HEARING IT, but I really needed to hear what you told me. Thank you." This was the response of a man whose boss had told him he wasn't getting a promotion. His boss explained the reasons the man had been bypassed, and instead of reacting defensively, he listened, accepted the truth, and made changes in his life.

One of the chief marks of maturity is the ability—in fact, the *desire*—to hear correction. Far too often, we pursue friendships with people who tell us only what they think we want to hear. They tell us that we're brilliant, gifted, and right, and if anybody (like a boss or spouse) tries to correct us, our "friends" take our side and tell us we're victims of injustice.

Nobody likes to hear correction, but think of it this way: When we're sick, we take medicine to make us well. Only a fool would insist he doesn't need it! In the same way, when our hearts are sick, we need the medicine of truth from a wise "physician of the soul" who speaks truth to us. If we listen, we take steps on the path of health and hope.

How do you normally respond to correction?

How is correction from a wise person like medicine?

"If what they are saying about you is true, mend your ways. If it isn't true, forget it and go on and serve the Lord." —H. A. IRONSIDE

STUMBLING IN DARKNESS

Do not rejoice over me, my enemy; when I fall, I will arise; when I sit in darkness, the LORD will be a light to me. MICAH 7:8

THE PROPHET MICAH had just issued a scathing condemnation of God's people. Their sins were unspeakable—murdering members of their own families, practicing bribery and corruption in politics, oppressing the poor, and defying their parents (see Micah 7:2-6). The sins of the people of God precipitated a very dark time in their history.

When the people heard Micah's rebuke, however, they responded with appropriate humility and courageous faith. Though they had stumbled in their self-made darkness, they believed the promises of God to forgive, restore, and give them light again. Their response is a powerful lesson for those who are stuck in their sins.

When we've gone down the wrong road for a long time, even destructive habits can feel very comfortable. Change is threatening, so we find excuses to stay in our darkness. We complain that nobody understands, or that change is too hard, or that we'll fail again so there's no use even trying. Any semblance of courage to change is washed away in a tidal wave of self-pity. An alcoholic explained that she felt more comfortable with the destruction of her addiction than the prospect of change: "It may be hell, but at least I know the names of the streets."

God's people, though, didn't use any excuses. They voiced their faith in God's mercy, and they took action to step out of darkness into His light. For people who have been deeply wounded or who stay stuck in sin or addiction for a long time, courage is the chief ingredient of change.

In what ways is staying in darkness easier and more attractive than taking positive steps toward change?

How can a person overcome feelings of self-pity and take steps forward?

"You can encounter many defeats, but you must not be defeated."
—MAYA ANGELOU

THE GREEN-EYED MONSTER

Saul was very angry, . . . and he said, "They have ascribed to David ten thousands, and to me they have ascribed only thousands. Now what more can he have but the kingdom?" So Saul eyed David from that day forward.

1 SAMUEL 18:8-9

SAUL WAS THE TALLEST, most handsome man in the land—straight off the *GQ* cover. His good looks, though, weren't as important as his status. Out of all the men of Israel, God had chosen him to be king. Saul had it made, but sadly, it wasn't enough for him.

By contrast, David was born in a relatively obscure shepherd family. He was only a young man, but he was as brave as a lion! When the Philistine giant Goliath threatened the army of Israel, little David stepped up and killed him with a rock from a slingshot. The army was spared, Saul still reigned on the throne, and the Philistine threat vanished. You'd think Saul would be grateful, but when the people sang to praise David's exploits, the green-eyed monster of jealousy rose in Saul's heart.

Jealousy warps a person's thinking, creating the illusion of threats that don't actually exist. Because people praised David, Saul concluded that David wanted his throne. His false perception justified his anger and further enflamed his jealousy.

One of the marks of a secure, mature person is to be thrilled that others receive praise and to join in. Jealousy is a sure sign of insecurity, and mental machinations that produce images of threats to ourselves only reinforce bitter feelings and jealous actions. The cure for jealousy isn't to control and condemn the other person. The solution is to step back, acknowledge the root cause of insecurity, and deal with it. The love, acceptance, and grace of God give us a firm foundation so that we don't have to be praised more than anyone else.

What are evidences of jealousy? How does it affect relationships?

What are some ways to address the root problem of insecurity?

"You will make a lousy somebody else, but the best you in existence." —ZIG ZIGLAR

HANDLE WITH CARE

I testify to everyone who hears the words of the prophecy of this book: If anyone adds to these things, God will add to him the plagues that are written in this book; and if anyone takes away from the words of the book of this prophecy, God shall take away his part from the Book of Life, from the holy city, and from the things which are written in this book. REVELATION 22:18-19

AN OBSERVANT TEACHER once said, "God created us in His image, and we've returned the favor. We've created Him in our image." All of us see the world through our own eyes, both physical and spiritual, and we tend to interpret biblical truth to make it fit our preconceived opinions. That's natural, but it's dangerous.

Early in the Bible, Moses instructs God's people not to add to or subtract from God's laws (see Deuteronomy 12:32). Here, at the end of the Bible, John gives us a similar warning, specifically about the prophecies in Revelation. For centuries, people have been fascinated with the dramatic vision of worldwide calamities that will occur before and when Christ comes again. Scenes of carnage that must have seemed unbelievable in the first century make sense in our day of mobile warfare and nuclear arms. Some of us try to fit our daily news accounts of the Middle East into the chapters of Revelation.

John warns us, though, to be careful—very careful—to avoid shoehorning prophecy into today's news or to interpret the scenes too specifically. Is it exciting to think about what prophetic scenes might look like in reality? Sure, but we need to hold God's message in the highest regard and read it with reverence. The Reformation teacher John Calvin wrote detailed commentaries on every book of the Bible—except for Revelation. He couldn't write about it, he explained, because he didn't understand it well enough.

How then should we read, interpret, and teach this spectacular book?

What does it mean to read it with reverence?

"No Scripture is exhausted by a single explanation. The flowers of God's garden bloom not only double, but seven fold: they are continually pouring forth fresh fragrance." —**CHARLES HADDON SPURGEON**

THE SHIRT OFF YOUR BACK

Jonathan and David made a covenant, because [Jonathan] loved him as his own soul. And Jonathan took off the robe that was on him and gave it to David, with his armor, even to his sword and his bow and his belt.

1 SAMUEL 18:3-4

JONATHAN HAD EVERY REASON to be wary of David. Jonathan was Saul's son, the next in line for the throne. He was going to be the king of Israel, with all the honor, wealth, and power of that preeminent position. But Jonathan was, first and foremost, a friend, not a prince. His dedication to David surpassed his desires for his own future.

Jonathan's commitment to his friend inspired him to initiate a covenant, a solemn pledge. To confirm the agreement, Jonathan gave David his royal robe. That was significant, but it wasn't all. Jonathan also gave him his armor, including his sword, his bow, and his belt. This act of remarkable generosity signified that Jonathan was acknowledging that David would take his place on the throne after Saul died.

Our friendships often are based only on mutual interests: You scratch my back, and I'll scratch yours. When the friendship threatens personal loss, it dissolves. Jonathan's example, though, is of a categorically different type of friendship, in which both parties are dedicated to the good of the other, no matter what the cost. These friendships are rare, but they are life changing for both people. Those who enjoy this level of friendship tell us that their friend made all the difference in their futures, most often because the friend remained loyal during the darkest, most difficult moments in their lives. That's the measure of true friendship, one that involves genuine love, sacrifice, and time.

Have you ever experienced a friendship like this? Explain your answer.

What would it look like if you were this kind of friend?

"Whatever you are, it is your own friends who make your world." —**WILLIAM JAMES**

ONE AT A TIME

Jesus turned around, and when He saw her He said, "Be of good cheer, daughter; your faith has made you well." And the woman was made well from that hour. MATTHEW 9:22

JESUS WAS IN A BIG HURRY. Well, actually, Jesus wasn't in a hurry—the disciples were. A synagogue ruler, Jairus, had asked Jesus to come to his house to heal his deathly ill daughter, and He had agreed to go (see Mark 5:22-24). The disciples thought this would be a great opportunity for Jesus to get some great press. *When He heals the guy's daughter,* they probably figured, *this movement will go somewhere!*

A huge crowd of people followed them. Suddenly, a woman who had been sick for years reached through the crowd to touch Jesus' cloak, and she was instantly healed. Jesus realized power had flowed out of Him, and He stopped to talk with her. The disciples and Jairus probably tapped their feet and coughed nervously to get Jesus' attention. A little girl was dying! But Jesus kept on talking to the woman.

Finally, Jesus finished His conversation with the woman, and He and the crowd moved on to Jairus's house. During the delay, the little girl had died, but that was no problem to the Lord of life. He spoke to her and brought her back (see Mark 5:41-42).

Who would stop to spend so much time with a chronically sick woman when a critically ill little girl needed help at once? Only One who knew that connecting with the woman at that moment was essential if she was to have a real relationship with Him. Death? That wasn't a problem. Jesus could deal with it later. But taking time to talk, to connect, to impart love as well as power to a woman who needed Him? That took priority.

What does this story tell you about God's priorities in His relationship with you?

Take some time now to respond to God's love and tell Him how you feel about Him.

"When you have come to the edge of all the light you know and are about to step off into the darkness of the unknown, faith is knowing one of two things will happen: there will be something solid to stand on or you will be taught how to fly."
—BARBARA J. WINTER

THREE THINGS GOD REQUIRES

He has shown you, O man, what is good; and what does the LORD require of you but to do justly, to love mercy, and to walk humbly with your God?

MICAH 6:8

THE PROPHET MICAH describes a tense courtroom scene as God accuses His people of being disloyal to Him and committing fraud against one another (see Micah 6:2-4, 9-11). God's tone, though, isn't harsh and condemning. He pleads with them as "My people," and He reminds them of many times when He rescued them from trouble. He doesn't want to judge them; He wants to build them up.

Like scolded teenagers, though, the people of Israel respond to God's correction with mock repentance. They complain, "What do you want from me? Okay, I'll give you everything you could possibly want. How about a thousand rams to sacrifice? And how about ten thousand rivers of oil? Not enough, God? Then I'll give you my firstborn child as a sacrifice. Surely that's enough for You!" (see Micah 6:6-7).

At this pressure-packed moment, Micah steps in and calmly speaks the truth, which cuts to the heart of the matter. "What does the LORD require?" he asks in response to their emotional, over-the-top offers of sacrifice to appease God. "God doesn't want rams or rivers or dead children. He wants only three things from you: to do justly, to love mercy, and to walk humbly with Him. That's enough, and that's plenty."

God is grieved when we rebel against Him or ignore Him, and like the parent of a defiant teenager, He is probably exasperated when we still don't understand and mock Him. Instead, God wants three things from us: good choices, rightly placed affections, and humility to embrace His love, acceptance, and forgiveness. That's enough, and that's plenty.

Have you ever responded to God in an over-the-top way like the people of Israel responded to Him? If you did, what were the circumstances?

What does it (or would it) look like in your life to make good choices, rightly place your affections, and humbly embrace God's love, acceptance, and forgiveness?

"Many times I have people come forth and say I have missed my calling, that I should have been a preacher. I find this both flattering and very humorous because, even though I'm not preaching, I am spreading the Word." —ZIG ZIGLAR

MAKE YOURSELF AT HOME

Jesus answered and said to him, "If anyone loves Me, he will keep My word; and My Father will love him, and We will come to him and make Our home with him." JOHN 14:23

IN ONE OF HIS LAST DISCUSSIONS with His closest followers, Jesus makes the same point three times in quick succession: Love for God is inextricably linked to obedience to Him, and God richly rewards our faithfulness (see John 14:15-18, 21, 23). In the last of the three statements, Jesus promises a rich relationship with God as the direct result of our love-spawned obedience. He says we'll feel "at home" with Him. What does that mean?

When a guest comes into your home, especially an important person that you don't know very well, you may find yourself on edge, making sure you do everything just right, but you're never quite sure if you've done enough. When a close friend comes over, however, everything is different. You prepare for the visit, but with a sense of anticipation, not fear. When you get together, you relax, talk, listen, unwind, and discuss things that are on your hearts. If an interruption happens, it's no big deal. You pick up where you left off. The time together feeds your soul because you feel deeply understood by someone you trust and who loves you the way you are—no pretenses, no masks, and no games.

Our love and obedience to God are steps toward a relationship like the one with a close friend. The more we obey Him, the more we realize that He is wise and strong beyond comparison. As we see Him work in our lives and the lives of others, we love Him even more. We trust Him more each time, and we learn to relax, to feel at home with Him. It's not that we take Him for granted or that we believe we're on the same level. That's the limitation in the metaphor of a friendship. Our relationship with God is never between peers. It's between King and ambassador, Master and trusted servant, powerful Father and dearly loved child.

What does it mean to you to be at home with God?

Are your love for God and your obedience to Him making you feel more at home with Him? Why or why not?

"It is the most astounding thing what happened to a tax gatherer, a fisherman, a farmer and a small business man—the disciples—when they lived with Jesus. They were transformed as the marvelous alchemy of His spirit had its way with them." —HENRY DRUMMOND

WHAT'S YOUR STORY?

[The man who was blind] answered and said, "Whether He is a sinner or not I do not know. One thing I know: that though I was blind, now I see."

JOHN 9:25 { MEMORY VERSE

THEOLOGIANS HAVE WRITTEN THOUSANDS OF BOOKS (some thrilling, some boring) about what happens when people trust in Christ and experience forgiveness. At that moment of conversion, their eternal address changes. All their sins are forgiven, and they become children of God. Guilt and shame are washed away by the unconditional love and acceptance of Almighty God.

Most of us, however, don't grasp these magnificent truths until we've been Christians and studied the Bible for a while. Even then, some aspects of the colossal transformation remain shrouded in mystery. They are simply too wonderful to grasp. Even from the first day we trust Christ, though, we know deep in our souls that something is different—very different.

One day, Jesus restored sight to a man who was born blind. The religious leaders questioned the man to find some reason to discount the miracle and to accuse Jesus of blasphemy. When they stated emphatically that Jesus was a sinner, the man must have laughed out loud. "There are some things I don't know," he told them, "but there's one thing I'm sure of: I was blind, but now I can see. That's enough for me."

We are wise to plumb the depths of God's truth to discover the different aspects of the incredible transformation we've experienced, but the deeper we go in our understanding, the more we realize that salvation is a genuine miracle of grace—a miracle that produces unmistakable and amazing changes in us from the inside out.

> **Describe the unmistakable transformation you've experienced because you trusted Christ.**
>
> **Is God's grace to save you still a wonder to you? Why or why not?**

> *"If you let yourself be absorbed completely, if you surrender completely to the moments as they pass, you will live more richly those moments."*
> **—ANNE MORROW LINDBERGH**

THE CURE FOR CONCEIT

I say, through the grace given to me, to everyone who is among you, not to think of himself more highly than he ought to think, but to think soberly, as God has dealt to each one a measure of faith. ROMANS 12:3 { MEMORY VERSE

PEOPLE HAVE AN AMAZING CAPACITY for self-deception—either thinking too highly of themselves or too lowly. Both bring a lot of trouble. Inflated egos lead to boorish behavior, hurt relationships, and using people instead of loving them. Crushed egos cause people to build walls around their hearts and drive them to prove that they aren't that bad after all.

To correct mistaken self-perceptions, Paul instructs us to "think soberly," that is, to have God's perspective of ourselves. Each of us contains the image of God, but that image is tarnished by sin. One writer said we are equal parts saint and beast, which explains the inner conflict we experience.

By faith, we realize that God created us the way He wanted to, and we accept our abilities and talents as gifts from Him. Sin, though, clouds our hearts and distorts our thinking. We desperately need God's grace to restore us, and we need His wisdom to lead us. We are wonderfully created, tragically fallen, deeply loved, and completely forgiven. That's a sober assessment of each of us who calls Christ our Savior and Friend.

What does it mean for you to think soberly, honestly, and truthfully about yourself?

How does the statement "We are wonderfully created, tragically fallen, deeply loved, and completely forgiven" give you a grasp on your self-worth?

"Very often when a person thinks too highly of himself, it is not a case of pride as much as it is a simple mistake." —IKE REIGHARD

"Conceit is a weird disease. It makes everyone sick except the one who has it." —ZIG ZIGLAR

GET BUSY

This is a faithful saying, and these things I want you to affirm constantly, that those who have believed in God should be careful to maintain good works. These things are good and profitable to men. TITUS 3:8

CONTRARY TO POPULAR OPINION, the Christian life isn't a spectator sport! Certainly, reflection and meditation are important elements of a life of faith, but not to the exclusion of action. Martin Luther called people who hid behind spiritual reflection to keep from taking a stand for Christ cowards. What would he say about some of us today?

Many of the commands in the Bible are simple, direct calls to action: Love sincerely, forgive those who hurt you, help the weak, associate with the lowly, study the Scriptures, give generously, speak words that build people up, and reach out to the needy, to name just a few.

When we take action, we take risks. With the risks, however, comes the opportunity to see God do amazing things, and seeing God work is the greatest thrill in our lives. Will we do it right and for the right reasons every time? Of course not, but we won't have the opportunity to fine-tune our actions and motives if we're not moving forward.

Don't miss out on the incredible joy of seeing lives change. Reach out, give a helping hand, and speak up for Christ.

What commands can you take action to obey today?

What can you expect from God and from yourself when you move ahead?

"Feelings follow actions. So when you don't really want to or feel like doing what needs to be done—do it and then you will feel like doing it." —ZIG ZIGLAR

RUDE LEADS TO RUDE

A wrathful man stirs up strife, but he who is slow to anger allays contention.

PROVERBS 15:18

WE DON'T NEED TO BE as wise as Solomon to see this proverb in action every day. The pace and pressures of life have escalated in recent years. Only two generations ago, most Americans lived on farms, where the pace was measured in seasons and the expectations were far lower than today's. A generation ago, many people still walked to work, and they enjoyed a stable family life, nightly dinners together, and minimal distractions. Today, we live in a whole new world. Greater mobility and high expectations create tremendous stress, and when stressed people don't get what they demand, the lid blows off!

We call them hotheads because the slightest provocation causes steam to blow out of their ears and produces fiery words. The people around them are just as stressed, so in reaction, they erupt like volcanoes! The cycle continues until somebody finally backs off, but they remain on "simmer," waiting for the next encounter that will trigger another explosion. Where do these people with short fuses live? Next door, in the next office, in the next bedroom, and next to us in bed.

Cooler heads, though, can reduce the fire and tension. God calls us to be peacemakers. That doesn't mean we're to be pushovers, but it means we can speak the truth calmly and pursue resolution instead of escalating the problem. To be a peacemaker, we first have to be at peace with God and not be stressed out ourselves. Our first task, then, is to take stock of the stresses in our lives and take steps to reduce them. Only then can we be slow to anger and reduce the fires of anger in people around us.

When have you seen tension escalate between angry people?

Are you a peacemaker? If not, what can you do to reduce stress so you can have a cool head?

*"Don't be distracted by criticism. Remember, the only taste of success some people have is when they take a bite out of you." —*ZIG ZIGLAR

EACH ONE REACH ONE

Walk in wisdom toward those who are outside, redeeming the time. Let your speech always be with grace, seasoned with salt, that you may know how you ought to answer each one. COLOSSIANS 4:5-6

MOST OF US are around unbelievers every day, but sadly, we often don't even think about the opportunities God gives us to touch their lives. We're so busy doing our own thing and so absorbed in our own stresses that we hardly notice them—unless they bother us!

Paul was acutely aware of his mission to reach as many lost people as possible, especially in parts of the world nobody else would visit. He saw every interaction as an open door to represent Christ to people. Touching them with the grace of God was on the front burner of his heart. He was convinced that every word he said and every attitude he expressed could make a difference in someone else's life.

In addition to reminding us to reach out to the lost, Paul reminds us to season our speech with salt. What does that mean? Throughout history, salt has been used for two purposes: to add taste and to preserve food. When our speech is seasoned with salt, we add flavor to people's lives. A painful but often accurate stereotype of a committed Christian is someone who is straitlaced, sober, and sad. Nothing should be further from the truth! Of all people, we should be the most creative, optimistic, compassionate, sensitive, and alive. And when the time is right, we can explain the reason for our spunk—the amazing grace of God that has been given to us in Jesus.

Very few of us have the role of an apostle Paul or Billy Graham, but God has put all of us in relationships with people who desperately need Him. We just need to be a little salty so that each one of us can reach one who needs Him.

At this point in your life, how salty are you? Explain your answer.

Who are some unbelievers God has put in your life? How can you be salty with them?

"I'm convinced that the lost person will respond to a sincere believer far better than to an insincere Bible scholar." —ZIG ZIGLAR

IF YOU KNOW, YOU'LL OBEY

We know that we have come to know him if we obey his commands.

1 JOHN 2:3, NIV

JOHN HAD HEARD JESUS say that we can identify the type of tree by the fruit it produces (see Luke 6:43-47). John explained that people who claim to know Christ demonstrate their faith by their obedience in following His commands. If they don't obey, and if there's no intent to obey, then we have reason to wonder whether their faith is genuine.

Simply knowing Christ, however, doesn't guarantee perfect obedience. Only a few verses earlier, John had written that those of us who claim to be without sin "deceive ourselves, and the truth is not in us" (1 John 1:8). Instead, true believers exhibit a general pattern of obedience, looking to Christ for guidance and often (if not always) doing what He says to do.

One of the evidences of a genuine commitment to Christ is a lifestyle of repentance. When God points out a sin of selfishness, apathy, or defiance, we respond by humbly admitting our sin and getting back on track with Him. In this way, the Spirit moves us ahead on our path of following Christ, and we take one step at a time.

Our obedience (or the lack of it) is most often seen by those closest to us, the ones we may take for granted. We may want to show what a fine Christian we are to those in our community and our church, but those under the same roof know best whether Christ is real to us. Simple acts of love such as helping with the dishes, taking out the trash, reading to a child, listening to a story, helping with homework, and countless other seemingly insignificant acts of love are, for some of us, dramatic steps of obedience to God.

Whatever God puts on your heart, follow Him and obey.

What does your level of obedience say about your faith in Christ?

Is there anything God has told you to do that you aren't doing? If so, when will you start?

"Read your Bible. It's easy to understand if you'll ask the Author to guide you in it. And He is always available." —ZIG ZIGLAR

CHEAP IMITATIONS

Shishak king of Egypt came up against Jerusalem, and took away the treasures of the house of the LORD and the treasures of the king's house; he took everything. He also carried away the gold shields which Solomon had made. Then King Rehoboam made bronze shields in their place, and committed them to the hands of the captains of the guard, who guarded the doorway of the king's house.

2 CHRONICLES 12:9-10

REHOBOAM WAS EMBARRASSED. He was the king of Israel, steward of the great Temple and all the riches amassed by David and Solomon, but he was a neglectful man, more interested in avoiding risk than trusting God. Because Rehoboam was disobedient, God sent the Egyptian army to defeat Israel and plunder its riches. To replace the gold shields, Rehoboam ordered bronze ones to be made. They looked pretty good on the outside, but they weren't the real thing. Who knew? From a distance, bronze looks a lot like gold, especially if it's polished. Maybe some of the people didn't realize the counterfeits, but the captains of the guard certainly knew. They had carried the gold ones, and now they had to carry cheap imitations. We can only imagine what they thought of the king.

One of the most attractive traits of any believer is authentic faith—genuine trust in God along with brutal honesty about our failures. Authenticity surfaces our continuing need for God's grace, and it builds trust with others. When people realize we are the genuine article, not wearing a mask of superspirituality that says, "I've got it all together," they let their guard down and open up to us, and in turn we pursue God together.

If Rehoboam had been honest with the guards, he would have won their respect. Together, they could have rebuilt the kingdom. Like the king, we may be tempted to cover up the truth so we look better to the people around us, but living a lie tarnishes our hearts and ruins our relationships.

It's better to be the real thing—with God and with those around us.

How do you respond to people who aren't authentic?

What are some things that tempt you to be less than genuine with God and with others?

"You cannot solve a problem until you acknowledge that you have one and accept responsibility for solving it." —ZIG ZIGLAR

ALWAYS WITHIN REACH

[God] has made from one blood every nation of men to dwell on all the face of the earth, and has determined their preappointed times and the boundaries of their dwellings, so that they should seek the Lord, in the hope that they might grope for Him and find Him, though He is not far from each one of us.

ACTS 17:26-27

IN HIS FAMOUS SPEECH to the Greeks in Athens, Paul didn't begin with the death and resurrection of Christ. Instead, he started by connecting with their culture and their beliefs, acknowledging their statue to "the unknown god" (Acts 17:23). "It's this God," he explained, "that I want to tell you about."

The Greeks had a long, rich history of philosophy, and Paul wanted to let them know he appreciated their culture. The history of nations, he explained, is the story of God's work to create man, populate the earth, and establish states. None of this was or is out of God's sovereign control.

Ultimately, God's design for human history isn't about governments, rulers, or philosophies; it's about salvation. Into every culture, God puts glimpses of grace to capture people's attention and prepare them to hear the message of Christ. Countless stories of missionaries are about people on riverbanks in the remotest jungles of the world and people in bustling cities whose hearts were prepared by God. Then, when a missionary brought the message of Christ's forgiveness, they were ready to embrace it.

On a local, personal level, God has put symbols of His grace in the lives of our neighbors, our friends, and our family members, so that He is always within reach of those with seeking hearts. Our job is to be like Paul, to study people, to ask a few questions to discover those glimpses of grace in each person's life, and then tell our story of finding Christ. He's not far from each person we know.

What are some glimpses of God's grace in people's lives around you?

What are some questions you can ask and topics you can discuss to connect them with God's grace?

"Many times people complain that God is not using them. God cannot do much through us until He gets in us." —ZIG ZIGLAR

AUTHENTIC LOVE

[Jesus said,] "A new commandment I give to you, that you love one another; as I have loved you, that you also love one another. By this all will know that you are My disciples, if you have love for one another." JOHN 13:34-35 { MEMORY VERSE

PEOPLE AROUND US aren't transformed by fancy church buildings, dramatic lighting, or exciting props in messages. They might be impressed by those things on a superficial level, but what they're really looking for is authentic love—the real thing. They want to know if the love Christians talk about touches hearts and changes lives. They want to see love in action, not just in slogans on the marquee. They have seen and heard too much hypocrisy to be fooled again.

Jesus said that believers' authentic love for one another is the litmus test of whether we follow Him or not—and people are watching us. When people are hurting, do we step in to mend a broken heart? When a tragic accident occurs, do we show up at the hospital the first day . . . or also at the house a week after the person leaves the hospital? When a marriage dissolves, do we help each person put the pieces back together and provide stability for the children? When needs surface, do we really care enough to step in and help? When someone is boring, do we continue to listen?

Jesus was saying that people have a right to wonder if our devotion to Him is real, and the true test of our loyalty to Him is our care for one another. God is invisible; needy people aren't. Platitudes don't cut it. Arm's-length programs can be sterile, but costly; glad service to those in need speaks volumes about the authenticity of the love of God in us.

Are you passing the litmus test?

How would you define "authentic love"? What does inauthentic love look like?

What is one thing you can do today to demonstrate authentic love to someone in need?

"Love each other as God loves each one of you, with an intense and particular love. Be kind to each other: it is better to commit faults with gentleness than to work miracles with unkindness." —MOTHER TERESA

"Learn to love and you learn to serve." —ZIG ZIGLAR

ALL THINGS ARE POSSIBLE

[Jesus] said, "The things which are impossible with men are possible with God."

LUKE 18:27

JESUS HAD JUST HAD AN ENCOUNTER with a rich man whose possessions and wealth were more important to him than experiencing God's love. As the man walked away, Jesus commented to His followers, "It's hard for rich people to enter the kingdom" (see Luke 18:24). His followers were shocked. Rich people had more time to pray, more resources to spend on religious rituals, and more of everything that seemed good in the world. They were highly respected. The confused disciples asked Jesus, "Who then can be saved?" (Luke 18:26).

Jesus changed the direction of the conversation. A changed heart, Jesus explained, is God's business. Wealth or poverty, health or sickness, academic brilliance or down-home simplicity—none of that matters. All these things can be roadblocks to a person's trusting in God, but God can easily overcome any obstacle.

Some of us need to hear Jesus' message again today. We've been praying for someone for years, and to be honest, we don't see any progress. We long for this person to come to Christ, to experience forgiveness and find peace and hope and joy. Every overture we've offered has been ignored or rebuffed, and we're close to giving up. Jesus is encouraging us, "Don't stop believing. It may look impossible, but all things are possible with God. Keep praying, keep believing, and keep watching for Me to work in this person's life."

Is there someone in your life who seems to be impossible?

What is Jesus saying to you about what's possible with God?

"I'm so optimistic I'd go after Moby Dick in a rowboat and take the tartar sauce with me." —ZIG ZIGLAR

A CONSUMING FIRE

Since we are receiving a kingdom which cannot be shaken, let us have grace, by which we may serve God acceptably with reverence and godly fear. For our God is a consuming fire. HEBREWS 12:28-29

THE WRITER TO THE HEBREWS began his letter by explaining that Jesus Christ is more exalted than angels and greater than their renowned leader Moses (see Hebrews 1:4; 3:3). Throughout his writing, he warned people to avoid complacency in their faith and to remain true to God. Now, at the end of the letter, he reminds them that they someday will enter heaven, and at that time of judgment, the whole earth will be shaken.

The proper response to the truth of Christ's supremacy, the hope of heaven for believers, and the certainty of judgment for unbelievers is to ask God for grace so that we may serve Him "acceptably with reverence and godly fear."

Fear? We think faith, hope, and love are appropriate, so what is this fear about? We make a mistake when we reduce God to a peer, someone we can take or leave depending on our mood and whether He makes us feel good at the moment. Throughout the Scriptures, however, we find that people who have any inkling of the greatness of God fall to the ground in abject awe. He isn't the sweet guy in many of our drawings of Him, and He isn't the fuzzy fellow we used to find in flannelgraph puppets in Sunday school. He is the Author of life, the Creator of the universe, the Alpha and the Omega, One whose presence was so terrifying that His best friend, John, fainted at the vision of Him in His glory (see Revelation 1:17). Our God is merciful and kind, it's true, but He is also a consuming fire. We will be wise not to forget that.

What happens to our faith when we lose sight of the awesome nature of God?

In your conception of God, is He both gracious and amazingly powerful? Explain your answer.

"The truth is, fear and immorality are two of the greatest inhibitors of performance."
—ZIG ZIGLAR

WHEN IT'S OKAY TO TEST GOD

"Bring all the tithes into the storehouse, that there may be food in My house, and try Me now in this," says the LORD *of hosts, "if I will not open for you the windows of heaven and pour out for you such blessing that there will not be room enough to receive it."* MALACHI 3:10

OUR FAITH IN GOD shouldn't be left in a devotional notebook or in the pew on Sunday. It should make a difference in the most basic areas of our lives—relationships, purpose, and money. Many of us gladly read the Bible and sing hymns, but we want to keep God out of our finances. *That's my business*, we think but seldom say to Him.

Our perspectives about money, though, cut to the heart of our values. Our use of money, in fact, reveals what we really believe about God, about His purposes and provisions, and about our relationship with Him. We are told to avoid testing God as a general rule because it demonstrates a lack of faith, but God invites us to test Him in our use of money.

Generosity is the hallmark of true faith, and God promises that He will reward generosity by opening the windows of heaven to pour out blessings on us! Will we take Him at His word?

Some Bible teachers say that the blessings are always "in kind"; that is, God rewards us financially for our generous giving of money to His work. Others say that God has many different ways to bless His generous children. Either way, the promise is that we'll feel enormously blessed if we open our hearts and our wallets to give gladly and liberally to God's mission.

The only reason we would fail to capitalize on this "sure thing" is that we simply don't believe God is trustworthy to fulfill His promise.

What does your level of generosity say about your trust in God's faithfulness?

What would it look like for you to test God by being generous?

"If we pack our measures down and run them over, that's the way they will come back. This applies to all areas of life: material, spiritual, and emotional. The evidence is overwhelming—those who give more, get more." —ZIG ZIGLAR

IT'S TIME

Jesus came to Galilee, preaching the gospel of the kingdom of God, and saying, "The time is fulfilled, and the kingdom of God is at hand. Repent, and believe in the gospel." MARK 1:14-15

IN THE ENTIRE SWEEP OF HISTORY, God could have chosen any moment or place for Christ to step out of eternity into time, but He chose a backwater Roman province two thousand years ago, before the era of mass communication. If it had been our decision, we might have chosen a time when we could see Christ's every move on CNN, but God had a different agenda. The pinnacle of human history took place at the time and place of His choosing, not ours, and people had the opportunity to believe in Him.

In the same way, every person has a time and place where the gospel comes to him or her, and a choice is offered. Paul later wrote that God gives enough light to every person to respond to God, so no one has an excuse (see Romans 1:19-20). Jesus didn't come with a slick, convincing advertising campaign. He came as a humble, itinerant preacher with a ragtag band of followers. And today, He comes to people in the form of a friend reaching out to say, "Hey, I care about you. Let me tell you the best news I've ever heard." And when they hear the news of God's love, it's time for a decision.

> Do you believe God orchestrates a moment (or several of them) for people to hear the gospel and respond, or is it just by chance?
>
> How will you know if it's time for your family members and friends to hear?

> *"I believe the greatest single mistake Christians make is not using sales knowledge and common sense in spreading the word about the benefits of walking through this life with Jesus Christ."* —ZIG ZIGLAR

THANK GOD FOR A SECOND CHANCE

Moses said, "I will now turn aside and see this great sight, why the bush does not burn." So when the LORD saw that he turned aside to look, God called to him from the midst of the bush and said, "Moses, Moses!" And he said, "Here I am." EXODUS 3:3-4

WE OFTEN THINK OF MOSES as the great leader of Israel who led God's people out of slavery in Egypt. We imagine him at the burning bush, and we think of him standing at the Red Sea when God parted it for the people to pass to the other side. Moses was one of the greatest leaders the world has ever known, but that's only half of the story.

We need to remember that the events we know so well happened after a tragic sin and many years of desolation. Moses had murdered an Egyptian (see Exodus 2:11-15). His motive may have been to help his people, but murder is murder. God sent him to the backside of nowhere for forty long, dusty, lonely years. During all that time, how many times did Moses think of giving up? How often did he think his life was over? Did he despair that his life would never have meaning again?

But God gave him a second chance. It didn't come when Moses wanted or expected it, but when it came, he responded. Even then, his response wasn't perfect. He hesitated, doubting his ability to do what God told him to do, but still, he chose to obey and move forward.

Many of us have blown it in a big way, either at work or at home, publicly or privately. We've experienced the consequences of our sins, and we feel like we've been exiled to a foreign land. Will we ever have a second chance? God is amazingly gracious. We don't deserve a second chance, but He gives it—and maybe a third and a fourth, too. We may wait for a long time, but when it comes, we need to be ready to respond.

Whom do you know who feels exiled and needs a second chance?

What are some ways we can be ready to respond when the second chance comes?

"Other people and things can stop you temporarily. You are the only one who can do it permanently." —ZIG ZIGLAR

DON'T BLUSH

[Jesus said,] "Whoever is ashamed of Me and My words in this adulterous and sinful generation, of him the Son of Man also will be ashamed when He comes in the glory of His Father with the holy angels." MARK 8:38

JESUS' HARSH WARNING is hard for us to hear. It's difficult to imagine our being ashamed of Christ. It's like a freed prisoner being ashamed of his rescuer, who risked his life to free him. But many of us are reluctant to speak up for Christ when we have the opportunity. How can that be?

At one point, Jesus told the religious leaders that their faith was weak because they "loved the approval of men rather than the approval of God" (John 12:43, NASB). That's the heart of the matter. When a flesh-and-blood person is standing in front of us, it's easy to rationalize and make excuses for being silent. Suddenly, we can think of lots of reasons we need to be quiet! But if Jesus was standing there and we had to choose between the two, we'd probably speak out for Him much more often.

The truth is that He *is* standing there. He is present in every conversation and in every place and moment. If we take a minute and reflect on what He has done for us, our boldness will return. We were lost, but He found us. We wandered in darkness, but He is our light. We were doomed to eternal condemnation, but He has given us eternal life. We were prisoners without hope, but He set us free.

Think about these things often, and when the moment of decision arrives, be certain that He is right beside you cheering you on. Don't let Him down.

When have you been bold for Christ, and when have you been ashamed?

How will reflecting on His grace and His presence help you be bold?

*"You do not have to be a theologian or a Bible scholar to share your faith and teach a class of small children. If we wait until we know everything before we start sharing, we will never share because no one knows all the mysteries of God." —*ZIG ZIGLAR

IN THE PIT

Benaiah son of Jehoiada was a valiant fighter from Kabzeel, who performed
great exploits. He struck down two of Moab's best men. He also went down into
a pit on a snowy day and killed a lion. And he struck down a huge Egyptian.
Although the Egyptian had a spear in his hand, Benaiah went against him
with a club. He snatched the spear from the Egyptian's hand and killed him
with his own spear. 2 SAMUEL 23:20-21, NIV

TUCKED NEATLY AWAY in these verses is the story of three difficult events
facing one man—Benaiah. He knew how to turn these three big problems
into three major platforms that elevated him to a place of prominence in
Israel's history. Scripture records how Benaiah at different times faced two
warriors from the land of Moab who were known for their fierce fighting
skills, a lion in a pit on a snowy day, and a well-armed Egyptian warrior who
was seven and a half feet tall.

We might question why Benaiah would be bold enough to chase down
a five-hundred-pound lion that could run twenty-five miles per hour down
into a pit during snowy conditions. The answer is simple: He had prepared
all throughout his life for situations like this. He took full advantage of what
others were running from and saw this as an opportunity for him to run
ahead full speed. Because of Benaiah's daring and courage, King David put
him in charge of his bodyguard; under King Solomon, he became the com-
mander-in-chief of the armies of Israel. Three thousand years later, we still
marvel at the courage, risk taking, and faith of this valiant warrior.

When we enter the last days of our lives, we will look fondly upon the
days when our faith was stronger than our fears and when our accomplishments exceeded our greatest aspirations. The times when we defeated our
warriors, chased our lions, and faced our giants will provide us with our
richest memories.

Today, seize your opportunities and keep in mind that your greatest
blessings may be masquerading as the biggest obstacles in your path!

**What are some of the events from your past that looked devastating at the
time, but turned out to be great blessings?**

Is there a lion that God is calling you to chase?

"Faith is taking the first step, even when you don't see the whole staircase."
—MARTIN LUTHER KING JR.

SIN CAN NEVER CATCH US

As far as the east is from the west, so far has He removed our transgressions from us. PSALM 103:12 { MEMORY VERSE

THROUGHOUT THE SCRIPTURES, God goes to great lengths to convince us that He completely forgives us. Why does God repeat Himself so often and describe His forgiveness in so many ways? The answer is because we're so slow to believe it.

In all the eras of human existence, people have lived with a strong sense of justice: People should get what they deserve. This perception is a God-given strength, one that we should value highly. Imagine what society would be like without it! This strong drive for justice, however, can effectively blot out the message of God's amazing grace. Over and over again, God reminds us in the Old Testament that the Messiah would come to pay for sins, and in the New Testament, we see Christ paying the price on the cross.

In a beautiful psalm, King David tells us that God's forgiveness is out of this world—"as high as the heavens are above the earth" (Psalm 103:11, NIV). God's grace, though, isn't only as high as the heavens; it's also as wide as the east is from the west. No matter how far east we travel, we never reach a stopping point on the globe. And no matter how far west we go, we can always go farther. When He forgave us, God removed our sin "as far as the east is from the west"—an infinite distance.

God longs to convince us that His grace trumps justice. Because of His immense, unending love for us, we don't get what our sins deserve. Instead of punishment, we receive forgiveness; instead of shame, we are filled with hope; instead of fear, God showers us with His love.

Do you have difficulty believing in the depths of your soul that God forgives you? Explain your answer.

What would it mean in your life for God's grace to trump justice?

"My own definition of the grace of God is this: the unlimited and unmerited favor given to the utterly undeserving." —R. G. LEE

"The Good News is not too good to be true, it's too good not to be true." —ZIG ZIGLAR

THE DANGER OF SITUATIONAL ETHICS

Let your "Yes" be "Yes," and your "No," "No." For whatever is more than these is from the evil one. MATTHEW 5:37

WE WANT TO SUCCEED and get ahead—there's nothing wrong with that, unless we take unethical shortcuts. In business and in all other relationships, we're tempted to tell people what they want to hear so that the deal will close, we'll get the promotion, our spouses will appreciate us, our kids will behave, and our friends will be more impressed with us. But telling people what they want to hear is, at its heart, manipulation, not integrity. Jesus didn't give a deep psychological explanation for manipulation or attempt to rationalize it. He said that manipulating people is from the pit of hell!

One of the marks of a person who is vitally connected to Christ is the courage to speak the truth—not to be obnoxious and blast people, but to speak the simple truth with clarity and grace. However, we're only human. When we're tempted to exaggerate to impress or withhold information to protect ourselves, we need to fight against it and say, "This is the truth. This is what happened."

Yes, we can certainly complain that "everybody shades the truth" from time to time, but that doesn't matter to Jesus. Every time we're tempted to manipulate people's responses by shading the truth, we have a choice: to follow the evil one or follow Christ.

What are some common situations in which you are tempted to shade the truth to manipulate people's responses to you?

What would it do for your self-esteem and your walk with God to choose the simple truth?

"It is amazing what happens when you recognize your good qualities, accept responsibility for your future, and take positive action to make that future even brighter." —ZIG ZIGLAR

THE THREE KEYS

Never be lacking in zeal, but keep your spiritual fervor, serving the Lord.
Be joyful in hope, patient in affliction, faithful in prayer.

ROMANS 12:11-12, NIV

IN A FEW PASSAGES in his letters to the churches, Paul boils down the walk of faith to simple, profound principles. In his letter to the Romans, he gives three keys to spiritual life. Practice these, he instructs, and you'll go far in your relationship with God.

The first key Paul tells us about is to "be joyful in hope." In the Bible, hoping isn't wishing, as in, "I hope my investment makes 40 percent this year." No, hope is a strong expectation of God's deliberate action. It's not wishing; it's confident believing. And with that confidence, our hearts sing as we anticipate God's divine work to accomplish His will in our lives.

The second key is patience in affliction. Difficulties are a part of life. We are fallen people living in a fallen world, and beyond that, God "prunes" fruitful believers so we will bear even more fruit—and pruning hurts! When we experience problems, our natural reaction is to try to get out of them as quickly as possible, but that's not how God wants us to respond. Whether He takes us out of them or through them, God wants us to look to Him for wisdom and strength during the difficulty so that our faith grows stronger.

Unfulfilled expectations, unforeseen difficulties, and waiting for God's answers can make us want to give up, but the third key is to continue praying with resolve. In difficult times, our prayers deepen and take on a new urgency. And if the delay continues, we stop asking and start listening, which may be the lesson God wanted to teach us all along.

Which of these keys is a strength in your walk right now?

Which needs some attention? What are you going to do about it?

"Most people who fail in their dream fail not from a lack of ability but from a lack of commitment." —ZIG ZIGLAR

DEFENDING HOPE

Sanctify the Lord God in your hearts, and always be ready to give a defense to everyone who asks you a reason for the hope that is in you, with meekness and fear. 1 PETER 3:15

YOU NEVER KNOW when it will happen. You might be on an airplane, at the office water cooler, in the backyard talking to a neighbor, in church, or in your child's room putting him or her to bed. Something—your kindness, the other person's need, an event in the news, a family problem—may prompt the person to ask you about your faith. Are you ready? What will you say? How will you say it?

Questions about our faith may come in all kinds of varieties—intellectual, ethical, or personal—but at the bottom of them all, people want to know if our faith experience is rich and real and if it makes a difference in how we live. They are also looking for hope. They long to know they are loved, forgiven, and accepted by God, and they need somebody to tell them that yes, it's true: God loves them, too.

When the question is asked, it's too late to prepare our hearts. We must get ready to answer the question by "sanctifying" Christ in our hearts, putting Him first, above all other affections. When our love for Him transcends everything else in our lives (and even if we're actively struggling to love Him more than anything else), we're ready. Our words will reflect our hearts, and authenticity is incredibly attractive to people.

We don't argue people into the Kingdom, and we don't intimidate them into becoming God's beloved children. Peter reminds us that our demeanor should be "with meekness and fear," realizing the awesome responsibility and privilege of communicating the light of the gospel to a darkened heart.

Are you ready?

If someone asked you about your faith today, what would you say and how would you say it?

What are some specific things you can do to "sanctify" Christ in your heart so you'll be ready?

"If knowing Jesus means a lot to you—and if you know Him, it does—then let me urge you to pray for God's guidance so that you might witness effectively, and for God's courage so that you will witness often." —ZIG ZIGLAR

GONE FISHING

Jesus said to them, "Follow Me, and I will make you become fishers of men."

MARK 1:17

SIMON AND ANDREW were professional fishermen in a family business. Like most people running small businesses, they had to hone their skills and use every ounce of their ability to make a living. By all accounts, they were good at their jobs and could have continued in their profession for many years. But Jesus came along and rocked their world. He showed them that there was something more valuable than catching and profiting from fish—people.

Christ's invitation to the brothers tapped into their previous passions and skills. Now, though, they'd be using those to fulfill God's purposes. God would use their discipline and teamwork in their new role of "catching" men. They had learned to read the water for signs of fish, but they would now learn to read the Spirit's leading as they pursued people with the good news of Christ.

What are the skills and passions in your life that God wants to use to build His Kingdom? You may be an entrepreneur who can dream big visions of God's work, or you may be a nurse whose tender care and thoroughness can be wonderful tools in God's hands. All of us have passions and skills God can use to build His Kingdom: plumbers and attorneys, salespeople and administrators, drivers and doctors.

Each of us is a repository of experiences, talents, and desires that God wants to use in the lives of people we touch each day. Will we let Him?

What are your top three skills, and how would you describe your passion over the past few years?

How might God tap into those skills and passion to use you to touch people?

"Those who learn prosper." —ZIG ZIGLAR

SAFE AND SOUND

[The Lord said,] "You shall observe My statutes and keep My judgments, and perform them; and you will dwell in the land in safety." LEVITICUS 25:18

ON A MOUNTAIN HIGHWAY, road signs aren't there for our amusement, to give a few people jobs, or to clutter up the beautiful landscape. They were put there for one reason: to keep us safe. If we obey them, we'll make it to our destination safe and sound, but if we disobey, we could be headed for trouble—big trouble.

God's laws weren't given to us to steal our fun and ruin our lives. God, the Creator of life and the wisest being in the universe, knows exactly what makes life work best. He gave us free will, but He also gave us clear directives to guide us. Sometimes we don't know what to do, but most of the time, His commands are unmistakably clear. When we obey them, God promises to bless us with safety.

In many cases, the pains we experience when we break God's laws are natural consequences. We overeat, and we get flabby. We stay up too late, and we feel tired the next day. We skip personal Bible study and prayer, and we become spiritually weak. We yell at our spouses, and we feel isolated. We drive when we're drunk, and we go to jail.

Sometimes, though, God intervenes and corrects our path without regard to natural effects. He is a gracious God who loves us too much to let us keep going in the wrong direction, and "whom the LORD loves He disciplines" (Hebrews 12:6, NASB) by bringing difficulties into our lives. When they occur, we wonder, *What's that all about?* If we pay attention, the Holy Spirit taps us on the shoulder and whispers, "I've given you plenty of warning, but you didn't listen. Maybe you will now. You need to stop sinning and start trusting." If we finally listen, we move toward obedience and safety again.

Do you usually view God's laws as beneficial or invasive? Explain your answer.

What kind of consequences does it take for you to notice and change your direction?

"Perhaps the most amazing thing about the Bible is the depth, richness, and hidden value that God will continue to reveal as we continue to prayerfully dig in."
—ZIG ZIGLAR

MASTER YOUR RESPONSE

Let every man be swift to hear, slow to speak, slow to wrath; for the wrath of man does not produce the righteousness of God. JAMES 1:19-20 {MEMORY VERSE}

ONE OF THE MOST IMPORTANT LESSONS any of us can learn (or need to learn) is to control our responses to difficult people and stressful situations. All of us remember (often with a wince of shame) times when we said too much, too intensely, and too often. In James's brief letter, he gave many insights and motivations about the power of words, but this lesson may be the most important of all for many of us.

When we face someone who is defiant or annoying, our natural response is to try to control. We may try to intimidate, we may run away, or we may appease the person to get the conflict over as quickly as possible. Those tactics work just fine—for a moment—but they don't create positive, healthy habits of communication.

In these situations, we often interrupt to say what we believe needs to be said. We fail to ask for the other person's point of view because, to be honest, we don't want to hear it! It takes only a few seconds for our anger to erupt like Mount Saint Helens, and then, all that's left is picking up the pieces after the relationship is shattered.

James offers a different way: Hush up, listen carefully, ask questions, don't jump to conclusions, and put a lid on your anger so you don't ruin the moment and, perhaps, the relationship. His solution is simple but challenging. We need to recognize the damage inflicted by our current responses to others, and then, with a fresh wave of motivation, take steps to change. Memorize a simple strategy: Don't jump to speak, ask questions and listen, watch your anger thermometer and keep the temperature down. You can do it. It just takes practice.

How would this strategy have changed your last difficult conversation? Imagine using it in that conversation. Imagine using it in the next one.

"Let your religion be less of a theory and more of a love affair." —G. K. CHESTERTON

"When you change your world for the better, you have positioned yourself perfectly to change the world of those around you." —ZIG ZIGLAR

TREASURE IN CLAY POTS

*We have this treasure in earthen vessels, that the excellence of the power may
be of God and not of us.* 2 CORINTHIANS 4:7

IN CORINTH and throughout that part of the Roman Empire, wealthy people
often concealed their valuables in ordinary, unadorned clay pots. These pots
were so common that, they hoped, thieves wouldn't think to look in them.
Paul picks up on this practice and uses it as an analogy of our faith. The treasure, of course, is Christ. Before verse 7, Paul describes in beautiful language
that the message of the gospel is the light that shatters the darkness of people's
hearts. The treasure, though, is carried by common, ordinary people—clay
pots that often have cracks!

Paul uses this stark contrast for two purposes: first, to show the difference
between the surpassing greatness of God and us so that we remain humble
and, second, to remind us of the incredible honor of being the vessels that
carry the greatest treasure ever known.

When God transforms our hearts, the miracle of change doesn't honor
us—it magnifies His infinite grace. And when we tell people what Christ has
done for us to forgive us and give us new life, our words don't focus on us—
they focus on His power and kindness. We are happy for people to look past
us to see Jesus in us. That's what matters. What a privilege! We have the inexpressible honor of carrying the message of Christ—by how we live and in the
words we say—to everyone around us. Never has a cracked, flawed, common
clay pot contained such a treasure!

**How do you feel about being a clay pot carrying the greatest treasure ever
known?**

Describe the privilege of carrying Christ for others to see.

*"Do the best you can with what you have, and God will take what you've done and
pass it on."* —ZIG ZIGLAR

SHARING SUCCESS

[David] died in a good old age, full of days and riches and honor; and Solomon his son reigned in his place. 1 CHRONICLES 29:28

AS FLAWED PEOPLE who try to walk with God, the best legacy we can leave our children is twofold: resources for success and honesty about our failures. When he died, David left both of these to his son Solomon.

Imagine being Solomon on the day David was buried. He could look back on his father's stunning successes: killing Goliath, conquering the Philistines, leading the Mighty Men, and uniting the kingdom. But as he stood at the grave, Solomon also thought of his father's tragic failures: adultery with Bathsheba, conspiring to murder Uriah, and the pride of numbering the people that led to thousands of needless deaths. A mixed bag, for sure.

David, though, had been painfully honest about his sins. He confessed them to God and to the entire nation. He even memorialized them in psalms of confession and forgiveness so that his repentance would be an example for others—including his son—to follow for centuries to come.

As we prepare our children for the time when we leave the earth, we, too, need to leave a legacy of success and integrity. When we tell our kids about our successes, we need to be careful to give God credit for blessing us and giving us the abilities to succeed. And when we tell them about our failures, we need to share them in an age-appropriate way, explaining the consequences we experienced, our deep remorse for being so foolish, and the refreshment of God's forgiveness.

Which will mean the most to our children? Both are essential for them to have success and integrity in their own lives.

As you think about leaving a legacy to your children, what successes will you tell them about? What sins will you share?

Why is it important to communicate both to them? What might happen if you focus on only one or the other?

"You can have everything in life you want if you will just help enough other people get what they want out of life." —ZIG ZIGLAR

SUCCESSION PLANNING

The contention became so sharp that they parted from one another. And so Barnabas took Mark and sailed to Cyprus; but Paul chose Silas and departed, being commended by the brethren to the grace of God. And he went through Syria and Cilicia, strengthening the churches. ACTS 15:39-41

EVEN AMONG COMMITTED CHRISTIANS, disagreements can cause divisions and necessitate a change in plans. Paul and Barnabas had been the Dynamic Duo of the early church. Together, they had formed an incredible team that took the gospel and established churches throughout the Eastern Mediterranean. On one of their trips, they took along a young man, John Mark, whose career was promising, but he deserted Paul at a critical point (see Acts 15:38). Barnabas wanted to give the young man a second chance, but Paul would have nothing of it.

The question here, like the question in so many disagreements among godly believers, wasn't between right and wrong. Was taking John Mark along again a risk? Yes, of course it was. Was Barnabas gracious to offer him a second chance? Certainly. The two men, though, couldn't agree, so they parted ways. Paul picked Silas and headed out. Barnabas and John Mark went in a different direction.

Leadership sometimes demands hard choices, especially about people. In many cases, these decisions aren't cut and dried. Different leaders have different perspectives. They can try to come to an agreement, but at the end of the day, someone has to make a decision so the work can move ahead. In this case, one team morphed into two, and their effectiveness doubled. That may not have been Paul's plan, and it probably wasn't Barnabas's first choice, but it was God's solution. He often has plans that we never considered. New plans may be found in the heat of disagreement, and ultimately, they produce more for the Kingdom.

Don't be afraid of disagreements. State your opinion and try to find common ground, but realize that God may have other plans for you and for others around you.

Would you have given John Mark a second chance? Why or why not?

What ground rules and expectations should be put in place when Christians disagree?

"If you want to move up the ladder of success, teach someone how to do your job better than you." —ZIG ZIGLAR

THANKSGIVING

Make a joyful shout to the LORD, all you lands! Serve the LORD with gladness; come before His presence with singing. Know that the LORD, He is God; it is He who has made us, and not we ourselves; we are His people and the sheep of His pasture. Enter into His gates with thanksgiving, and into His courts with praise. Be thankful to Him, and bless His name. For the LORD is good; His mercy is everlasting, and His truth endures to all generations.

PSALM 100:1-5

IN OUR ADVANCED SCIENTIFIC and technological age, people have made amazing discoveries in every field. Medicine, telecommunications, and computers are only a few areas in which we've seen astounding progress in a short span of years. Our advancement has been so startling that it's easy for us to think that we are the creators and sustainers of the universe. This perception, though, is out of focus and, in the end, dangerous.

Even our ability to think, dream, and invent comes from God. Our God-given capacity to earn a living puts food on the table and provides money to pay the mortgage for the roof over our heads. In fact, everything good comes from the hand of God.

When we focus our attention too much on human abilities, we praise ourselves and forget God. From time to time, we need a refresher course, and this psalm is a good tutor. All we have, all we can do, and every creative thought ultimately originates in God. Without Him, nothing exists at all. When we realize that all the blessings we enjoy—including our amazing abilities to create, invent, and discover—come from a loving God, we respond like the psalmist: shouting for joy, singing about God's blessings, thanking Him, praising Him, and committing ourselves to live only and always for Him.

What happens when we give people too much credit for the advances of the modern age?

Describe the right perspective, one that gives people the right amount of credit but ultimately goes back to God as the source of all good things.

"It has seemed to me fit and proper that the gifts of God should be solemnly, reverently, and gratefully acknowledged with one heart and one voice by the whole American People." —ABRAHAM LINCOLN

SHARING YOUR FAITH

Continue earnestly in prayer, being vigilant in it with thanksgiving; meanwhile praying also for us, that God would open to us a door for the word, to speak the mystery of Christ, for which I am also in chains, that I may make it manifest, as I ought to speak. COLOSSIANS 4:2-4

PAUL UNDERSTOOD that evangelism is successful only if God leads us, opens doors, and motivates us by reminding us of the wonder of the gospel message. Paul was tough as nails, but he recognized that telling others about Christ is a partnership between us and God, and God has to do the heavy lifting!

Throughout his career, Paul had learned to be sensitive to the Spirit's leading. He went to Macedonia because the Holy Spirit led him, and he didn't go other places because the Spirit blocked the door (see Acts 16:6-10). An open door, Paul realized, is essential, and it wasn't good enough for him to use a bulldozer to knock the door down. He had to pray, listen intently, and follow the Spirit's directions.

Paul was gripped with the wonder of the gospel. He never got over his encounter with Christ on the road to Damascus, and it shaped his life until the day he died. The love and forgiveness of God weren't neat, formulaic doctrines; they were life and breath imparted to him by Jesus—truths that propelled him from city to city to tell anyone who would listen about Christ, no matter what the consequences, which included beatings, whippings, and imprisonment.

In our lives, it's easy to leave evangelism to the professionals. Certainly, we can bring people to church to hear a great message, but we can also ask God for open doors with family and friends. When the time is right and the Spirit leads us, we can tell people what Jesus has done in our lives. We may not be as articulate as the preacher, and we may not be able to answer all the questions, but that's okay. People just want to know if our faith is real—and we're the only ones who can show them it is.

Take a few minutes to ask God for an open door to share your faith with particular people who are on your heart.

Write an outline of what you will tell them when God opens the door. Write about what your life was like before you trusted Christ, the event when you trusted Him, and the difference He has made in your life.

"Since the Lord in the great commission clearly tells us to 'Go ye therefore into all the world, teaching and preaching,' I felt that not only was I instructed to do so but I wanted to do so. As a believer I felt I needed through my own life to be an example of my belief." —ZIG ZIGLAR

LEADERS ARE LEARNERS

As you therefore have received Christ Jesus the Lord, so walk in Him, rooted and built up in Him and established in the faith, as you have been taught, abounding in it with thanksgiving. COLOSSIANS 2:6-7

ONE OF THE MOST ATTRACTIVE TRAITS of a powerful leader is getting excited about learning a new skill or gaining fresh insights. Conversely, one of the most discouraging characteristics of some in leadership is a know-it-all mentality that walls them off from new ideas. Leaders who love to learn add enthusiasm and creativity to every meeting and every relationship, and they are great examples to others in the organization.

Spiritual life, like all other aspects of life and leadership, requires a rigorous commitment to learning and growing. When we stop growing, our momentum quickly fades, and we start the process of atrophy. Paul used three metaphors to describe the importance of continuing to learn in our spiritual lives: walking, being rooted, and being built up. The Christian life is often called a walk. A slow, steady, consistent pursuit of God and His will characterizes our lives. And, like the roots of a tree, we reach down deep into the truth and grace of God to find nourishment. Soaking up sustenance never stops, and even in times of drought, we find sources of strength if we've gone deep enough. And finally, like a sturdy building, each choice we make to honor God is a block in the structure of our spiritual experience. We grow stronger with each God-honoring decision.

How much is enough? When can we coast? Don't bother to ask for Paul's answers to questions like these. He never quit his relentless pursuit of God, and he warned that we can never put our lives on cruise control. Learning was central in his life until the day he died. In his last letter to Timothy shortly before he was executed, Paul told him, "Bring me the books I left with you" (see 2 Timothy 4:13). He was probably reading them as the ax fell.

What happens to us when we stop learning?

What are you doing right now to keep walking, going deeper, and growing stronger?

"Life is a classroom. Only those who are willing to be lifelong learners will move to the head of the class." —ZIG ZIGLAR

GETTING BACK TO WORK

It happened, when our enemies heard that it was known to us, and that God had brought their plot to nothing, that all of us returned to the wall, everyone to his work. NEHEMIAH 4:15

IF THE MEASURE OF A MAN is how much it takes to get him to quit, then Nehemiah would rank near the top of anyone's list. Nothing could keep this guy down! He began with an almost impossible task, and his "staff members" were all demoralized. He had rallied them to get them started rebuilding the walls of Jerusalem, but they soon encountered betrayal from their own ranks and opposition from outside.

At one point, some locals insulted the builders to discourage them. When that didn't work and the building continued, they plotted to attack Nehemiah's builders. The people got wind of the impending danger, and they came close to panic. Nehemiah, though, coolly and calmly gave orders to deploy the people so that they felt responsible for those near them. "Don't be afraid," he told them. "Remember the greatness of God and fight for your families!" (see Nehemiah 4:14).

Nehemiah's leadership saved the day. He had kept them working through all the opposition until now, but at this critical moment, he told them to focus their attention on defending their families from attack. The enemies found out that Nehemiah had put steel in the backbones of his people, so they gave up. Immediately, Nehemiah told the people to go back to work on the walls.

Couldn't they take a break? How about a few days off to celebrate and regroup? No, Nehemiah knew that the best thing for them was to get back to work. They wouldn't be safe until the walls were rebuilt, and they couldn't afford to waste time.

As leaders, our first instinct shouldn't be to take a break after a success. Sometimes, it's appropriate, but often, people need to get back to work so they can capitalize on their success.

When is taking a break a good thing to do? When is it best to get back to work immediately?

Describe Nehemiah's leadership style.

"The degree of hope you manifest by persevering through obstacles becomes a measure of your passion." —ZIG ZIGLAR

INTEGRITY

[The Lord] chose David His servant, and took him from the sheepfolds; from following the ewes that had young He brought him, to shepherd Jacob His people, and Israel His inheritance. So he shepherded them according to the integrity of his heart, and guided them by the skillfulness of his hands.

PSALM 78:70-72

WE KNOW KING DAVID as one of the most gifted leaders the world has ever known. His bravery inspired incredible exploits by the Mighty Men, his battle strategy won many conflicts, and he welded the divided kingdom back together with his diplomatic skill. If we look back to his younger years, we find that his leadership skills and character were shaped during years of obscurity on the hillsides tending sheep.

During those seemingly empty years, how many times did David wonder if his life would ever amount to anything? Day after day and night after night, he paid attention to the task before him. He led the sheep to better pastures and fresh water, and he killed a lion and a bear that attacked them. Alone with his thoughts, he prayed, reflected, and developed literary skill as he wrote his prayers to God. When the time came for David to act to rescue Israel from Goliath and the Philistines, his heart was strong and his hands had been trained. He was ready.

Some of us find ourselves living and serving in obscurity. Many of our friends and colleagues have passed us up, and we're tempted to feel abandoned and quit trying. David's example helps us stay in the game, to sharpen our skills and strengthen our hearts so we're ready when the time comes to act.

Will you be ready?

Describe times in your life when you felt passed by. How did you respond?

What are some things you can do to sharpen your skills and strengthen your heart?

"Integrity gives you real freedom because you have nothing to fear, since you have nothing to hide." —ZIG ZIGLAR

HE MADE IT ALL

All things were made through Him, and without Him nothing was made that was made. JOHN 1:3 { MEMORY VERSE

WHEN JOHN PENNED THESE WORDS in the first century, he and some of his readers had been eyewitnesses to the life of Christ. One of their tasks of faith was to hold Christ's humanity in one hand and His divinity in the other, something we also must do. We must remember that the One who was born in a stable, grew up in a carpenter's house, and walked among people on earth—eating, sleeping, sweating, and ultimately dying a horrible death—is the same One who created the entire universe and existed long before the earth was formed! Our faith is stunted if we fail to grasp both aspects of His nature.

When we allow both Christ's humanity and His divinity to amaze us, our trust in God soars. When we focus on God's stooping so low as to become a human being because He loved us and wanted to connect with us on our level, we're astounded. The Creator of the universe subjected Himself to abuse, ridicule, misunderstanding, betrayal, physical pain, spiritual abandonment, and ultimately death. This King of kings argued with rigid, self-righteous leaders who should have known better, and He defended the weak and powerless. By looking at His amazing life on earth, we can conclude that He genuinely understands the pain we experience, and we can believe that He must really love us.

Christ, the Son of God, wasn't limited by time, space, and a human body before He became a man, and He isn't limited in any way today. His power is infinite, His knowledge complete, and He is present everywhere in the universe all the time.

Humanity and divinity. The combination amazes us, and both are essential to our faith.

What amazes you about Christ's humanity? about His divinity?

How is your faith challenged and strengthened by both of these traits?

"All I have seen teaches me to trust the Creator I have not seen."
—RALPH WALDO EMERSON

"Time in the civilized world is measured by His birth. It's either BC or AD. This is proper because He is Alpha and Omega—the beginning and the end."
—ZIG ZIGLAR

ULTIMATE ACHIEVEMENT

My dear brothers and sisters, stay true to the Lord. I love you and long to see you, dear friends, for you are my joy and the crown I receive for my work.

PHILIPPIANS 4:1, NLT

SOMETIMES WE THINK OF PAUL as a grim, determined adventurer who kept going no matter what dangers and obstacles he encountered. Certainly, he was fiercely dedicated to the cause God had given him, but from time to time, he gives us a glimpse of another side of his personality. As he concludes his letter to the Philippians, he tells them that they mean the world to him. How does he communicate his heart? Twice in the same verse, he shares that they are "dear" to him, and he says that they are his joy and crown. They were his *joy* because their faith in Christ and their generosity to him delighted him, and they were his *crown* because on the day Paul stands before Christ to give an account for his life, he can point to them as evidence of his faithfulness.

What are the messages we give those around us? Some of us communicate warmth and affection, but many of us feel uncomfortable telling people we love them. Paul, perhaps the toughest guy in the New Testament, exuded affection for people. He wasn't the least bit threatened by displays of love.

Statements of love, though, have to come from the heart. If they're fake, they result in resentment, not trust. We need to focus on God's love for us and for the people around us, asking God to give us His eyes to see them, and then we can take steps to communicate the love He gives us for them. That's not phony. It's the real thing, and it changes lives.

At this point in your life, who is your "joy" and "crown"?

If you have difficulty expressing affection for people close to you, how would it help to see them the way God sees them?

"Christians are like the flowers in a garden, that have each of them the dew of Heaven, which, being shaken with the wind, they let fall at each other's roots, whereby they are jointly nourished, and become nourishers of each other." —JOHN BUNYAN

ACCOMPLISHING HIS WILL

After David had done the will of God in his own generation, he died and was buried with his ancestors. ACTS 13:36, NLT

WHAT A WONDERFUL EPITAPH: David served according to the will of God, and then he died. If we are Christians, on the day that our eyes close for the last time, we'll be ushered into the presence of Christ, and we'll celebrate as never before! At some point, He will ask us to give an account of what we did as believers on earth, and hopefully, each of us will be able to say, "Lord, I served according to Your will."

Our service, even for the most dedicated of us, is checkered. David was a man after God's own heart (see 1 Samuel 13:14) who conquered nations, led the Mighty Men in battle, and unified the divided nation, but he also committed adultery and murder. And by all accounts, he was not the best father in the world. God doesn't demand perfection from us, but He desires our love, loyalty, and passion.

From looking at the life of David, we can surmise that God is very gracious to overlook our flaws if we follow Him with our whole hearts. Like the patient mother of an overactive toddler or the gracious father of an adolescent who is longing for independence, God overlooks our excesses and focuses on the big picture: Do we desire, more than anything in the world, to please Him, honor Him, and serve Him? If that's our heart, we'll accomplish God's will, and He'll be delighted.

Do you agree or disagree that passion is more important than perfection? Explain your answer.

What do you need to do to rekindle or inflame your passion for Christ?

"History judges a man not by his victories or defeats but by their results."
—WINSTON CHURCHILL

THE GOD OF INCREASE

I planted, Apollos watered, but God gave the increase. So then neither he who plants is anything, nor he who waters, but God who gives the increase.

1 CORINTHIANS 3:6-7

IT'S EASY TO GET MIXED UP about the role we play in the Kingdom of God. The Lord has given us the inexpressible privilege of being partners with Him in the greatest venture of all time: reaching every person on the planet with the message of Christ. He could have used angels, rocks, or volcanic plumes of sky-writing, but He chose to use us. He wants us to look for opportunities to touch lives, to love people unconditionally, and to explain the message of the Cross. When God transforms a life, though, we may think we made it happen!

We aren't the power source; God is. We don't change lives; God does. We can't make spiritual life occur from a dead heart; only God can do that. We need to recognize the privilege and the limitations of our role. Yes, God calls us His ambassadors (see 2 Corinthians 5:20), but we represent Him, not ourselves. And in the metaphor Paul uses in this passage, God gives us the privilege to plant seeds of the gospel and water them with truth and grace, but the transformation of a human heart requires divine intervention. We're just the gardeners. God is still the Creator.

Understanding our role and limitations humbles us, refocuses our faith on God instead of our own abilities, promotes prayer for God to work, and lifts the burden of changing lives from us and puts it on God, where it belongs.

What problems can occur when we take credit for God's work to change lives?

Describe your role and limitations in the Kingdom. How are you doing with them?

"It is not enough to do God's work; it must be done in His way and for His credit."
—ERWIN LUTZER

CALLED TO COUNT

Let each one remain in the same calling in which he was called.

1 CORINTHIANS 7:20

"BLOOM WHERE YOU ARE PLANTED." These famous words from a 1960s poster are just as pertinent today as they were then. Many of us look at our lives and wish things were different—really different. We wish we were married, or we wish we were married to someone else. We wish we'd taken another job, or we wish we'd gone in a completely different direction in college. We wish this, and we wish that. We live in a cloudy world of "if onlys" and "what ifs."

Paul's encouragement for people to remain in their calling was written to—get ready for this—slaves (see 1 Corinthians 7:21). He told them not to worry about their freedom. If they could become free, they should go for it, but if not, they didn't have to worry about it. Either way, they were told to follow God with passion and whole heart. If slaves could bloom where they were planted, maybe we can, too.

In our nation, we have phenomenal opportunities to change our lives in many ways, but not all changes are necessary or even helpful. Most of us would benefit from honest reflection about the level of contentment in our lives, followed by a rigorous assessment of what we demand out of God, out of other people, and out of ourselves. Quite often, we'd find that we have bought into the dream of more and better. We'd be wise to back away, think hard about where God has placed us, and maybe, just maybe, put our energies into blooming exactly where we've been planted.

Take a minute to reflect on your contentment and demands for more. Is anything out of line? Explain your answer.

What would it look like for you to bloom where you're planted?

"The awareness of a need and the capability to meet that need; this constitutes a call." —JOHN R. MOTT

THINGS GOD WILL NEVER TAKE BACK

The gifts and the calling of God are irrevocable. ROMANS 11:29

ULTIMATELY, on a national or a personal level, God's purposes can't be side-tracked. In the middle of his letter to the Romans, Paul leaves his teaching about how to grow in Christ and turns to answer questions many people had asked: So many Gentiles are coming to Christ, but what about the Jewish people? Has God abandoned them?

Paul's answer is an emphatic no. God chose the Jewish people to represent Him to every nation, but they failed. Since they hadn't followed His directions, God, in essence, put them on the shelf. His plan for them, though, isn't finished. They might have been enemies of the gospel of Christ in Paul's day or might be in ours, but a moment in history is coming when many Jews will turn to Christ as their promised Messiah. God's gift of truth and His calling to follow Him are still pure and strong, even if the Jewish people have walked away for a while.

God's patience and persistence with the Jews is a picture of His relationship with us. Over and over in the Scriptures, we read of God's promises, people's rejection of God, and God's grace to restore them. Our disobedience grieves God, but He doesn't wring His hands and wonder, *What in the world am I going to do now?* He has complete knowledge of all of history, and He possesses wisdom and power to accomplish His purposes. Nothing confuses Him, and nothing can ultimately block His purposes.

When we think about the incredible patience of God, we are reassured that He never takes back His gifts to us and His calling in our lives.

What are God's gifts and His calling in your life?

What are some ways God has shown His patience to keep pursuing you?

"Each honest calling, each walk of life, has its own elite, its own aristocracy based on excellence of performance." —JAMES BRYANT CONANT

MODELED PRAYER

*As [Jesus] was praying in a certain place, when He ceased, . . . one of His
disciples said to Him, "Lord, teach us to pray, as John also taught his disciples."*

LUKE 11:1

EVERY DAY, before and after every conceivable situation, the followers of
Jesus saw Him pray. Sometimes when they were cooking breakfast, He wandered in from the hillside, where He'd been praying all night. At other times,
they saw Him burst out in spontaneous praise to God, and they watched
Jesus labor as He prayed about pressing needs. As they observed Him, they
saw something about His time with the Father that captured their hearts and
made them thirsty to learn from Him.

In the ancient Jewish culture, famous rabbis and teachers often com-
posed prayers for their followers. The disciples now asked Jesus to compose
one for them. He didn't miss a beat. Communication with the Father was such
an integral part of His life that He was ready to give them a model of prayer
before they even asked. We know it as the Lord's Prayer, but it could accurately
be called the Disciples' Prayer because it was a pattern for them to follow (see
Luke 11:2-4).

The prayer is elegant in its simplicity. It begins with the affirmation of the
majesty of God the Father and the desire that His will be done on earth. The
requests are for daily sustenance, forgiveness, protection, and direction.

How do we pray? Do we focus on the Father and ask for the things Jesus recommended in His prayer? Jesus gave us a wonderful pattern, not a straitjacket.
The Lord's Prayer is a template and a jumping-off point to explore each element
in more depth. Consider using it for the next week to shape your prayers.

**Why is it important to begin prayer by focusing on the greatness and the
will of God?**

**Use the prayer today as a model. Paraphrase each section and make it
your own.**

*"I asked Him to give me the prayers He wants me to pray and to give or withhold
anything according to his plan for me. Nothing is too big to ask of Him, not even
an ocean lot. It is God's business to decide if it is good for me. It is my business to
obey Him."* —ELISABETH ELLIOT

THE FIVE *P*'S OF PRAYER

When you pray, go into your room, and when you have shut your door, pray to your Father who is in the secret place; and your Father who sees in secret will reward you openly. MATTHEW 6:6

PRAYER HAS ALWAYS BEEN A MYSTERY to those who pursue God. It is our way of connecting with the One who created us and loves us, but in some ways, prayer is nothing like any other type of communication in our lives. Here are some tracks to keep us going toward God as we pray, the five *P*'s of prayer:

- Primacy. Connecting with God is the most important thing we can do each day. From Him we gain wisdom to make better decisions and courage to follow through.

- Period. We need to carve out a time so that prayer is a priority to us. The pressures we face each day will threaten to crowd out our time with God, so we need to guard our time of prayer.

- Privacy. Some of us pray publicly, but all of us first need to go to God alone, with no audience and no distractions to pour out our hearts to Him and to listen.

- Person. Prayer isn't just a self-improvement exercise. When we pray, we are connecting with a living Person who loves, grieves, laughs, and hears.

- Promise. Jesus assures us that our Father will reward our efforts to connect with Him. That doesn't mean He promises to give us everything we want. More importantly, God will gradually change our hearts so that what we want most of all is Him.

In which of these *P*'s are you doing well? Which need some attention?

What is one thing you can do in the next week to deepen and strengthen your connection with God through prayer?

"It seems universally true that people who have direction in their lives go further and faster and get more done in all areas of their lives." —ZIG ZIGLAR

FORGIVEN TO FORGIVE

Whenever you stand praying, if you have anything against anyone, forgive him, that your Father in heaven may also forgive you your trespasses.

MARK 11:25

FORGIVENESS MUST BE A REALLY BIG DEAL to God. It lies at the heart of the gospel message: The Good News is that God has paid the price to forgive sinners. We enter a relationship with God only because Christ took away the barrier between us, and our spiritual growth rests on the strong foundation of gratitude that we have been freed from sin. Forgiveness, then, is the crux of Christian life.

In human relationships, however, love can evaporate as quickly as a cutting word is spoken. Offenses, great or small, require the healing salve of forgiveness. Forgiving other people is central to spiritual life, and our prayers are hindered if we refuse to forgive.

Jesus explained that we continue to enjoy God's grace and forgiveness only when we have forgiven people who hurt us. His forgiveness has already been bought by Christ two thousand years ago, but our experience of His forgiveness is blocked when we harbor resentment. We may have a seemingly good reason to withhold forgiveness: He did it on purpose, she isn't sorry she did it, he'll do it again, she doesn't even care, he has done it repeatedly, or she is vicious and doesn't deserve to be forgiven. All these reasons, however, mean very little in light of God's command to forgive and His promise to bless us if we do.

Resentment secretly (or not so secretly) wants revenge. Give it up. Choose to forgive, and enjoy God's peace and love more deeply than before.

What are some things that happen to us (emotionally, physically, relationally, and spiritually) when we harbor resentment?

Is there someone you need to forgive? Tell God about it.

"He who cannot forgive others breaks the bridge over which he must pass himself."
—GEORGE HERBERT

SOLITUDE IN THE MORNING

In the morning, having risen a long while before daylight, [Jesus] went out and departed to a solitary place; and there He prayed. And Simon and those who were with Him searched for Him. When they found Him, they said to Him, "Everyone is looking for You." MARK 1:35-37

IT'S EASY TO THINK OF JESUS' LIFE as very different from ours. We see Him in stained glass serenely holding a lamb, or we think of Him hanging out with His followers around a campfire. Ahh, the good life. But actually, the Gospels tell us that Jesus experienced incredible pressures. Everybody wanted a piece of Him. Sick people came to Him for healing, confused people asked for wisdom, and religious leaders wanted to kill Him. And we think we've got it rough!

Early in Mark's account of Christ's life, Peter and the other disciples searched frantically for Him early one morning. Where could He have gone? "Everyone," an exasperated Peter told Jesus when he finally found Him, "is looking for You." The people had enormous demands, and the disciples had equally high expectations of Jesus. At that point, they didn't really understand that the Father had even higher goals for Jesus: to die for all of us.

Under enormous pressure, Jesus opted for sanity. He got up very early and headed out to be by Himself so He could clear His head and pray. He could easily justify working twenty hours a day—so many sick people, so many lessons to be taught, and so many leaders to refute—but instead, He had a different priority. To keep on track with the Father's plan, He had to spend time with the Father, pour out His heart, gain needed perspective, and get the game plan for the day.

Do you and I need those things less than Jesus did?

When you feel most stressed, do you pray more or pray less? Explain your answer.

How would finding solitude in the morning help you?

"Prayer is the highest intelligence, the profoundest wisdom, the most vital, the most joyous, the most efficacious, the most powerful of all vocations." —E. M. BOUNDS

SOLITUDE IN THE EVENING

When [Jesus] had sent the multitudes away, He went up on the mountain by Himself to pray. Now when evening came, He was alone there.

MATTHEW 14:23

IT HAD BEEN A REALLY BAD COUPLE OF DAYS. Jesus learned that Herod had beheaded His cousin, John the Baptist. He tried to get away to grieve, but an enormous crowd of five thousand men—probably a total of twenty thousand, including women and children—followed Him and found Him. Jesus had compassion for them, healed the sick, and fed them miraculously with a boy's lunch (see Matthew 14:10-21). Now He tried again to get away.

Jesus sent the crowd home, and He sent His disciples to the other side of the lake in a boat. He was finally alone with His thoughts and His sadness about John the Baptist.

There are times in our lives when success distorts our perspective. Success—especially miracles—can be intoxicating. It's easy to think we have some magic power or that we're indispensable. But when we feel stressed, we need perspective more than we need one more success. Jesus had His priorities straight. He knew He had to get away so He could feel the weight of the loss of His cousin, sense the Father's comfort, and prepare for the next day.

His solace and solitude didn't last long, though. Around three in the morning, the boat carrying the disciples was being blown by a storm. Rising from His grief, He stepped out onto the water to help His friends (see Matthew 14:25).

No matter what we do, we can't keep some of the stresses of life away from us. When stress levels reach their highest, we need to carve out time to be alone for a few hours in the evening, in the morning, or whenever we can find the time.

When is it necessary to be alone for a while, and when is it selfish?

What are some patterns of solitude you need to build into your schedule? How will it help?

"Times of isolation with God will precede the times of inspiration we receive from God." —IKE REIGHARD

GOD'S FORMULA FOR STRESS RELIEF

You will keep him in perfect peace, whose mind is stayed on You, because he trusts in You. ISAIAH 26:3 { MEMORY VERSE

"PERFECT PEACE"? You've got to be kidding! Most of us wonder what that looks like, but we might not recognize it if we saw it. Our lives are full of stress, and for some reason, we keep turning off the alarm as we feel increasingly busy, hurried, and overwhelmed with responsibilities. We find a semblance of peace when we turn on the television and escape for a few minutes or when we take a much-needed vacation, but our lives certainly aren't always characterized by God's peace.

Isaiah's promise of peace was given to men and women whose lives made ours look like a first-class cruise! The people of Israel had been defeated in battle, and most of them had been marched off into slavery. Stressed? They felt completely out of control, but God promised to rescue them and restore them—not just physically, but spiritually and emotionally, too.

The key to perfect peace isn't in keeping a finely tuned schedule and hitting all green lights. The key is to rivet our minds on God's goodness, strength, kindness, and purpose—not just to know these things are true, but to trust Him, delight in Him, and experience His leading each day. Then, when stresses come, we have a benchmark of peace, and we can say yes or no according to God's design for our lives, rather than acquiring more possessions, positions, or pleasures.

Is perfect peace possible? Yes, even in our rapid-paced, stress-producing world, we can fix our minds and our hearts on God, and He gives us peace.

What are some things that rob you of God's peace?

What are some ways you can fix your mind and heart on God's character and His will for you?

"Peace is such a precious jewel that I would give anything for it but truth."
—MATTHEW HENRY

"Surely it makes sense that the Lord who knew how to create the world knows how to run it—including even your life." —ZIG ZIGLAR

WHEN YOU DON'T KNOW HOW TO PRAY

The Spirit also helps in our weaknesses. For we do not know what we should pray for as we ought, but the Spirit Himself makes intercession for us with groanings which cannot be uttered. ROMANS 8:26

A MAN REMEMBERED WISTFULLY, "I always knew my grandmother was praying for me—when I was at my best and when I was at my worst, I knew she was praying that I'd follow God." It's tremendously encouraging to know that somebody loves us enough to spend time in prayer for us, and Paul tells us an amazing fact: The Holy Spirit continuously prays to the Father for us!

Sometimes, we want to pray but we are confused. Conflicts in marriage or with our kids, problems at work, an unexpected diagnosis of disease, or some other calamity boggles our minds and clouds our hearts. We know we need God's intervention, but we don't know how to pray. During those times, we can feel lost, empty, and helpless. But at those very moments, the Spirit of God, who knows us better than we know ourselves, brings our needs to the Father's throne of grace.

The Spirit's prayers for us aren't glib, meaningless ramblings. He groans in His intercession for us, with passion, intensity, and deep concern for our welfare.

On most days, we have a good idea of God's plan for us in our interactions and decisions that day, and the Spirit is praying along with us. On those days when we don't have a clue what to pray, we can rely on the Spirit's loving concern to either give us insight about what we can pray or to pray for us when we feel completely overwhelmed. Either way, we feel encouraged that He is our Advocate in a difficult situation.

How does it encourage you to know that the Spirit prays for you?

Is there any situation right now that baffles you and you don't know how to pray about it? Thank the Holy Spirit for His prayers and love.

"To the individual believer indwelt by the Holy Spirit, there is granted the direct impression of the Spirit of God on the spirit of man, imparting knowledge of His will in matters of the smallest and greatest importance. This has to be sought and waited for." —G. CAMPBELL MORGAN

HE SEARCHES HEARTS

He who searches the hearts knows what the mind of the Spirit is, because He makes intercession for the saints according to the will of God.

ROMANS 8:27

EARLIER IN THE CHAPTER, Paul had explained that the Holy Spirit prays for us, even when we don't know what to pray. Now he amplifies the encouragement by telling us that the Spirit's prayers are directed by the Father's complete knowledge of every detail of our lives, even into the crevasses of our hearts.

The Father knows everything. He understands us better than we understand ourselves! Because the Father also is one with the Holy Spirit, they are in constant and complete agreement as the Spirit prays for us. The Spirit's prayers are always in perfect alignment with the will of the Father.

Some of us think we have a good grasp of God's will for our lives—and we sometimes think we know God's will for other people too! Certainly, many aspects of God's divine direction are clearly spelled out in the Bible. But more often than we care to admit, our desires for an *easy* life overshadow God's desire for us to live an *abundant* life. We want fun, excitement, happiness, and wealth—and God often gives us those things—but far more, God's will is for us to learn to trust Him, to lean on Him when times are tough, and to gain wisdom by going through confusing or difficult times. In these cases, God's will isn't to get us *out of* trouble, but to take us *through* it so we learn valuable lessons.

When the Spirit prays to the Father for us, His requests focus on these deeper, richer lessons of life. We are wise to learn to pray along with the Spirit's purposes for us.

What are some ways we might confuse our wants with God's will?

Does it comfort you or disturb you that the Father searches your heart? Explain your answer.

"God always answers our prayers according to our good and His glory."
—IKE REIGHARD

THE WORLD'S BEST GUIDANCE COUNSELOR

When He, the Spirit of truth, has come, He will guide you into all truth; for He will not speak on His own authority, but whatever He hears He will speak; and He will tell you things to come. JOHN 16:13

IF YOU HAD IMMEDIATE AND CONTINUOUS ACCESS to the brightest mind in your field, would you use that resource? Would you call that person to ask for insights several times a day, or would you think, *No, I'd better just call once a week for about five minutes; that's enough*?

The fact is that the brightest mind (and most loving heart) in the universe is on call 24/7 for every believer. Jesus calls the Holy Spirit "the Spirit of truth" because He directed the writers of Scripture as they recorded God's thoughts, and He promises to guide us so that we grasp and apply God's truth in every situation. We can hardly imagine a better guidance counselor!

But do we value Him? Do we pursue Him? Do we ask Him questions and then patiently listen for His directions? Sadly, many of us would answer, "No, I'm too busy." Too busy? If Warren Buffett offered to be available for a day to give us advice on investments, we'd spend a month carefully crafting questions and preparing for the conversations. In our appointment with him, we'd soak up every word like a sponge.

The Spirit of God has given us access to Him all day every day. We can take advantage of this monumental opportunity by preparing our hearts to value Him, crafting our questions to get at the root issues, and listening intently to Him as He reminds us of passages of Scripture we've read or as He whispers to us to give us direction.

Those who value Him and listen become wise; those who don't . . .

Do you treat the Holy Spirit like you'd treat the best mind in your field? Explain your answer.

How can you value Him more? What difference will it make?

"Be assured if you walk with Him, and look to Him, and expect help from Him, He will never fail you." —GEORGE MÜLLER

MOVED BY THE SPIRIT

Knowing this first, that no prophecy of Scripture is of any private interpretation, for prophecy never came by the will of man, but holy men of God spoke as they were moved by the Holy Spirit. 2 PETER 1:20-21

FAR TOO OFTEN, people read the Bible with all the enthusiasm they'd have if they were reading last week's news or another city's phone book. They think it sounds so old, so outdated, so out of touch with real life. Certainly, the Scriptures were written years ago, but though they were written in another era in a farming society, the Bible is for all cultures—even our high-tech environment. The truth of God's Word is the most challenging, most dramatic, and most comforting the world has ever known. If it doesn't blow our socks off by its power, we're just not paying attention!

Some people complain, "Yeah, but it's just men writing what they thought about God. What difference can that make to my life today?" Great question! It makes all the difference in the world because every word was written under the direction of God's Spirit. Each writer was prompted, guided, and inspired to write God's message, which applies to every person for all time.

If we take our blinders off, we'll see that certain passages give us the most wonderful promises we can imagine. God offers forgiveness and cleansing to the worst of sinners, and He promises His Spirit's presence and power if we'll only ask. When we doubt, God's Word gives hope. When we feel crushed under the weight of guilt, the Scriptures teach that God forgives. When we don't know where to go, God's promises and commands guide us. And when we close our eyes for the last time, God leads us to a glorious place He has prepared for us, a place He described in His Word.

The Bible doesn't speak to every conceivable situation in our technological age, but it speaks boldly and clearly about the condition of the heart, the nature of relationships, and the hope we can experience if we follow God. That should be enough to keep us interested.

> **When you read the Bible, what are your expectations? Explain your answer.**
>
> **Since every word was written under the leadership of the Spirit, what could (or should) your expectations be?**

> *"Nobody ever outgrows the Scriptures; the Book widens and deepens with our years."*
> —CHARLES HADDON SPURGEON

GIVING IS LIVING

I have shown you in every way, by laboring like this, that you must support the weak. And remember the words of the Lord Jesus, that He said, "It is more blessed to give than to receive." ACTS 20:35

CHRIST'S MESSAGE turned everything upside down when He lived on the earth. To become great, He told His followers, become a servant of all. To rise up, stoop low. The last shall be first, and the first last. To be significant in the Kingdom, become like a little child. And as Paul related to the leaders of the church in Ephesus, we are filled up when we give out.

Our culture, like every culture throughout history, is remarkably self-absorbed. Selfishness transcends time, race, and societies. But because we have more disposable income than any other people in history, we have more that we can spend to indulge ourselves. Everywhere we look, ads tell us that our lives are deficient if we don't have this car or that perfume. Though we claim to be shrewd, we are all infected by at least a light case of consumerism, and we clutch things more tightly than we should.

The promise of advertising is that the product or service will give us fulfillment in our lives! People who have walked with God for a while, though, understand the danger in this lie. We know that having more stuff only fills us for a short time, and soon we thirst for even more. And we know that we *really live* only when we *really give*. Heartfelt fulfillment, and in fact, the deepest thrill of our lives, comes when we pour out our lives to help those who can never invite us to a dinner party, take us out on their boat, or make us look good in any way. When we help the weak, the poor, and the sick—expecting nothing in return—we are most like God, and He blesses us beyond anything the world can offer.

What act of giving or service has brought you the most joy?

In what way is it really "more blessed to give than to receive"?

"Gratitude is a fruit of great cultivation. You do not find it among gross people."
—SAMUEL JOHNSON

DO YOU BELIEVE?

Jesus said to him, "If you can believe, all things are possible to him who believes." Immediately the father of the child cried out and said with tears, "Lord, I believe; help my unbelief!" MARK 9:23-24

MOST OF US READILY IDENTIFY with this distraught father, who desperately wanted Jesus to help his demon-possessed son but struggled to find the faith to trust Him. The demon threw the boy into a convulsion, and the dad turned to Jesus. "If you can do anything, help us!" (see Mark 9:17-22).

The problem in this situation, like all problems we encounter, isn't a limitation of the power of God but a limitation of man's faith. God can do absolutely anything, but He often waits for us to wrestle with our faith until we truly believe. (And of course, no matter how much faith we have, He may still choose to act in ways that are different from our request. We can't make Him do what we want.)

Jesus quickly refocused the man's attention and reminded him, "All things are possible to him who believes." The man, painfully aware of his weak faith, acknowledged the little faith he had and pleaded with Jesus for more. At any point in our walk with God and at any moment of crisis in our faith, we can follow this man's example. God delights in our honesty, and He responds to our cries for help. Whether in a flash of insight or a long process, Christ answers our prayer to build our faith. Perhaps we see Him perform a miracle in the moment we cry out to Him, or perhaps He gives us faith to trust Him through a long illness or a strain in a cherished relationship. Whatever our situation, we first admit that our faith is flawed, and we ask Him for help.

Describe a time when you felt like the man in this story.

Do you need God to build your faith so that you can trust Him for something significant? Explain your answer.

"Our belief at the beginning of a doubtful undertaking is the one thing that assures the successful outcome of any venture." —WILLIAM JAMES

THE SON OF GOD

In the beginning was the Word, and the Word was with God, and the Word was God. He was in the beginning with God. JOHN 1:1-2 { **MEMORY VERSE**

IN ONE OF THE MOST BEAUTIFUL and powerful preambles in literature, John reminds us that Jesus was unlike anyone who ever lived, categorically different and utterly unique. The man—who was born as a baby, grew up in a carpenter's shop, taught and healed people, and died a martyr's death outside Jerusalem—was flesh and blood, but He was from another realm. He was, in fact, God incarnate.

Even in the prescientific world, people understood that time went back a long way. Today, we have a clearer grasp of the age of the universe: some 14.6 billion years old! The age and distances are staggering. Most of us have to strain to remember things that happened thirty, forty, or fifty years ago. But Jesus, God's Son, was alive before Creation began—infinitely before!

We live in an information age, and we like to think that we have everything figured out (or at least, we're close to having everything figured out). But when we contemplate the wonder of God becoming a man, mystery comes back into our world, and we're amazed at the nature of God.

Being amazed is a good thing. In fact, wonder is essential to real faith. Creation reminds us that God is great beyond all imagination, and the Cross convinces us again that He loves us more than we'll ever fathom. The Son of God is truly amazing.

How does thinking about Christ living in eternity past stretch your faith?

Are Christ's greatness and goodness amazing to you? Why or why not?

"God is pursuing with omnipotent passion a worldwide purpose of gathering joyful worshippers for Himself from every tribe and tongue and people and nation. He has an inexhaustible enthusiasm for the supremacy of His name among the nations. Therefore, let us bring our affections into line with His, and for the sake of His name, let us renounce the quest for worldly comforts and join His global purpose." —JOHN PIPER

BELIEVING IS SEEING

We walk by faith, not by sight. 2 CORINTHIANS 5:7

IN THE MIDDLE OF A BEAUTIFUL DESCRIPTION of heaven, Paul reminds us that our confidence in God's promises must be the product of faith in His trustworthiness to fulfill His promises, not visual observation. When we enter the gates of heaven, our bodies will be transformed. The bodies we dwell in today will be destroyed. In their place, we'll have strong, healthy, beautiful bodies (see 2 Corinthians 5:1-8). The change will be so dramatic that we can hardly conceive it!

We have a taste, though, of the heaven to come. When we trust in Christ, the Holy Spirit takes up residence in our bodies. As we grow in our relationship with God, we give more attention to the Spirit's whispers and nudges, and we respond in increasing faith and obedience. The Spirit's presence is a down payment for the future and a guarantee that God's promises will be fulfilled one day.

We live by our five senses in this world. Every interaction, every activity, and every meal comes through our God-given sensory organs. But spiritual life is different. It operates in the unseen realms and is based on faith, not feelings. It's focused on God's promises, not tangible things.

Spiritual growth comes as we pay attention to the Holy Spirit's activity reminding us that God's promises are true and that we can trust Him to do what He says He will do. Some of us are like Thomas, who said he wouldn't believe unless he could touch Jesus' wounds (see John 20:24-25), but as we grow in our faith, we gradually become more aware of the presence of an unseen world that is just as real as what we can touch, taste, smell, hear, and see.

How much are you like Thomas, needing to see to believe?

What are some of the most important of God's promises to you?

"Sight is not faith neither is feeling faith; but believing when we neither see, hear, nor feel is faith, and everywhere the Bible tells us our salvation is to be by faith. Therefore we must believe before we feel and often against our feelings, if we would honor God by our faith." —HANNAH WHITALL SMITH

CHRIST'S MISSION

God did not send His Son into the world to condemn the world, but that the world through Him might be saved. JOHN 3:17

SOME OF US HAVE AN IMAGE OF GOD as the meanest schoolteacher we've ever had, someone who demands perfection and delights in punishing us when we don't measure up to that standard. We live with the faint hope that this time we'll do better, but in our hearts, we're sure we'll fail and get blasted again.

Jesus shattered that false image of God. His heart, His delight, His passion was to impart the love of God to every person on the planet. He moved toward the people others condemned so He could demonstrate His grace to them. He touched lepers, befriended prostitutes, and stopped to give attention to sick women. All these were condemned by others, but not by Jesus.

Was Jesus ever tough? Yes, He reserved harsh language for those who condemned the poor and oppressed the needy. He was angry that anyone would get in the way of God's desire to rescue, redeem, and restore broken people.

Jesus' love for people wasn't just sentimental feeling. He took initiative and action to connect with people, touch them physically and spiritually, and make a difference in their lives. A mean schoolteacher? No, not at all. He's the most loving parent and dearest friend anyone can ever have.

Why do you think many people see God as harsh and condemning?

What would (or does) it mean in your life to see Him as loving, kind, and active in His grace toward you?

"I can't understand how God could love us so much that two thousand years before we were born He sent His Son into the world to die on the cross for the sins we were going to commit. But just because I don't understand that love doesn't mean I can't accept it." —ZIG ZIGLAR

BEING RIGHT BY DOING GOOD

Let us not grow weary while doing good, for in due season we shall reap if we do not lose heart. Therefore, as we have opportunity, let us do good to all, especially to those who are of the household of faith. GALATIANS 6:9-10

WE SOMETIMES HEAR someone cynically say, "No good deed goes unpunished." Occasionally, there's a measure of truth in the statement. When we try to do the right thing, it can backfire and get people upset with us. But our good deeds never backfire with God. We have the promise that He always rewards us for doing the right thing when we help others.

"Doing good" is an exceptionally broad category. We do good when we notice something positive in a person's life and affirm it, when we take time to listen, when we love someone enough to speak the truth and confront him or her about a sin, when we set aside our agenda to offer a helping hand, and countless other ways. Paul said we should do these things "as we have opportunity," which is all day every day!

Paul also identifies the priority of doing good to those in God's family. The world is watching to see if we really love one another. If they see that we genuinely support one another with actions, not just lip service, they may become convinced that faith in Christ makes a difference.

And it does.

> Who are some people you know who are examples of those who do good?
>
> What are some things you can do today for others?

> *"We must first be made good before we can do good. We must first be made just before our works can please God."* —HUGH LATIMER

CAN'T LOVE YOU MORE

Greater love has no one than this, than to lay down one's life for his friends.

JOHN 15:13

IT'S EASY TO TALK a good game. We say we're committed to our spouses, our kids, and our friends, but the measure of love is the depth of sacrifice we are willing to make for them. How often are we willing to forgo our own pleasures, comforts, and desires for the good of another person?

We see genuine love in times of crisis, when a person risks life and peace to help someone in need. Soldiers have difficulty putting words to the bond they build in combat when the men next to them are willing to give their lives for one another. Did they die for their country, for democracy, for their unit? Yes, but more than that, they died for their friend in the foxhole with them.

Caring for a chronically sick relative is another demonstration of authentic, "greater love," as are patience with an annoying person, forgiving a habitual offender, and speaking truth when it would be easier to run away and hide.

We live in a self-absorbed world where personal rights reign supreme, but every society has been selfish to one degree or another. Self-sacrifice is as rare as it is powerful; however, it's the inherent nature of believers who follow the example of the One who risked all and gave all for those who didn't understand or appreciate what He was doing. His life and His death are the ultimate models of love. We are wise to think deeply and often about His patience, His tenacity, His single-minded focus, and eventually His supreme sacrifice for us.

What does authentic love look like to you?

In what ways was Christ's life as much of a sacrifice as His death?

"The greatest enemy of Christianity may be people who say they believe in Jesus but who are no longer astonished and amazed." —**MIKE YACONELLI**

LEAVING A LEGACY

Let this mind be in you which was also in Christ Jesus, who, being in the form of God, did not consider it robbery to be equal with God, but made Himself of no reputation, taking the form of a bondservant, and coming in the likeness of men. PHILIPPIANS 2:5-7

WE USUALLY THINK of someone's legacy as a stellar achievement or an accumulation of wealth. Christ's legacy, though, is quite different. His life is remembered as one of service instead of power, one of giving instead of achieving earthly success.

At the heart of Jesus' legacy is selfless love that values others over Himself. He had it made in heaven. He lived in the fullness of glory, attended by angels and without a care in the world. Because He loved us, He made a choice to stoop to our level, to connect with us in a way we could understand (if not always accept), and to serve us to the nth degree by dying as our substitute.

The more we grasp how much Christ gave up and how much He gave, the more we'll be amazed at His love, and the more we'll want to emulate Him. Who are the people around us who need our love? They are the people we see everywhere we look: next to us in our beds, down the hall in our homes, in the next office, next door in our neighborhoods. They're the people we talk to on the phone and those we e-mail. Leaving a great legacy is pouring out our lives for them, speaking truth to them, encouraging them to do the right thing for God's sake, celebrating when they do, and forgiving when they don't.

Thankfully, our lives are peppered with people who are leaving a legacy like this. It could be a gracious grandmother, a loving nurse, a faithful friend, a forgiving dad, or a generous boss. These people are leaving a powerful legacy of selfless care. We can too.

What kind of legacy does God want you to leave?

What steps can you take today to forge that legacy?

"No individual has any right to come into the world and go out of it without leaving behind him distinct and legitimate reasons for having passed through it."
—GEORGE WASHINGTON CARVER

THE FULLNESS OF TIME

We, when we were children, were in bondage under the elements of the world. But when the fullness of the time had come, God sent forth His Son, born of a woman, born under the law, to redeem those who were under the law, that we might receive the adoption as sons. GALATIANS 4:3-5

THE PROMISE OF THE MESSIAH had been given many times by many prophets for over two thousand years, but for generations, He didn't appear. People longed for Him to come, but God refused to be hurried. Then, when the moment was right, Christ stepped out of eternity into time to pay the ultimate price to rescue us.

Why did He appear at that precise moment and at that particular place? We don't know the mind of God, but when we look at the vast sweep of history, we notice some amazing "coincidences" in first-century Palestine. We can identify three factors as CPR: communication, *Pax* Romana, and roads.

Communication: Until the Roman Empire conquered virtually all the known world, people existed in local tribes and roaming bands of hunter-gatherers. Rome stamped its image on every culture under its banner, and two languages, Latin and Greek, became the lingua francas ("common languages") of the empire.

Pax Romana ("the Roman peace"): Rome's military victories were won because the Romans had superior armor, weapons, tactics, and leaders. As new lands were conquered, fighting ceased and peace spread throughout the land.

Roads: Trade and commerce thrived in the Roman Empire, at least partly because the Romans built the most extensive and finest transportation system the world had ever seen—and would see for the next fifteen hundred years. Roman roads are still in use today in parts of the ancient empire.

Christ came, lived, and died at a time and place where the gospel message could explode across miles and cultures to reach every person. He could have come at any time, but from a historical point of view, few other periods have offered as many advantages for the spread of the gospel.

Why are these three factors important to the spread of the gospel after Jesus came?

What are some similar factors today that make it convenient to tell people about Him?

"A pregnant virgin gave birth to the promised Son of God at a time when the world was pregnant with possibilities." —IKE REIGHARD

THE VALUE OF FRIENDSHIP

A friend loves at all times, and a brother is born for adversity.

PROVERBS 17:17 { MEMORY VERSE

JOE HAD SEEN his comfortable, stable, happy life crumble over the last few months. Demands of his in-laws created tension with his wife, and the tension continued to escalate. He found himself figuratively kicking the dog and literally yelling at the children. The strain spilled over into his work because he was so preoccupied with the problems at home. He noticed that his circle of friends gradually diminished. It seemed that few of them wanted to hang around somebody who wasn't much fun anymore.

"I've never felt so lonely in my life," he reported later. "I thought they'd all leave, but Phil stayed. When I was at my worst, he didn't walk away. You have no idea what that meant—and still means—to me."

All significant relationships are tested by disputes and difficulties. It's easy to walk away when friends no longer give as much as they take, but a true friend moves toward someone who is hurting. He or she provides stability when life is out of control and a listening ear when no one else wants to understand. A true friend doesn't jump in to fix problems. He or she offers advice sparingly.

We all want friends like this. To *have* a friend who cares about us during difficult times, we need to *be* this kind of friend.

In your life, who has been this kind of friend?

Who needs you to be this kind of friend today? What will you do to show support?

"Be slow in choosing a friend . . . even slower in leaving a friend." —IKE REIGHARD

"The best way to have more friends is to be a friend." —ZIG ZIGLAR

POWER TO LIVE

God both raised up the Lord and will also raise us up by His power.

1 CORINTHIANS 6:14

THE CORINTHIAN BELIEVERS were very young in their faith, and they were, to say the least, earthly. Paul spoke to them on their level, and in his first letter to them, he addressed two issues that concerned him very much: food and sex (see 1 Corinthians 6:12-13). Spiritual growth sometimes has to pass through physical territory, and for the Corinthians, Paul had to start with the basics.

The Corinthians believed that since we have natural, normal urges for food and sex, those urges must have come from God. (Great reasoning, don't you think?) Paul told them, "No, no. You've got it wrong. Everything we have and everything we are, including our bodies, is *for* the Lord." Natural appetites for food and sex aren't meant to enslave our bodies. Instead, our bodies are to be dedicated to God, to be used to honor Him in everything we do.

To make his point even more pronounced, Paul explained that the physical body is so important that Christ's body was raised from the dead, and one day our bodies will be resurrected too. The power of God works in and through our bodies today to enable us to accomplish His purposes. Yes, we have natural urges, and yes, our bodies aren't perfect in this life, but they are vital instruments we can use to honor God and help others. Bodies that will one day be resurrected and glorified should be considered sacred, not used for immoral behavior. They're too valuable for that.

In what ways are you using your body to honor God? In what ways are you failing to use it for that purpose?

What are some choices you can make today to use your body more effectively for Christ?

"If Christ was not raised, His death was in vain. Your faith in Him would be pointless, and your sins would still be counted against you with no hope of a spiritual life."
—JOHN MACARTHUR

PURE AS GOLD

When He works on the left hand, I cannot behold Him; when He turns to the right hand, I cannot see Him. But He knows the way that I take; when He has tested me, I shall come forth as gold. JOB 23:9-10

IN THE FIRST CHAPTER OF JOB, we find out what's going on behind the scenes in his story. Job, however, doesn't have a clue. He can't figure out why he is experiencing such tragic loss, and his friends are no help; they tell him it must be his fault!

Job wants to talk to God directly to ask Him a few questions, but like everything else in his life at this point, God doesn't cooperate. Whether Job turns to the left or the right—whatever he does—he feels lost, abandoned by God.

Some difficulties we experience are, in fact, the natural consequences of our sins and bad choices. Others, though, come from a completely different source. God tests us, not to make us fail, but to strengthen our faith as we trust Him through difficult times. Jesus called this process "pruning" so that we bear more fruit (see John 15:1-5). Job compared it to purifying precious metals in intense fire to burn away the impurities and leave only pure silver or gold.

When we experience hard times, we need to look for the source. If we can trace our problem back to a selfish or foolish decision, we can make appropriate changes. But if we can't connect those dots, we need to accept the problems from the hand of God as a test, pruning shears, or the refiner's fire. These trials aren't meant to harm us, but to make us stronger. Recognizing the source shapes our response.

What are some ways God tests, prunes, and refines believers?

How has He done this in your life? How did you respond?

"Trial is God's alchemy by which the dross is left in the crucible, the baser metals are transmuted, and the character is enriched with gold." —**WILLIAM MORLEY PUNSHON**

CALLING ON GOD

What great nation is there that has God so near to it, as the LORD our God is to us, for whatever reason we may call upon Him? DEUTERONOMY 4:7

WHEN GOD PREPARED THE PEOPLE OF ISRAEL to enter the Promised Land, He gave them laws to direct their steps and signs to remind them to trust Him. The laws prescribed their choices and the consequences for disobedience. Unlike any other country ever created, the nation of Israel would be guided by God's decrees. For many years, God had also given them two undeniable signs—the Tabernacle in the camp and the pillar of fire and smoke over the Tabernacle—to reassure them of His presence and guide them on their journey. These signs were an open invitation to come to Him in prayer, day or night, formally or informally, collectively or individually.

Our nation's laws are derived from a long history of Judeo-Christian ethics. They provide an amazing balance of freedom and direction, reward and punishment. Throughout our history, secular and Christian leaders have called us to pray in difficult times of wars, famines, floods, and earthquakes and to give thanks for God's wonderful blessings of peace, prosperity, family, and homes.

Many of our nation's founders looked to God for direction as they crafted the Declaration of Independence and the Constitution, and they thanked Him for leading them as they saw the nation begin to flourish. But how quickly we can forget Him! Today, as never before, we enjoy God's blessings, and we need His continued care. We need to remind one another to call upon Him in the good times and the bad so that we don't forget the One who has given us so much.

What leader do you know of who called on people to pray to God in either good times or bad?

What are some ways you can remind yourself and others to pray more often for our country?

"The price of freedom is eternal vigilance." —THOMAS JEFFERSON

BIG CHOICES

Behold, I set before you today a blessing and a curse: the blessing, if you obey the commandments of the LORD your God which I command you today; and the curse, if you do not obey the commandments of the LORD your God, but turn aside from the way which I command you today, to go after other gods which you have not known. DEUTERONOMY 11:26-28

IN HIS EXPLANATION of the benefits of following His law, it's as if God is saying, "You have a choice. You can have a thousand dollars in cash or a poke in the eye with a sharp stick. Which one do you want?" Sadly, the history of the children of Israel is that they often chose the poke in the eye. We look at this choice and we think, *How could anybody make the wrong decision? It looks so clear!* But they did, and quite often, so do we.

God has made Himself abundantly clear, but like Eve in the Garden, we question His motives, His authority, and His purposes. Satan came to Eve and asked, "Did God really say not to eat of that tree?" (see Genesis 3:1). The correct answer, of course, was, "Yes, but He gave us all the rest of these, and that's plenty!" But the subtle questioning of God's authority and goodness was enough to drive a wedge into Eve's heart. Doubt grew, and she walked away from God.

In the same way, we experience temptations every day to doubt God's goodness and His central place in our lives. We think having sex with that person sounds really good, and nobody will ever know. Blowing off this responsibility won't hurt anybody. Lying about that person may help us get the promotion, and he wasn't going anywhere anyway. Having one more toy won't hurt anything. Another double cheeseburger and large fries? What can it hurt? But all these thoughts (and countless others, great and small) cast doubt on God and question the benefits of obedience.

We face big choices every day. Each one may seem small, but together, they are steps in a direction toward God or away from Him, toward wonderful blessings or in the direction of painful curses. It's our choice.

What are the choices you face each day that question or affirm God's authority in your life?

Which path are you on? How much progress are you making?

"There is no failure in God's will, and no success outside of God's will."
—GEORGE W. TRUETT

SPRINGTIME FOR THE SOUL

Lo, the winter is past, the rain is over and gone. The flowers appear on the earth; the time of singing has come, and the voice of the turtledove is heard in our land. SONG OF SOLOMON 2:11-12

ROMANTIC RELATIONSHIPS, as well as our relationship with God, go through seasons. Sometimes, we feel as if we're in the midst of winter, mustering the discipline to keep going even though there's little warmth. The deadness of plants in late winter symbolizes the barrenness of our hearts, but it doesn't last forever. Soon, the first signs of spring appear, warmth returns, and hope fills our hearts.

We can learn a lot about walking with God by observing mature marriages. They began with the heat of passion and the idealism of pure love, but when the honeymoon ended, reality hit husbands and wives hard. A time of reassessment was necessary but challenging. If they failed to rebuild their relationship based on realistic expectations and good communication, the marriage became an empty shell. However, if the winter of discontent ultimately led to richer conversations and deeper affection, the marriage flourished as never before.

In the same way, many of us began our Christian experience with great joy and high hopes. In those early days, God gave us wonderful experiences to confirm our faith, then sooner or later, He chose a more difficult curriculum for us. Struggles, disappointments, and misunderstandings about the nature of the Christian life threatened our fledgling faith, but the winter season provided the opportunity to go deeper and grow closer to God.

In the seasons of the year, in romantic relationships, and in our walks with God, the beauty of spring doesn't come without the dormancy of winter. If we develop greater trust when it's cold and dark, we'll experience more love in the warmth of spring.

How have you observed seasons in relationships with people and God?

In both kinds of relationships, what are some things we can do in winter to prepare for spring?

"Destiny is not a matter of chance, it is a matter of choice. It is not a thing to be waited for; it is a thing to be achieved." —WILLIAM JENNINGS BRYAN

INDEX OF DAILY
SCRIPTURE REFERENCES

*Memory verse

ABOUT THE AUTHORS

ZIG ZIGLAR is a motivational teacher and trainer who has traveled the world over delivering his messages of humor, hope, and encouragement. As a talented author and speaker, his international appeal has transcended every color, culture, and career. Recognized by his peers as the quintessential motivational genius of our times, Zig Ziglar incorporates a unique delivery style and powerful messages that have earned him many honors, and today he is considered one of the most versatile authorities on the science of human potential. Ten of his twenty-eight books have been on the best-seller lists, and his titles have been translated into more than thirty-eight languages and dialects. He is a committed family man, a dedicated patriot, and an active church member. Zig lives in Plano, Texas, with his wife, Jean.

DR. DWIGHT "IKE" REIGHARD is a pastor, an author, and a speaker and trainer in the corporate world who strives to breathe life into the dreams of others. Ike and his wife, Robin, have two adult children and reside in Georgia.

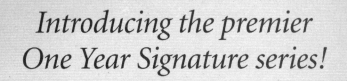
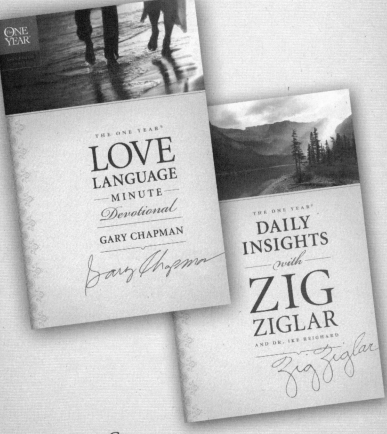